DATE DUE

NOV 1 5 2012	
DEC 0 8 2012	
3-6-13.	
JUL 2 4 2014	

NOMONHAN,
1939

STUART D. GOLDMAN

NOMONHAN, 1939

THE RED ARMY'S VICTORY THAT SHAPED WORLD WAR II

Naval Institute Press
Annapolis, Maryland

The statements of fact, opinion, or analysis expressed in this book are those of the author and do not reflect the official policy or position of the Department of Defense, the U.S. Government, or the U.S. Navy.

Naval Institute Press
291 Wood Road
Annapolis, MD 21402

ISBN 978-1-59114-329-1

Printed in the United States of America.

FOR MY SISTER CAROL,
WHO CHEERED ME ON FROM THE SIDELINES
THROUGH THE DOUBLE MARATHON OF THIS BOOK, AND
PASSED AWAY JUST BEFORE I CROSSED THE FINISH LINE

Contents

LIST OF MAPS

Acknowledgments

The first glimmering of this project came in the summer of 1965 when I happened upon a footnote in *Barbarossa*, Alan Clark's masterful history of the German-Soviet struggle in World War II. Clark cited Georgy Zhukov's 1939 defeat of the Japanese at Khalkhin Gol as an important battle. With a brand-new master's degree in history and the naïve belief that I was something of an expert on the Second World War, I was dubious that there could even have been a major Soviet-Japanese conflict in 1939 of which I was unaware. Finding myself in Washington, D.C., with time on my hands, I went to that cathedral of learning, the Library of Congress, and for the first time in my life undertook a serious research project that was not an academic requirement. I discovered that Khalkhin Gol (aka Nomonhan) was indeed a major conflict and the Library of Congress had a lot of unpublished material on the subject. I was struck by the fact that the peak of the fighting coincided with the conclusion of the German-Soviet Nonaggression Pact and wondered, even then, if there might be some connection. I could hardly imagine that this modest quest would shape my career, or that I would later spend thirty years as a research analyst in the Library of Congress.

A year later I was back in school, a PhD candidate at Georgetown University. For Tom Helde's research seminar on modern European diplomatic history, I wrote a paper on the Soviet-Japanese conflict and its possible link to the nonaggression pact. Professor Helde, chairman of the History Department, said, in effect, "Goldman, you have the makings of a doctoral dissertation here." For that, and Helde's role in securing for me a university fellowship, I will always be grateful. I also had the good fortune of having Prof. Joseph Schiebel as my dissertation adviser. Academe is notorious for its pettiness. Joe Schiebel took the highly principled—and unusual—position that "even though I disagree with your underlying interpretation of Stalin's foreign policy, the argument you make in support of your thesis is as plausible as my own, and I will be proud to have my name associated with your work."

A broad-based work of scholarship necessarily stands on the shoulders of others. My interpretation of Soviet foreign policy in the 1930s generally follows Adam Ulam's magisterial *Expansion and Coexistence*. I am also indebted to George A. Lensen's multivolume chronicles of Soviet-Japanese diplomatic relations in the interwar period. I cannot fail to mention the Japanologist, Alvin D. Coox, whose exhaustively detailed books on Changkufeng (*The Anatomy of a Small War*) and especially *Nomonhan: Japan Against Russia, 1939*, made him the acknowledged American expert on these battles. The many footnote references to his work in this book acknowledge his mastery. When I was a graduate student, Professor Coox graciously offered research guidance. He later paid me the "compliment" of viewing me as a competitor and rival.

When I was still a young assistant professor of history, John K. Fairbanks, dean of American Asian scholars and president of the American Historical Association, saw promise in my project and helped me win an AHA grant to begin Japanese language study at Columbia University's East Asian Institute. Two years later, a Japan Foundation Fellowship provided for a year in Tokyo studying Japanese and doing research on Nomonhan, which proved invaluable for this project. There I had the help of a brilliant young research assistant, Kose Nariaki, who guided me through the intricacies of prewar Japanese writing and the labyrinth of Japanese archives. Nariaki died tragically in a mountaineering accident at age twenty-seven. A former Library of Congress colleague, Nobuko Ohashi, generously helped me as interpreter, interviewing retired Japanese army officers in Tokyo. Later, Natella Konstantinova put in countless hours helping me comb through Soviet-era documents.

The renowned military historian, John Toland (Pulitzer Prize for *The Rising Sun*), was kind enough to read an early version of this manuscript and encourage me to stick with it and seek publication. My friend, David L. Robbins (author of *War of the Rats, Last Citadel, Liberation Road, The End of War, Broken Jewel*, and many other novels) has been unstinting in his advice and encouragement.

Imanishi Junko, associate director of the Atsumi International Scholarship Foundation, provided invaluable support for my participation in an international symposium on Nomonhan in Ulaanbaatar. The Sekiguchi Global Research Association of Japan and the Aratani Foundation of Los Angeles provided generous financial support for this symposium and my travel. My five-day adventure driving across the Mongolian steppe and touring the Nomonhan battlefield would have been impossible without my loyal interpreter, "Tom" Urgoo, and resourceful driver, Enkhbat.

My friend, Sambuu Dawadash, a Mongolian diplomat and adviser to the prime minister, was tireless and enterprising in his support of this project and rendered invaluable assistance in the United States and Mongolia. Former Mongolian ambassador to the United States, Dr. Ravdan Bold, whose father was at the Battle of Khalkhin Gol, provided valuable information on the events of 1939 and helped me gain access to the battlefield. Ambassador Khasbazar Bekhbat, who succeeded Dr. Bold as ambassador in Washington, has also been most helpful.

My friend, Capt. John Rodgaard, USN (Ret.), historian, intelligence officer, and technical expert, provided invaluable advice and support, not least of all by introducing me to Rick Russell, director of the Naval Institute Press—one of a handful of people who, years ago, had actually read my doctoral dissertation on which this book is based. What are the odds of that? Thanks also to Adam Kane, my editor at Naval Institute Press, who made the process of turning a manuscript into a book remarkably painless.

Finally, to all my beloved family and friends who believed in me, encouraged me, and waited patiently through an absurdly long gestation period for a book I've talked about for years and years—Thank You!

INTRODUCTION

The Halha River flows from south to north near the tip of a flat, grassy finger of Mongolian territory that pokes eastward into Manchuria. In the 1930s Manchuria's Japanese masters regarded the river as an international boundary line: Manchuria to the east, Outer Mongolia—the Mongolian People's Republic (MPR), then a protectorate of the Soviet Union—to the west. Those on the Mongolian side claimed that the border ran some ten miles east of the river, roughly parallel to it, near the tiny hamlet of Nomonhan. While the precise location of the border meant little to the Mongol nomads who had led their herds back and forth across the river for centuries, the Kwantung Army, the elite Japanese force that occupied Manchuria, had a different view.

In April 1939 Major Tsuji Masanobu of the Kwantung Army's operations staff drafted an inflammatory set of "principles" for dealing with the skirmishes that had been troubling the border region since Japan had seized Manchuria in 1931 and created the puppet state of Manchukuo. Tsuji's border principles declared that "if the enemy crosses the frontiers . . . annihilate him without delay. . . . To accomplish our mission, it is permissible to enter Soviet territory, or to trap or lure Soviet troops into Manchukuoan territory. . . . Where boundary lines are not clearly defined, area defense commanders will, upon their own initiative, establish boundaries. . . . In the event of an armed clash, fight until victory is won regardless of relative strengths or of the location of the boundaries. If the enemy violates the borders, friendly units must challenge him courageously . . . without concerning themselves about the consequences, which will be the responsibility of higher headquarters."[1]

In mid-May, the Kwantung Army officer responsible for the Halha River area, Lieutenant General Komatsubara Michitaro, commander of the 23rd Division, was meeting with his division staff to discuss implementation of the new border principles when he received word of an incursion by MPR cavalry across the Halha River near Nomonhan. In keeping with the new orders, the usually cautious Komatsubara reacted sharply. Irked by the bothersome skirmishes and hoping that a tough response would get the Mongols (and Soviets) to back off, Komatsubara decided on the spot to destroy the invading Outer Mongolian forces.[2] That snap decision and the conflict it ignited would have far-reaching consequences.

General Komatsubara followed up on his decision with action. After a series of indecisive small-unit skirmishes in mid-May, he dispatched a two-thousand-man force under Colonel Yamagata Takemitsu to crush the Mongolian/Soviet "intruders." Yamagata's detachment was built around a 23rd Division infantry battalion, a regimental artillery unit of 75-mm guns and smaller rapid-fire guns, and a two-hundred-man truck-borne reconnaissance unit under Lieutenant Colonel Azuma Yaozo.

Yamagata found that the enemy had constructed a pontoon bridge across the Halha River and taken up positions less than a mile west of Nomonhan. He decided to trap the enemy east of the river and destroy them there. He ordered Azuma's recon unit to push south along the east bank of the river to the bridge, cutting off the enemy's escape route. Yamagata's infantry, with artillery support, would attack frontally, driving the enemy toward the river and the waiting Azuma unit. There the enemy would be trapped between the two Japanese forces and destroyed.

Because of faulty intelligence, Yamagata believed that the bridgehead was held only by MPR border troops and light cavalry. In fact, the Mongolian forces had been reinforced by Soviet infantry, combat engineers, armored cars, and artillery, including a battery of self-propelled 76-mm guns. The combined force totaled about a thousand men.

On the morning of May 28, Yamagata's main force hit the Soviet-Mongolian units near Nomonhan. The attack achieved some initial success, pushing the enemy back toward the bridge. But Yamagata's advance was checked as Soviet artillery and armor came into action. The attackers were soon forced to dig in for protection from Soviet shelling. Meanwhile, Azuma's recon unit was startled as it approached the bridge to find its objective held by Soviet infantry with armored car and artillery support. The Soviet armored cars mounted the high-velocity 45-mm gun of a medium tank. Azuma had no artillery or antitank weapons and was wholly incapable of dislodging the Soviet force. When Yamagata's assault bogged down, Azuma found himself caught between two superior enemy forces.

As the day wore on, the Soviet 149th Infantry Regiment, which had recently been deployed to the area, was trucked to the combat zone and thrown against Azuma. Yamagata, pinned down several miles to the east, was unable to relieve him. The outcome was inevitable: Azuma's unit was annihilated. Only four men managed to escape that night; the rest, including Lieutenant Colonel Azuma, were killed or captured. In the words of Kwantung Army's official history, "remorse ate at the heart of General Komatsubara."[3]

Spurred on by Major Tsuji and other hotheaded staff officers at headquarters, the Kwantung Army command resolved to avenge this defeat with a major ground and air offensive across the Halha River, into indisputably Mongolian territory. The assault force was built around Komatsubara's 23rd Division, reinforced by a regiment from the crack 7th Division, several hundred attack planes, and the Imperial Army's only independent tank brigade. But the Japanese buildup again was detected by their Soviet-MPR foes. Moscow too dispatched powerful reinforcements to the region, designated as First Army Group, under the command of an as-yet-untested leader named Georgy Zhukov. The Japanese offensive in early July was repulsed by Zhukov, with heavy losses on both sides.

Kwantung Army continued to escalate the conflict but was checked each time by ever-more-powerful Soviet forces. Josef Stalin decided to send massive reinforcements to Zhukov's First Army Group, which launched a decisive counteroffensive in August. Intermittent fighting continued into mid-September 1939.

This conflict was no mere border clash. Nearly 100,000 men and a thousand armored vehicles and aircraft engaged in fierce combat for four months. Thirty to fifty thousand were killed or wounded. This small undeclared war is known in Japan as the Nomonhan incident and in Soviet Union and Mongolia as the Battle of Khalkhin Gol. Tsuji and Zhukov would go on to play critical roles in the Second World War and after—Tsuji as a famous and notorious soldier in the Pacific War and a member of parliament in postwar Japan; Zhukov as the architect of victory over Nazi Germany and later Soviet minister of defense.

But even more surprising, this little-known conflict fought in remote inner-Asia helped pave the way for Adolf Hitler's invasion of Poland—and all that followed. Indeed, the height of the fighting at Nomonhan coincided *precisely* with the conclusion of the German-Soviet Nonaggression Pact (August 23, 1939), which gave Hitler the green light to invade Poland, triggering the Second World War one week later. This was no coincidence. The Nomonhan conflict is directly linked to the German-Soviet Nonaggression Pact and the outbreak of the war in Europe. The nonaggression pact assured Hitler he would not have to fight Britain, France, *and* Russia, so he felt safe in attacking Poland. The pact (temporarily) kept Russia out of this intracapitalist war in Europe. It also isolated Japan from Germany. This gave Stalin a free hand to deal decisively with Japan at Nomonhan—which is exactly what he did.

Yet the standard histories of the origins of the Second World War make little mention of the Soviet-Japanese conflict and its connection to the events in Europe. This book does not presume a wholesale reinterpretation of those events. It does suggest, however, that a small but important piece, the Nomonhan conflict, has been overlooked or misplaced in most attempts to piece together the jigsaw puzzle of the origins of the war. This thesis is strongly supported by documents readily available soon after the end of the war, starting with the published volumes of German, British, French, and U.S. diplomatic documents. The *Documents on German Foreign Policy* provided an especially important window onto the secret German-Soviet negotiations leading to the 1939 nonaggression pact, a record that the Soviet government attempted for decades to deny and conceal. The military history section of the U.S. occupation forces in Japan produced approximately two hundred volumes on Japan's military experience in Manchuria, including many that focus specifically on the Nomonhan conflict. These monographs, prepared primarily by former Japanese military officers and then translated into English by the U.S. occupation authorities, provided an early, albeit fragmentary, record of the conflict, showing that it was provoked and escalated by the Japanese. The *Proceedings of the International Military Tribunal for the Far East* documents Moscow's allegations of Japanese aggression at Nomonhan.

Some forty years ago I marshaled evidence from such sources to support a doctoral dissertation arguing a causal link between the Nomonhan conflict, the nonaggression pact, and the outbreak of the war in Europe.[4] I could not then read Japanese. In the absence of reliable official Soviet documents, I augmented my interpretation of Soviet foreign policy by deconstructing Comintern publications of the period. Three years after earning my degree, while on the faculty of the Pennsylvania State University, I was fortunate enough to be awarded a postdoctoral research fellowship by the Japan Foundation that allowed me to spend a year in Tokyo studying Japanese and doing further research on Nomonhan. This led me to write a more fully documented and nuanced version of my Nomonhan thesis, which wound up, however, as an unpublished academic exercise. A few years later I left academe and embarked on a thirty-year career as a specialist in Russian political and military affairs in the Congressional Research Service of the Library of Congress—a splendid institution.

Upon retiring from CRS, I decided to return to my work on Nomonhan. I was encouraged in this by the release in post-Soviet Russia of a growing number of Soviet-era documents that not only confirm but strengthen my interpretation of the influence of the Nomonhan conflict on Soviet foreign and military policy. In addition to the official two-volume set of Soviet Foreign Ministry documents for 1939[5] and such collections of documents as *God Krizisa 1938–1939* (*Year of Crisis, 1938–1939*),[6] *1941 God Dokumenty* (*The Year 1941, Documents*),[7] more documents from the archives of the Communist Party, various government ministries, and intelligence services have been released or ferreted out, despite the efforts of the Vladimir Putin regime to check this flow and salvage the reputation of Soviet foreign and defense policy.

The idea of a connection between Nomonhan and the nonaggression pact, however, still has not received adequate attention from scholars. The two published studies in English that focus on Nomonhan treat it as an obscure East Asian military episode, ignoring its connection to the coming of the war in Europe.[8] Many Japanese and Russians have written about this conflict. The Japanese authors, however, show little interest in the complex European diplomacy. And in Putin's Russia, the Hitler-Stalin Pact remains a sensitive, if not downright dangerous, subject for Russian scholars.[9] Most U.S. and European analyses of the origins and outbreak of World War II ignore or briefly gloss over the Soviet-Japanese conflict.[10] Several historical studies contain tantalizing references to a possible connection between the Nomonhan conflict and the German-Soviet pact,[11] but none have developed the idea fully. This book is intended to fill that gap.

The organizational scheme for this book is chronological, but not linear. It has two stories to tell: a military history of the Soviet-Japanese conflict on the Mongolia-Manchuria border, and a diplomatic history of the coming of the war that is Europe-centered and global in scope. To avoid creating an ungainly two-headed monster, the narrative shifts back and forth between the disputed inner-Asian borderland and the political/diplomatic maneuverings of the major powers, highlighting the relationships among these events. The analysis does not stop in September 1939 with the end of the fighting at Nomonhan and the outbreak of the war in Europe. The Soviet-Japanese conflict at Nomonhan influenced decisions in Tokyo and Moscow in 1941—Japan's decision for war with the United States and the Red Army victory in the Battle of Moscow—that helped shape the conduct and the outcome of the war. Appreciating the significance of this seemingly obscure East Asian military episode and placing it in the broader geopolitical context sheds new light on, and provides a more complete understanding of, the Second World War. Nomonhan is, arguably, the most important World War II battle that most people[12] have never heard of.

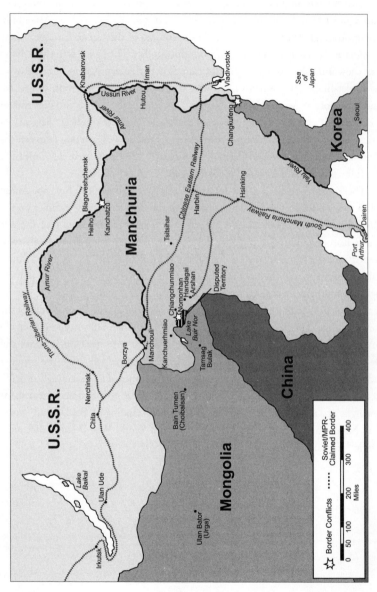

Map 1. Manchuria and Environs in the 1930s

CHAPTER 1

THE LEGACY OF THE PAST

War and Revolution

The year 1853 was a momentous one in Japan and Russia. Few could have predicted that events set in motion that year would put the two on a collision course leading to war a half century later. In 1853 American Commodore Matthew Perry's squadron of "Black Ships" steamed imperiously into Tokyo Bay, precipitating the end of Japan's feudal regime and ushering in a rush toward modernization the spectacular success of which would become one of the wonders of the modern world. Also in 1853 Russia invaded the Turkish-controlled Danubian Principalities, triggering the Crimean War, in which an ineptly led Anglo-French force humiliated the Russian army on its own soil. This defeat too spurred modernization. Russia's temporary diplomatic isolation in Europe also led the Tsarist government to redirect its attention toward Asia in order to reassert its great-power status.

Russian expansion into Asia had begun in earnest in the sixteenth century and proceeded eastward through the Eurasian corridor until checked by Manchu China a hundred years later, deflecting Russia northeastward to the sparsely populated North Pacific rimland. By the nineteenth century, however, the Manchu empire had entered into a period of decline and was beset by the seafaring European imperialist powers and by Russian pressure from inner Asia.

Only a few years after its defeat in the Crimean War, Russia forced the Manchu court to sign the Treaties of Aigun (1858) and Peking (1860), whereby China ceded the huge swath of territory north of the Amur and east of the Ussuri Rivers to Russia. Russia then began applying pressure on China's faltering control of Manchuria and Korea, a policy both symbolized and accelerated by the construction of the Trans-Siberian Railway. The Tsarist push toward Manchuria and Korea aroused suspicion and hostility not only from Russia's traditional western rivals, but from a new competitor for power in East Asia—Japan.

From the very inception of the new regime in Japan, its leaders determined to see their nation take its place among the great powers. The logic of geopolitics dictated that if Japan were to expand, it was in the direction of Northeast Asia that she first must move—at the expense of the crumbling Chinese empire and in competition with Imperial Russia. This became clear during the Sino-Japanese War of 1894–95, when Japan successfully fought China for control of Korea and South Manchuria, only to have Russia intervene, at the head of the so-called Triple Intervention, depriving Japan of one of the most important fruits of her victory, the Liaotung (Kwantung in Japanese) Peninsula in South Manchuria. Russia further antagonized Japan by taking control of that peninsula itself in 1898, by occupying most of the rest of Manchuria in 1900 in the wake of the Boxer Rebellion, and by penetrating Korea economically, politically, and militarily.

Tokyo viewed this Russian thrust with anger and alarm. Not only was the Russian bear encroaching on what the Japanese considered to be their sphere of influence, but also Russia's push into Korea also threatened what the Japanese saw as their own legitimate defense perimeter. After securing a military alliance with Great Britain in 1902, Japan sought an agreement with Russia for the division of the Northeastern Chinese empire. The Russians demanded all of Manchuria as a Russian sphere of influence, northern Korea as a buffer zone between them, and southern Korea as a Japanese sphere, with certain limitations. Tokyo found these proposals unacceptable and in 1904 decided on war. In the David-and-Goliath–like struggle, the upstart Japanese, whose warrior class had relied on swords, bows and arrows, and spears only fifty years earlier, astounded the world by vanquishing its huge foe.

In the 1905 Treaty of Portsmouth, Russia recognized Japan's "paramount political, military and economic interests" in Korea and ceded to Japan its leasehold (from China) on the tip of the Liaotung Peninsula—renamed Kwantung Leased Territory by the Japanese. Russia also ceded to Japan the southern half of Sakhalin Island and a 150-mile section of the South Manchuria Railway. Both powers agreed to evacuate Manchuria, which had been the principal battleground, and to return that province—temporarily—to Chinese administration.

The strategic 1,300-square-mile Kwantung Leased Territory commanded the seaward approach to Peking and contained the port of Dairen and the fortress/naval base of Port Arthur. In 1919 Japan established a special force, the Kwantung Army, to administer and defend the Kwantung Leased Territory. The Kwantung Army would become the spearhead of Japanese expansion on the mainland.

Less than two years after the end of the Russo-Japanese War, the former combatants concluded a secret treaty recognizing Korea as a Japanese sphere of influence. In return, Japan acknowledged a Russian sphere of influence in Outer

Mongolia. Manchuria was to be divided roughly in half, with Japan exercising dominant influence in the south and Russia in the north. Such new and far-reaching cooperation between nations that had recently been at war was made possible, in part, because Russian foreign policy had taken a periodic swing back toward a primarily European focus. Also, both nations were suspicious of the Asian ambitions of the Western European powers and the United States. Finally, the imminent demise of the Chinese empire offered the prospect of enough territory to satisfy both Russian and Japanese imperialists. Russo-Japanese cooperation would be paid for in Chinese coin. Naturally, neither Russia nor Japan consulted their intended victims, nor did they delay implementing their agreement. In 1910 Japan formally annexed Korea. A year later, Outer Mongolian leaders, with the assistance of Russian agents and Russian guns, proclaimed the independence of Outer Mongolia from China. By 1912 Outer Mongolia was, de facto, a Russian protectorate.

There remained the question of Manchuria. With the waning of central authority in China, it seemed inevitable that Russian and Japanese forces, encroaching from opposite directions, would meet—and perhaps clash—at some point in central Manchuria. As it happened, the outbreak of the Great War in 1914 and the subsequent upheavals in Russia intervened, so that when the collision finally came in the 1930s, the point of impact was not in central Manchuria but many hundreds of miles north and west, along the Manchurian–Outer Mongolian frontier.

The second decade of the twentieth century presented extraordinary opportunities for Japanese expansion. The disintegrative end-of-dynasty syndrome in China entered its critical phase in 1911–12 with the onset of revolution, the abdication of the Manchu imperial house, and the establishment of rival successor regimes. Then, just as the "Great Game" in China appeared to be reaching its climax, Europe descended into its great bloodletting of 1914–18, with the result that the German colonial empire in China and the Pacific fell into Japanese hands, while Britain and France, wholly absorbed by the struggle in Europe, faded as East Asian powers. The Russian empire seemed to disintegrate no less dramatically than that of China in the revolutions of 1917 and the subsequent civil war and foreign intervention. In the course of a few years, nearly all of Japan's traditional rivals—with the notable exception of the United States—had been seriously weakened, paralyzed, or liquidated.

These developments emboldened Tokyo's continental ambitions. Japan's Twenty-One Demands, a clumsy attempt in 1915 to make China a vassal state, aroused anti-Japanese nationalist passions in China and fixed the image in the public mind of Japan bullying a helpless China, an image that would bedevil Japan's relations with the West for years to come.

Japan's intervention in Siberia during the Russian Civil War was a more far-reaching and, ultimately, costly failure. Japan sent some 70,000 troops into the

Russian Far East, by far the largest foreign contingent to intervene in the Russian Civil War. This Siberian expedition, which brought Japan little profit and no glory, did bear some fruit—mostly bitter.[1] Japan's involvement prolonged the Russian Civil War, in which some 13 million people perished. It provided little combat experience for the Japanese army but it did initiate some young staff officers, future leaders of the Kwantung Army, into the world of political manipulation, intrigue, and insurgency, which would be put to fateful use later in Manchuria. Japanese troops remained in eastern Siberia until 1922, by which time the Bolsheviks had triumphed throughout Russia and Japanese hopes of acquiring control of the Russian Far East had faded.

The recall of Japan's Siberian expedition in 1922 was the first step in a Soviet-Japanese detente. Three years later, they reached a broad diplomatic settlement providing for the withdrawal of Japanese forces from Northern Sakhalin, the recognition by the Soviet government of certain Japanese commercial interests in Northern Sakhalin and on the Soviet Maritime Coast, and the establishment of formal diplomatic relations between the two nations.[2]

The profound hostility of Japanese authorities toward communism, and the Soviet government's deep-seated suspicions of Imperial Japan's intentions in Northeast Asia, did not disappear. But for the next five years, Soviet-Japanese relations were "proper." The largest issue between them during the 1925–30 period, literally as well as figuratively, was China. And in those years the influence of the China question on Soviet-Japanese relations was not entirely negative.

Both Japan and Russia felt threatened by an upsurge of militant Chinese nationalism, which demanded abrogation of the hated "unequal treaties" and the driving out of all imperialists, be they Western, Soviet, or Japanese. Chinese Nationalist leader Chiang Kai-shek's near extermination of the Chinese Communists during the 1927–28 period led to the rupture of diplomatic relations between Moscow and the Nationalist government in Nanking. The Nationalists then tried to take Peking, the traditional capital. Japanese forces twice moved into the Shantung Peninsula during the 1927–28 period, temporarily blocking Chiang Kai-shek's advance. Moscow did not protest these Japanese actions.

Similarly, Tokyo did not object to a Soviet military action in Manchuria directed against Chinese nationalism. The "Young Marshal," Chang Hsueh-liang, warlord of Manchuria, launched a vigorous anti-Soviet and anti-Communist campaign in 1928, with Chiang Kai-shek's blessings, and in July 1929 seized the Soviet-owned Chinese Eastern Railway (CER) and arrested its Soviet personnel.[3] The Red Army promptly invaded northern and western Manchuria, routed the warlord's poorly equipped troops, and forced him to restore the status quo ante on the

CER, whereupon Soviet forces promptly left Manchuria.[4] The civilian-led Japanese government maintained a benevolent neutrality throughout the affair.

By the late 1920s, however, the winds of political change, of strident nationalism and militarism, were rising in Japan and would grow through the next decade to typhoon strength. At the same time, the "Stalin revolution" would radically transform the USSR economically, politically, and militarily.

Stalin's Industrial Revolution

In 1928 Josef Stalin emerged victorious from the succession struggle of the twenties and promptly put his stamp on Soviet Russia with his policies of forced collectivization of agriculture, rapid industrialization, and ruthless terror. In Stalin's view, collectivization was necessary to bring the agricultural sector under state control and harness it to support his industrial policy. Massive rapid industrialization, he argued, was necessary not only for modernization, but also for survival. The first Five-Year Plan did not emphasize military production, focusing instead on basic industries and industrial infrastructure. But it laid the foundation for the subsequent militarization of the Soviet economy. In a famous speech to factory managers, in which Stalin urged completion of the first Five-Year Plan in four years, he warned,

> It is sometimes asked whether it is not possible to slow down the tempo somewhat, to put a check on the movement. No, comrades, it is not possible! The tempo must not be reduced! On the contrary, we must increase it. . . . To slacken the tempo would mean falling behind. And those who fall behind get beaten. . . . One feature of the history of Old Russia was the continual beatings she suffered because of her backwardness. . . . Now we are fifty or a hundred years behind the advanced countries. We must make good this distance in ten years. Either we do it, or we shall be crushed.[5]

The plan was predicated on short-term peaceful relations and economic cooperation with capitalist states, but it also foresaw ultimate conflict with hostile capitalist forces. The plan was drafted during the golden years of Weimar democracy in Germany and the brief flowering of parliamentarianism in Japan. On the day of its completion, however, the entire capitalist world groaned in the throes of the worst depression in history, fascism was on the march across Eurasia, Japanese armies in Manchuria threatened three thousand miles of the weakly defended Soviet Far Eastern frontier, and Adolf Hitler was thirty days from being appointed Reich chancellor.

When the plan was officially declared completed in December 1932, electric power generation in Soviet Russia had increased 165 percent, coal and oil production by 81 percent and 83 percent, and iron and steel output by 112 percent and 47 percent, respectively. Assessments of the first Five-Year Plan tend to vary according to whether one emphasizes its considerable achievements—gross industrial production more than doubled in four and a quarter years, its staggering human and material costs, or such long-range consequences as the creation of an industrial base that made possible the defeat of Nazi armies in World War II. But even many who were hostile to Soviet goals and who abhorred Stalin's methods paid grudging tribute to this raw industrial achievement.

To many contemporary observers, Soviet economic accomplishments were all the more impressive in contrast to the near paralysis of the capitalist economic order. Conservative political and economic leaders the world over, confused and alarmed by the unprecedented scope of the Great Depression, were genuinely frightened by the implications of the Soviet achievement, both in terms of growing Soviet power and of the potential political impact on their own impoverished working class. It is ironic that the very success of the Five-Year Plan and its attendant propaganda contributed not only to the prestige of the Soviet Union and communism, but also to the rapid growth in many countries of violent, right-wing, anti-Communist movements, pledged to protect society from the Bolshevik menace. This theme is well known to Western readers in the context of German politics and the rise of Nazism. In Japan too, the depression and the perception of the danger of Bolshevism, as well as an upsurge of Chinese nationalism, led to traumatic and ruinous political developments.

The Depression, Ultranationalism, and Militarism in Japan

In 1927 Japan experienced a preview in miniature of the worldwide depression that struck two years later. This was the result of an unsound credit system that led to a chain reaction of bank failures, including the state-related Bank of Taiwan, one of the largest in the country. As credit contracted, many small and medium-sized firms were forced into bankruptcy or taken over by the *zaibatsu*, the giant conglomerates that dominated Japan's economy.[6] Simultaneously, 1927 brought the first of four successive bumper rice crops. The precipitous decline in the market price of rice added to the burden of overtaxed farmers who had already borne much of the cost of Japan's modernization. Thus, two years before the Wall Street crash, Japan was already experiencing hard times—which rapidly worsened.

The depression immediately ruined the silk industry, the second-most-important agricultural product in Japan, as well as her leading export commodity. The year 1930 also saw the largest of the four huge rice harvests. The already-depressed rice market plummeted another 33 percent in four months. By the end of 1931, average farm income had dropped to roughly 50 percent of the already depressed 1929 level. In the autumn of 1931, an early severe frost destroyed most of the rice crop in the northeastern five provinces, bringing famine to that region. Desperation gripped the countryside as rural indebtedness rose rapidly, taxes fell into arrears, and daughters were sold into prostitution.[7]

International trade contracted worldwide in the first phase of the depression and then came almost to a standstill as protectionist tariffs walled off one national economy from another. For resource-poor Japan, which had to buy heavily abroad in order to live and therefore was critically dependent upon a large volume of export trade, this was disastrous. This was further compounded by Japan's rapid population growth, which was sending nearly half a million new workers annually into the labor market.

Premier Hamaguchi Osachi, like most of his contemporaries, was unprepared for the economic crisis. The politically liberal but economically conservative Hamaguchi, who had come to power in July 1929, pledged to a balanced budget and reduced government spending, reversing the heavy military spending and aggressive foreign policy of his predecessor, General Tanaka Giichi. Hamaguchi cut government salaries by 10 percent, reduced military spending, and returned the Japanese yen to the gold standard, which had been abandoned during the First World War. Such measures of fiscal austerity were the standard, orthodox governmental response to economic depression and were being instituted around the world. But they deepened the depression in Japan, as elsewhere. The government's inability to cope with the economic crisis was evident.

Economic ineptitude was compounded by political failings. "The main parties in the Diet dug their own graves," wrote historian Richard Storry. The two scandal-ridden major political parties each were backed by one of the giant, and increasingly resented, *zaibatsu*, Mitsubishi and Mitsui. Bribery at election time was exceeded only by the "gifts" that politicians received from business interests. The party in office was invariably attacked on charges of corruption by the opposition, which, in turn, was open to the same accusations. Diet proceedings sometimes degenerated to rowdy brawls. This offended the Japanese public, which valued decorum and at least the appearance of harmony, further undermining the authority and prestige of the Diet and the concept of parliamentary democracy.[8]

This scandal-plagued political ineptitude, coupled with the government's failure to deal with the depression, might have been enough to sink Japan's fragile young democratic experiment.[9] But the perfect storm that drove Japan to dictatorship, war, and ultimately to ruin was further fueled by ultranationalism, militarism, and international crises.

In its first half-century, Japan's new Imperial Army had been dominated by men of the samurai class. By the 1920s, however, that dominance, and the iron discipline it instilled, was challenged by newcomers. By 1927 some 30 percent of the junior officers were of non-samurai origin, sons of small farmers and tradesmen. From this strata came hundreds of officers sensitive to the economic plight of the little man, officers who, despite the imperial prohibition against the participation of active-duty officers in politics, would be receptive to ultranationalist propaganda, agitation, conspiracy, and even insurrection.[10] The political, economic, and social malaise in Japan, compounded by the growing sense of urgency regarding developments in China and the Soviet Union, seethed mostly beneath the surface throughout the 1920s. This violent energy was released in a series of upheavals beginning in 1930.

The Hamaguchi government aroused the hostility of the Japanese military establishment and nationalists in 1930 by acceding to U.S. pressure at the London Naval Conference to accept a ratio of 10:10:6 for American, British, and Japanese heavy cruisers respectively, despite the vehement opposition of the Navy General Staff, the Supreme War Council, the major opposition party, the Privy Council, countless nationalist societies, and much of the popular press. The iron-willed Hamaguchi succeeded in pushing the London Naval Treaty through ratification—but at great political and personal cost. "Hamaguchi's vigorous stand released such a torrent of reaction from his opponents that in the long run the cause of parliamentary government suffered a disastrous blow—from which it was unable to recover until after Japan's defeat in 1945."[11] Within months of the ratification of the treaty, the admirals who had supported the government's position were forced into retirement by the angry naval establishment. On November 14, 1930, six weeks after ratification, Hamaguchi was shot and mortally wounded by a young "patriot," a member of one of the ultranationalist societies that so despised his policies. This was the first of a series of murderous assaults and coup attempts that prompted an American journalist in Japan to characterize the situation as "government by assassination."[12]

The top military brass ultimately found a simpler way of bringing government fully under its control. An Imperial Ordinance dating back to 1900 stipulated that the army and navy ministers must be active-duty generals and admirals. Either service could thus cause the government to fall simply by withdrawing its service minister and refusing to put forward a replacement. By the late 1930s, this expedient effectively brought civilian government under military control. Before long, generals and admirals themselves headed the government.

One ordinarily associates the notion of military rule—let alone military dictatorship—with very strict discipline. This was certainly what Japan's military rulers imposed on the civilian population. But within the military there was a peculiar and distinctively Japanese aberration, known as *gekokujo*. The word literally means "rule from below"; more broadly, it is the usurpation and exercise of authority by subordinates. *Gekokujo* was at the center of Japan's involvement in the Nomonhan conflict in 1939. It eventually helped lead Japan down the path to the Pacific War.

Gekokujo sprang partly from traditions of extreme deference to people of high social status and advanced age, which tended to place such men in positions of nominal authority regardless of their ability. Real power often flowed elsewhere—below. This tendency was intensified as Japan leaped into the process of modernization, which suddenly put a high premium on specialized knowledge and technical skills, attributes not abundant among the venerable old men nor the scions of the great families who occupied so many positions of authority. This was particularly true in the army. This tradition fostered a strong sense of self-reliance among the elite young staff officers who were designated, or imagined themselves designated, the stewards of such great authority.

These mid-level staff officers came to play a dominant a role in policy making. Many of them attended official military preparatory schools from the age of twelve or thirteen. The next step was the National Military Academy, which graduated about five hundred young lieutenants annually. These young officers then spent several years in regimental duty, after which some fifty of the most promising were selected annually to enter the Army War College. Graduates of the war college were the army's elite, destined for important staff positions, with potential for high command. Their education and training stressed moral/spiritual strength in contrast to material factors and logical, critical thinking. This was partly a legacy of the Sino-Japanese and Russo-Japanese Wars, in which the Japanese army triumphed despite its often-inferior numerical and material strength. Army authorities maintained that moral and spiritual power—the samurai spirit of Bushido—rather than material strength, was the key to victory. However, Japan's experiences in those conflicts would not apply in a struggle against an army qualitatively comparable to its own. Japanese military doctrine and training ignored this fact.

The military academy's curriculum that dealt with concrete strategy and tactics was skewed in a different way, focusing on complex strategies that might be useful to the cadets as division commanders twenty or thirty years later, rather than the tactics appropriate to the command of an infantry platoon or company. Similarly, at the war college the emphasis was on the command of whole armies, rather than medium-sized units. Thus, the army consistently prepared young officers to think in terms of command responsibilities far beyond those appropriate to their rank. This intensified the tendency toward *gekokujo*. The result, according to an expert on the Imperial Army, was a situation in which the influence of these mid-level staff officers constantly grew "until, by the late 1930s, they occupied the controlling positions in the decision-making process. Consequently, the sense of superiority and the dogmatism, irrationality and recklessness bred in them by their military training came to dominate policymaking within the army."[13]

Staff officers in Japan's Kwantung Army stationed in southern Manchuria came to exemplify *gekokujo* in its most extreme form. Manchuria was very attractive to Japan economically. In the 1920s Japan imported from Manchuria huge amounts of soy, bran, flour, and other food stuffs, as well as increasing amounts of coal, iron ore, and timber.

On the night of September 18, 1931, a clique of staff officers of Japan's Kwantung Army staged an explosion on the tracks of the Japanese-controlled South Manchuria Railway near Mukden. They then used this provocation as a pretext to unleash a preplanned invasion of Manchuria. Within a matter of months, Japanese troops occupied all of Manchuria and set up a puppet government—Manchukuo, nominally ruled by "Emperor" Henry Pu Yi—all controlled by the Kwantung Army.

Many accounts have detailed the clandestine plotting among Kwantung Army staff officers, the complicity of senior Army General Staff (AGS) officers in Tokyo, Kwantung Army's night attack on the Chinese army barracks in Mukden and its rapid expansion of the combat zone throughout South Manchuria, and, finally, the government's inability to reverse or even slow Kwantung Army's operations in Manchuria in the face of that army's open defiance and the complicity and/or sympathy of many key AGS and Army Ministry officers. After the Manchuria incident, the term "Kwantung Army" came to be applied in Japanese army circles to any force in the field that ignored central authorities' orders.

That the Manchuria incident was a decisive event in world history is beyond debate. Some historians view it as the start of the Pacific War. This study will focus on the impact of Japan's seizure of Manchuria on Soviet-Japanese relations and the less well-known conflict between those powers.

Deterioration of Soviet-Japanese Relations

Japan's occupation of Manchuria profoundly altered its relations with the Soviet Union. To the north and east, Manchuria shared a long border with the Soviet Far East; to the west lay the Mongolian People's Republic. The Japanese empire had suddenly and violently acquired a three-thousand-mile border with the Soviet empire.

In late 1931 and early 1932, while Japanese military operations were under way in Manchuria, Stalin, aware of his military weakness in the Far East, adopted a policy of strict neutrality. Not only was there no Soviet military intervention, but also the Red Army even refrained from mounting a show of force along the border. Moscow also refused to participate in the League of Nations' Lytton Commission, which investigated the conflict and barred its members from crossing Soviet territory en route to Manchuria. Soviet appeasement of Japan went further. In December 1931 Foreign Minister Maksim Litvinov proposed a nonaggression pact to the Japanese ambassador, which was rejected by Tokyo. Sensing Russian timidity, the Japanese demanded and obtained the right to have their troops transported across Manchuria on military missions by the Soviet-owned Chinese Eastern Railway. Moscow denied use of the CER to Chinese forces to avoid being accused by Japan of a breach of neutrality. Acquiescing to the Japanese demand not only vitiated Soviet "neutrality," but it also facilitated the very invasion that increasingly imperiled Soviet security. As a final indignity, the Japanese refused to pay for their use of the railroad and soon owed millions of rubles to the CER.[14] Both the balance of power in East Asia and the perception of that balance had shifted dramatically, to the disadvantage of the USSR.

By mid-1932 Japan had overcome all organized military resistance in Manchuria. The army was blooded but not exhausted. To some Japanese, it seemed that the time had come to deal decisively with the Russian menace while the Soviet Far East was still relatively weak. At a roundtable discussion, prominent Imperial Army generals unanimously supported a quick preventive war against the Soviet Union. This sensational news was reported in the Japanese press.[15] It was not just empty talk. Japan's war minister, General Araki Sadao, enthusiastically supported the idea. Araki's service in Siberia during the Russian Civil War had led him to detest Bolshevism. Araki and several like-minded senior officers in the AGS and War Ministry spoke openly of the inevitability and desirability of war with the Soviet Union. This talk also appeared in the Japanese press and sparked a war scare. The Soviet ambassador to Japan expressed his alarm in a series of urgent cables to Moscow.[16] The U.S. and British ambassadors informed their governments of the apparent war danger.[17] The war scare was reported in newspapers from Mukden to Moscow to Milwaukee. The Araki clique's advocacy of immediate war against the Soviet Union sparked a full-scale—and secret—policy debate within AGS. Most of the senior staff officers vigorously opposed the idea, and it was—secretly—rejected in May 1933.[18] But the war scare lingered in public discussion for another year. Soviet attempts to improve relations with Japan were rebuffed by Tokyo. As the Japanese chargé d'affaires in Moscow put it to the British ambassador in November 1932, "Soviet-Japanese relations are good, but Japanese-Soviet relations are not so good."[19]

There are good reasons why the term "ill-defined" is so often applied to the three-thousand-mile border that separated the rivals in the 1930s. As recently as the 1850s, Korea, Manchuria, the Maritime Province, Inner and Outer Mongolia, and that vast expanse of eastern Siberia forming the northern watershed of the Amur

River were all parts of the "Middle Kingdom," either part of the Chinese empire proper or tributary states recognizing the suzerainty of Peking. Boundaries between these entities were not always precise, as most were not international borders. That changed in 1858–60, when China was forced to cede the Maritime Province and trans-Baikal Siberia to Russia. The new Russo-Chinese border was mostly riverine, following the Amur River eastward to its confluence with the Ussuri, thence south along the Ussuri/Sungacha system to Lake Hanka and beyond, to a point where the boundaries of Korea, Manchuria, and the Russian Maritime Province meet.

The new boundaries, however, were ambiguous. The Chinese border was said to be the southern and western banks of the rivers, while the northern and eastern banks were the Russian border. This had the effect of making the rivers themselves neutral territory and said nothing about the sovereignty of the hundreds of islands within the river systems. At the western and southern extremities of the new border there were no convenient rivers to use as boundaries. Red lines were drawn on the negotiators' often-inaccurate maps, across desert wastes, over obscure mountain ridgelines, and through swamps. On the basis of these maps, wooden boundary markers were erected. However, some of the map markings were unclear and the elements eroded many of the boundary markers. In some remote areas no boundary markers were erected at all.[20] Thus, when Japan seized Manchuria from China in 1931, the international boundary was subject to dispute in many places.

Japan suggested several times to the Soviet Union that they create a commission to establish precise international boundaries. Moscow rebuffed these offers, replying, not without sarcasm, that the border problems could be overcome most efficaciously if the Japanese only would return to Japan.[21] Under these circumstances, it is hardly surprising that border disputes arose. Alleged border violations reported by one side or the other for the period 1932 to 1939 number well over one thousand, ranging from low comedy (charges that Soviet border guards stole fish from the lines of Manchukuoan fishermen) to bloody conflicts. Major military clashes that occurred in the summers of 1937, 1938, and especially 1939 are major foci of this book.

According to Japanese military sources, while Kwantung Army was mopping up the last armed resistance in Manchuria, the Soviet Union began bolstering its defenses in the Far East. By the time Japanese forces turned their attention to the international boundary, the Soviets had made substantial progress in strengthening their defenses. These measures included double-tracking the Trans-Siberian Railway, constructing large-scale border fortifications, increasing the number of border garrison units from two or three in 1932 to twenty in 1934, and relocating border-area inhabitants.[22]

In response, the Japanese began a major program of border fortification. In addition, new railroad lines were constructed in Manchuria, generally following military

YEAR	Soviet Forces in the Far East				Japanese Forces in Manchuria			
	Military manpower	Infantry divisions	Aircraft	Tanks	Military manpower	Infantry divisions	Aircraft	Tanks
1931	?	6	?	?	65,000	1	?	?
1932	100,000	7	160	250	94,000	4	100	50
1933	?	8	300	300	114,000	3	130	100
1934	230,000	11	500	650	144,000	3	130	120
1935	240,000	14	950	850	164,000	3	220	150
1936	300,000	16	1,200	1,200	194,000	3	230	150
1937	370,000	20	1,560	1,500	200,000	5	250	150
1938	450,000	24	2,000	1,900	220,000	7	340	170
1939	570,000	30	2,500	2,200	270,000	9	560	200

rather than economic criteria. This was one aspect of a Japanese program to secure and develop Manchuria as an integral part of the empire. Production of coal and ferrous metals in Manchuria doubled between 1931 and 1939 as Manchuria's mineral wealth was mobilized to feed the industries of the home islands. In 1936 the Japanese government announced the goal of resettling one million Japanese farming families (approximately five million people) in Manchuria over a twenty-year period, a plan to "nipponize" Manchuria, sponsored by the Kwantung Army and the War Ministry.

Moscow perceived the Japanese presence in Manchuria as a threat that necessitated the strengthening of its Far Eastern army. The Japanese interpreted the increase of Soviet forces in the region as a threat warranting the further strengthening of Japanese forces in Manchuria, which, in turn, resulted in redoubled efforts to reinforce the Red Army in the Far East, and so forth. The resulting increase in the armed forces of both powers in that region is illustrated in the preceding chart.[23]

These figures, however, create a false impression of Soviet preponderance. Geography strongly favored Japan. Japanese forces in Manchuria could be reinforced quickly and securely from the homeland and, after 1937, from Japanese armies in Northern China. Conversely, Soviet Far Eastern forces were spread over an immense area, 2.4 million square miles, two-thirds the size of the continental United States. And because of the remoteness of the Soviet Far East from the industrial and population centers of European Russia, Moscow had to make its Far Eastern forces as self-sufficient as possible. Even double tracked, the Trans-Siberian Railway was highly vulnerable in the event of war with Japan, because long stretches of its track ran so close to the Manchurian frontier that the Japanese easily might have cut it.[24]

The Japanese probably enjoyed an overall strategic advantage vis-à-vis the USSR until 1937. In July of that year, however, with Japan's invasion of China, the military balance began to shift, a fact that many Japanese military leaders, especially in Kwantung Army, failed or refused to recognize. But this carries the narrative a bit too far. Before considering the impact of the China War on Soviet-Japanese relations, there are several other related pieces of this jigsaw puzzle that must be put in place.

CHAPTER 2

THE GLOBAL CONTEXT

Winston Churchill's famous characterization of Russia as a riddle wrapped in a mystery inside an enigma aptly describes Soviet foreign policy in the 1930s. Josef Stalin's diplomacy has been portrayed variously as a pursuit of world revolution, a defense of collective security, an exercise in balance-of-power politics aimed mainly at avoiding war, and a malevolent instigation of war. Stalin has been cast as a Russian nationalist, an international revolutionary, and a paranoid megalomaniac. Perhaps one reason why Stalin's diplomacy evokes so much controversy and confusion is the common practice of considering Moscow's European and Far Eastern policies as distinct, almost unrelated, entities. This chapter will examine the development of Soviet foreign policy as a unified whole.

The Emerging Fascist Threat and the Popular Front/United Front

Soviet Russia's relations with the other major powers were inherently hostile. From the outset, foreign military intervention in the Russian Civil War was matched by Vladimir Lenin and Leon Trotsky's shared conviction that for the revolution to survive in Russia, it had to spread to the West. After the foreign armies withdrew from Russia, having failed to oust the Bolsheviks, and Moscow's early attempts to spread revolution to the West—by example, by subversion, and by war—also failed, the two camps gradually worked out a modus vivendi. But the underlying antagonism remained. Soviet relations with the capitalist world, particularly the major powers, in the 1920s and early 1930s generally ranged from surly to acrimonious.[1]

This was reflected in the policies that Moscow imposed on foreign Communist parties, which were ordered to vigorously oppose their respective regimes, be they fascist dictatorship, monarchy, or bourgeois democracy. The principal instrument by which the Soviet Union controlled foreign Communist parties was the Communist International, or Comintern.[2] Soviet authorities claimed that, although the Comintern was headquartered in Moscow, it was not controlled by the Soviet government. This was a fiction. The Communist Party of the Soviet

Union (CPSU), the only ruling Communist party, was absolutely dominant in the Comintern from the outset.[3]

Long before the selective opening of Soviet archives in the 1990s, a lot could be learned about Soviet foreign policy priorities by studying the Comintern's instructions to foreign Communist parties. These were conveyed not only in secret communications and closed and open meetings of the Comintern leadership in Moscow, but also in Comintern publications, widely distributed in many languages to the party faithful worldwide. The most ubiquitous of these was the Comintern's news weekly, *International Press Correspondence* (*Inprecor*), renamed *World News and Views* in 1938.

Through the 1920s and into the early 1930s, week after week, *Inprecor* spouted the orthodox Bolshevik line that the Communists' main enemies were their competitors for proletarian and leftist support—trade unionists and socialists. This began to change with the rise of militant, stridently anti-Communist parties and regimes on Soviet Russia's flanks. The winter of 1932–33 brought both the completion of Japan's conquest of Manchuria and the rise of the Nazi Party to power in Germany. The advent of Manchukuo and the Third Reich near the eastern and western frontiers of the USSR posed threats that Stalin could not ignore. Moscow's response to these threats resulted in a reversal of basic Comintern and Soviet policies. In late 1932 Moscow reestablished diplomatic relations with the government of Chiang Kai-shek, a man who, since his coup of 1927, had been reviled by *Inprecor* as the archenemy of international Communism. Also in 1932 the Soviet Union concluded five nonaggression treaties: with France, Poland, Finland, Estonia, and Latvia. In November 1933 Moscow established diplomatic relations with Washington, partly to create the impression of Soviet-American solidarity against possible Japanese aggression. A year later the Soviets joined the League of Nations, which they had denounced for years as the "league of imperialists." At the same time, Moscow ended the vehement campaign against socialism, which had been denounced as "social fascism" for a decade. Yet, despite these operational shifts, symbolized by Foreign Minister Maksim Litvinov's oratory at Geneva, Stalin's goals remained fundamentally unchanged. In 1935, as in 1925, his paramount objective was to prevent the formation of a grand capitalist alliance directed against the Soviet Union.

The Kremlin sought to avoid war with any powerful state, particularly if it involved the threat of combat on Soviet soil. Other objectives included the weakening of the capitalist powers (particularly by encouraging revolution in their colonial empires), and the fostering of conflict among the capitalist states. What seems to have changed in the transitional period of 1932–34 was Stalin's perception of the immediacy of the international dangers threatening his regime and the means required to achieve the goals that had been pursued since coming to power.

As the grim decade of the 1930s continued to unfold, the international situation confronting the Soviet Union grew increasingly menacing. The Japanese conquest of Manchuria and the Nazi triumph in Germany were followed by disturbing developments in France. On February 6, 1934, a new coalition government of leftist parties enjoying a strong parliamentary majority and headed by Edouard Daladier, was overthrown by the violent rioting of several militant groups of the extreme right. Although the French Republic itself may not have been in immediate danger, the events of February 6 had important repercussions. Daladier's leftist coalition was replaced by a conservative "National Government" headed by a former president of the republic, Gaston Doumergue. Moderate and leftist elements perceived a threat, partly real, partly chimerical, of a fascist coup in France.[4] Militant fascism appeared to be on the march. Its unchecked spread threatened to bring into being that situation most dreaded in the Kremlin: a unified Europe—and Japan—joined in an aggressive anti-Communist alliance. Such an alliance spelled doom for Stalin and the Soviet Union. Consequently, international affairs were accorded a new priority in Moscow. The top priority was to check the spread of fascism. This is the context in which Moscow's new popular front/united front policy should be understood.

The popular front/united front policy often is represented as a Soviet attempt to forge a powerful antifascist bloc, or even an antifascist military alliance, with itself at the head. Soviet leaders and historians and their post-Soviet successors have promoted this view. However, Soviet actions contradict that conclusion. Instead, they seem to suggest that Soviet objectives were of a more defensive character. The same can be said of the Franco-Soviet mutual assistance pact of 1935. Its greatest value to Moscow was not its faint promise of joint French-Soviet military action against a German threat, but that it placed an obstacle in the path of a future Franco-German rapprochement. Despite Soviet and Comintern rhetoric of the popular front era, this interpretation of Soviet policy is supported by the instructions passed on from Moscow to the Communist parties of foreign states.

The popular front policy in its full and mature form was officially articulated at the Seventh Congress of the Communist International in Moscow, July–August 1935. The records of that meeting illuminate the objectives of the popular front/united front.[5] Communist support for anticolonial liberation, which had been a central dogma of the Bolshevik Party since 1917, was played down. As a gesture to Britain, where Soviet anticolonialism rubbed a particularly raw nerve, no delegates from India were invited. Instead, the congress focused on cooperation with the "healthy" political elements of the center and left in opposition to fascism.

If Stalin was really intent upon forging a firm antifascist bloc, and if he contemplated the possibility of joint military action against "international fascism," he should have wanted the Western democracies to be militarily strong and prepared for war. However, the instructions given to the European Communist parties in 1935 indicate that Stalin was not overly concerned about the bourgeois democracies' military preparedness. Although he did order the French Communists to drop their virulent antimilitarist and antinational defense campaign,[6] he did not instruct them to support fully their government's rearmament and defense plans. Maurice Thorez, head of the French Communist Party, declared at the Comintern congress that "we continue to fight in the name of the working class of France against the enslavement of the people, and against the return to the two-year term of military service."[7] Yet the instructions to the French Communists were generous when compared to those given to other European Communists. The unanimous voice of international Communism decreed that "the Communist Parties of all capitalist countries must fight against military expenditures . . . against militarization measures taken by capitalist governments, especially the militarization of youth."[8]

Even after the election of a popular front coalition government in France in May 1936, the French Communist Party did not come out wholeheartedly in favor of a strong program of rearmament and national defense. In fact, as late as the spring of 1939, the Comintern news weekly was still strongly denouncing Western military measures, such as Neville Chamberlain's proposal for peacetime conscription.[9]

This lack of solicitude on Stalin's part toward the military preparedness of the West gives credence to a darker interpretation: that Stalin was actively conspiring to involve the West and the Axis in war, and like a shrewd racetrack handicapper, he was inhibiting Western rearmament vis-à-vis the still-weak Wehrmacht so as to promote a more evenly matched and exhausting struggle. There can be little doubt that such an outcome would have been much to Stalin's liking. Indeed, it is arguable that any thoughtful strategist in charge of Soviet foreign policy, confronted with that array of powerful capitalist states, *should* have sought to incite conflict between the bourgeois-democratic capitalists and the fascist-militarist capitalists. But to suppose, as some have,[10] that for five, or fifteen, years Stalin had been working unwaveringly toward that one goal underestimates the flexibility of Stalin's diplomacy. The mutual destruction of the Western democratic regimes and the Axis regimes would have been the ideal, maximum achievement of Soviet policy, but the minimum vital task was to thwart a broad capitalist anti-Bolshevik crusade, or, perhaps only slightly less nightmarish to Stalin, a coordinated German-Japanese assault. It is reasonable to assume—although it must remain an assumption—that Soviet energies were divided between these maximum and minimum programs as one would expect, between that which one would hope to achieve and that which one must have for survival.

Another insight that can be gleaned from the 1935 Comintern congress is Stalin's perception of the relative acuteness of the threats posed by Germany and Japan. The outlawed German Communist Party was not called upon to sabotage the Nazi regime nor to attempt to organize armed resistance, but was instructed to "work inside the fascist mass organizations" to achieve higher wages and more decent working conditions for the laboring masses.[11] Almost all speeches at the congress bespoke a fervent desire for peace. There was no talk of a preventive war against Adolf Hitler. In marked contrast, the one party at the congress that received really belligerent orders and that evinced a desire to come to blows with the enemy of the international proletariat was the Chinese Communist Party. The CCP was told to fight the Japanese aggressors with every means at its disposal.[12] The Chinese delegate, Wang Ming, spoke emotionally of "the earnest desire of the Chinese people to take up arms against the Japanese oppressors."[13]

Yet, during that very period, July–August, 1935, the Chinese Communists were in the last stage of the exhausting "Long March" and were fighting for their very existence against the anti-Communist campaign of Chiang Kai-shek's Nationalist Army. Nonetheless, the Chinese Communists were instructed to embrace their would-be exterminator, Chiang, and to make common cause with him against Japan. Such a strategy, if successful, would have the effect of inciting conflict between China and Japan and of distracting General Araki Sadao and his clique from their anti-Soviet course. The utility of this Moscow-dictated popular front policy for the interests of the Chinese revolution was much more problematic, and it was accepted by the CCP only grudgingly and after much hesitation.[14] The priorities established at the 1935 Comintern congress suggest that the Far East was in the forefront of Stalin's mind as a danger area and that the popular front/united front policy was conceived and implemented at a time when Japan was perceived as the most immediate threat.

If the Seventh Comintern Congress inaugurated the popular front/united front policy, the Spanish Civil War enshrined it in the hearts and minds of Western liberals. The Spanish generals' insurrection against the popular front government in Madrid, and the aid their insurrection immediately received from Benito Mussolini and Hitler, is a well-documented tale. Soon after Italian and German aid was extended to the rebels, the Soviet Union began supplying the Republican forces with war materiel. While Soviet aid to Spain never reached the scale of that provided by Italy and Germany, it was a substantial contribution without which Republican opposition quickly would have been overcome.

Why did Stalin send large numbers of Soviet tanks, planes, guns, and "volunteers" to fight in Spain? One can discount the Soviet contention that they were motivated primarily by the altruistic desire to help defend the freedom-loving people of the Spanish Republic. Conversely, it seems unlikely that Stalin seriously contemplated the establishment of a Soviet republic in Spain at that time. Whatever benefits might have accrued from a Soviet satellite in agrarian Iberia would have been greatly outweighed by the hostility such an enterprise would have engendered in France and Britain. There are a number of plausible explanations for Stalin's substantial military aid to the Spanish Republican forces. To have refrained from assisting the socialist-oriented Republic against the assault of the fascist-supported Nationalists would have given credence to the accusations of the exiled Trotsky and his adherents that Stalin had turned his back on the international proletarian revolution. If the Madrid government—the first popular front government elected anywhere—were quickly and easily subdued by the very forces the popular front had been designed to combat, it might be taken symbolically and psychologically as the triumph of fascism over the whole popular front idea. As the conflict grew, the struggles and exploits of the Republicans captured the imagination and fired the spirit of millions of Western liberals who earlier had been opposed only passively to the regimes of Hitler and Mussolini. The Spanish Civil War has been credited by some with the conversion of the British Labour Party from pacifism in 1936 to militant antifascism by 1939.[15] The protracted combat in Spain tied down a considerable amount of Italo-German military resources in a remote corner of Europe, and, to that extent, provided the Soviet Union with an added measure of military security at a fairly cheap price.

These factors alone were probably sufficient justification for Stalin's Spanish policy. But the evidence suggests that he was playing for higher stakes. By buttressing the Republican forces, Stalin fostered a prolonged and extensive Italo-German military presence in Spain, which in turn threatened France's previously secure Pyrenean frontier. The Communist-controlled press hammered away week after week at the theme of the peril to France in Spain. It is a reasonable inference that Stalin hoped this would arouse the French government to take a firmer stand against the rapidly rearming Germany. This then would cause Hitler to direct his attention westward, rather than toward the Soviet borders. It even might lead to a war on the westernmost extremity of Eurasia between the fascist powers and the democracies, a conflict from which the Soviet Union might abstain. However, as in the analysis of the popular front policy in general, it would be a mistake to conclude that the instigation of an intracapitalist war was the sole raison d'être of Stalin's Spanish policy. Long before the fall of Madrid in February 1939, it became clear that France would not be roused to resist Mussolini and Hitler in Spain. Despite that, Stalin was well served by his Spanish policy. In view of General Francisco Franco's stubborn independence after 1939 and Spain's neutrality in the Second World War, it might not be too much to say that Stalin derived more profit from the losing cause of the Republic than did Mussolini and Hitler from Franco's victory.

As a complement to the strategy in Spain, Soviet policy in East Asia was, in Adam Ulam's succinct appraisal, "a masterful blend of appeasement, sufficient firmness to impress Japan that a war would be extremely costly and risky, and encouragement of the Chiang Kai-shek regime to resist further Japanese encroachments and not to reach a modus vivendi with Japan."[16]

Soviet appeasement of Japan, especially in the years 1931–35, was discussed in the preceding chapter. Soviet firmness toward Japan began cautiously in the mid-1930s with the Soviet military buildup and reached its peak at the Battles of Changkufeng and Nomonhan, which will be treated in detail in subsequent chapters. The Soviet policy of playing off China against Japan, introduced earlier, can be pursued a bit further here.

The declarations and resolutions of the Seventh Comintern Congress suggest that Moscow perceived a clear and present Japanese threat to the Soviet Far East. The instructions to the Chinese Communist Party also illustrate Stalin's hope of deflecting the Japanese army away from the Soviet borders and toward China.[17] The greatest obstacle to the achievement of that goal was Chiang Kai-shek, who at that time was pursuing a policy of temporary accommodation with Japan in order to consolidate his control in the interior and destroy his rivals, notably the Chinese Communists.

The factors that brought Chiang to completely reverse his policies between 1935 and 1937 are still shrouded in mystery. The voluminous Communist propaganda denouncing Chiang's "collaboration" with the Japanese imperialists and urging a Chinese popular front against Japan, while useful in revealing the main thrust of Soviet policy, was hardly influential with Chiang. There is evidence to suggest that the Chinese Communists did exercise considerable influence with the "Young Marshal," Chang Hsueh-liang (son of the assassinated Chang Tso-lin, and former warlord of Manchuria), and with his officers, and that this influence was instrumental in precipitating the Xian incident.[18] In December 1936 Chiang Kai-shek, visiting the northern city of Xian, was incarcerated by the Young Marshal, creating a political crisis. The ensuing negotiations between Chiang and representatives of his Nationalist government, the Communists, the Young Marshal, and several other warlords, remain shrouded in mystery and provoke controversy among scholars to this day. By most accounts, the imprisoned generalissimo is believed to have pledged to end the civil war against the Communists and adopt a hard line against the Japanese.

At the same time, the Soviet government was engaged in negotiations with Chiang's Nationalist government in Nanking for a treaty that would ally China with the USSR in opposition to Japan. The main drift of these negotiations can be glimpsed from a conversation between the United States chargé d'affaires in Moscow and the Chinese ambassador. The Chinese diplomat told his American colleague that D. V. Bogomolov, the Soviet ambassador to Nanking, "had been free in making oral assurances of Soviet readiness to assist China in case of war with Japan. . . . Bogomolov and influential groups in China friendly to the Soviet Union continued during the spring and summer of 1937 to endeavor to make the Chinese Government believe that if it would undertake to offer armed resistance to Japan it could confidently expect the armed support of the Soviet Union."[19]

During the course of the concurrent Chinese Communist and Soviet Russian negotiations with the Nationalist government in Nanking, there occurred the Marco Polo Bridge incident of July 7, 1937, which soon grew into a full-scale Sino-Japanese War. Naturally this overcame any lingering reservations in Nanking, and in rapid succession Chiang agreed to a united front treaty of friendship and nonaggression with the USSR (August 21) and a popular front alliance with the Chinese Communists (September 22). However, simultaneous with these negotiations in China, and immediately prior to the Marco Polo Bridge incident, a sharp border clash occurred between Soviet and Japanese forces on the Amur River. This little-known conflict adds to our understanding of the international context in which the China War began.

The Amur River Incident

By the end of 1936, the Soviet Far Eastern Army had grown to sixteen infantry divisions supported by 1,200 tanks and an equal number of aircraft. Although this force had to cover an immense territory, it was, nonetheless, a formidable array. As the year 1937 wore on, however, it became evident that all was not well with the Red Army. The great purge that Stalin had begun two years earlier was growing in scope and ferocity and was spreading to the armed forces. On June 11, 1937, *Pravda* announced the startling news that Marshal Mikhail Tukhachevsky, the guiding spirit behind the modernized Red Army, together with seven other high-ranking generals, had been found guilty, in secret trial, of "habitual and base betrayal of military secrets to a certain hostile fascist power, and working as spies to accomplish the downfall of the Soviet state and to restore capitalism." On the following day it was revealed that the eight men had been shot. These eight generals had held some of the most important posts in the armed forces. Their execution implied that the security of the Red Army—in more ways than one—was gravely compromised. In the next two years, Stalinist purges, also known as the Great Terror, wrought havoc throughout the Soviet armed forces.

Of the five marshals of the Red Army, three were shot, as were all eleven deputy commissars for defense. Seventy-five of the eighty members of the Military Collegium perished. Every military district commander was liquidated, as were the heads of the Army Political Administration and the Frunze Military Academy. Of the fifteen army commanders, only two survived. Fifty-seven out of eighty-five corps commanders were shot, as were 110 of the 195 division commanders. At the brigade level, only 220 of the 406 colonels survived. In the Soviet Far Eastern forces the attrition rate was even higher, with 80 percent of the staff being removed in one way or another. According to some sources, between one-fourth and one-third of the entire officer corps was executed, imprisoned, or discharged within a period of eighteen months.[20]

The purge led many outside observers to believe that the Red Army had been severely, and perhaps mortally, wounded. As early as June 28, 1937, Major General Homma Masaharu of the Japanese AGS, just back from a trip to Moscow, concluded in a report published in an Osaka newspaper that the recent executions in its high command were threatening the Red Army with disintegration and, therefore, it need no longer be considered a threat to Japan.[21] Only two days after the publication of this analysis, there occurred the most serious Soviet-Japanese border fighting up to that time.

On June 30, 1937, Japanese forces fired on three Soviet gunboats in the Amur River, between Manchuria and the USSR, sinking one, damaging the others, and causing considerable loss of life. There is still debate over who fired the first shots, but the significance of this clash and its portents for subsequent Soviet-Japanese relations are clear.

The Russo-Chinese Treaties of Aigun and Peking (1858, 1860) dealt vaguely with the technical aspects of the river boundaries. However, in accordance with a common international practice known as the thalweg doctrine, the median line of the river's principal navigable channel was taken as the boundary, with the sovereignty of islands determined on the basis of their relation to the main channel. Islands north of the Amur's main channel were considered Russian, while those south of the main channel belonged to China. There seem to have been no serious disputes over the status of these hundreds of mostly small river islands before 1931.

When Japanese troops replaced Chinese along the southern bank of the Amur, tension increased along the great waterway whose Chinese name means "black dragon." One of the principal causes of the tension was of natural rather than political origin, because in the seventy-five years since the Treaties of Aigun and Peking, the main channel of the Amur River had shifted in several areas as a result of storms, floods, and other natural causes. Such phenomena caused political problems. When, for example, the main channel of the river that had run along the southern shore of an island shifted and began to pass the island on its northern shore instead, the sovereignty of the island might be called into question. Furthermore, the northern channel, which previously had been an internal waterway of the nation possessing the northern shore, now might be considered an international waterway open to free navigation.

Just such a case arose among a group of small islands some seventy miles southeast of the Soviet city of Blagoveshchensk. There, to the chagrin of Soviet authorities, the main channel had shifted from the southern to the northern side of the islands. The Soviets argued that the shift of the main channel was transitory and did not affect the sovereignty of the islands. They constructed ferroconcrete barriers in the northern channel, closing it to navigation, in keeping with their interpretation of the international boundary.[22] In the spring of 1937, ice floes from the thaw of the Amur carried away some of the barriers the Soviets had erected. Seizing upon this opportunity, on May 31 several vessels of the Manchukuoan River Defense Flotilla steamed through the northern channel in the vicinity of the largest (3.5 by 5 miles) of the disputed islands, called Kanchatzu Island by the Manchurians, Bolshoi Island by the Russians. This feat was given wide publicity throughout the Manchukuoan press. The Soviet side did not resist this "forcing" of the northern channel, but on June 19 a detachment of some twenty Soviet soldiers occupied Kanchatzu Island, chasing away some Manchurians who had been panning for gold. The next day, Manchukuoan police and soldiers tried to come ashore to investigate but were driven off by Soviet gunfire. On June 22 more Soviet troops arrived and were seen digging defensive positions. A squadron of Soviet gunboats appeared in the area.[23]

Local Japanese forces sent a report to Kwantung Army headquarters of what they viewed as a Soviet invasion of Manchukuo. On June 22 the Army General Staff in Tokyo received the news and seemed to take a strong stand. AGS sent the following message to the Kwantung Army chief of staff, General Tojo Hideki (who would become Japan's wartime leader from 1941 to 1944): "If territory clearly belonging to Manchukuo has been seized illegally by Soviet troops, we believe that the effects upon our future operations could be serious; therefore, you are instructed to take appropriate steps to restore the previous situation."[24] Kwantung Army thereupon dispatched elements of the 49th Infantry Regiment (1st Division) to the vicinity of the trouble, with orders to drive the Soviet troops from the disputed island. At the same time, a stiff diplomatic protest was sent to the Soviet consul in Harbin and the foreign ministry in Moscow.

It was hotheaded young officers of the 1st Division who had led the notorious Tokyo Army mutiny of February 26, 1936, a bloody attempted coup d'état that had strong ties to right-wing anti-Soviet circles in Japan. In the aftermath of the abortive coup, the proud 1st Division was posted (exiled) to Manchukuo, where it had served uneventfully for more than a year. Now suddenly it was again poised for action, ready to strike a blow against the hated Bolsheviks.

In this highly charged atmosphere, events moved rapidly. In Tokyo on June 28, a tense conference was held at AGS. Faced with the possibility of large-scale combat in Northern Manchukuo, the General Staff reversed its earlier decision, concluding that, "the problem of these islands located so remotely did not warrant risking a major commitment of the national strength." ASG decided, instead, to try to resolve the dispute through diplomatic channels. Orders were sent to Kwantung Army headquarters canceling the earlier sanctioned attack by the 1st Division.[25]

On June 28 in Moscow, when Japan's ambassador, Shigemitsu Mamoru, met with Deputy Foreign Minister Boris Stomonyakov, the two diplomats stated their governments' respective positions. The next day, however, in a meeting between Shigemitsu and Litvinov, the foreign commissar took a surprisingly conciliatory position. While maintaining that the islands were indeed Soviet territory, he stated that, "*apart from the matter of principles,* the USSR has no objection to a withdrawal from the disputed points; hence the Japanese troops should pull out also" (italics added).[26] This was a more forthcoming response than the Japanese might have expected, because previous Soviet practice had been to refuse any compromise concerning the sovereignty of Soviet territory. Did this apparent concession by Litvinov derive from Soviet doubts as to the validity of their case, or their ability to back it up with force? The latter seems more likely, with the purge about to annihilate Red Army leadership. In any case, on the next day, June 30, before word of the talks in Moscow reached the scene of the dispute, fighting erupted.

On June 30 resentment and frustration was intense at Kwantung Army headquarters and in the 1st Division. Ever since the order from AGS canceling the imminent counterattack planned by the 1st Division, "a sense of humiliation knifed through Kwantung Army, which felt that it had suffered a loss of prestige in its command prerogatives toward its subordinate units."[27] On the afternoon of the June 30, three small Soviet gunboats[28] steamed into the southern channel between the disputed islands and the Manchurian shore. The Soviets considered this the main channel of the river, hence an international waterway, while the Japanese maintained that it was an internal waterway of Manchukuo. The Soviet show of force in the contested waterway infuriated the Japanese troops on the southern shore, who were smarting under what they considered the unjustified constraint imposed by AGS. Despite the cautionary instructions from Tokyo, the local units would not be restrained. Employing rapid-fire 37-mm artillery, a battery of the 1st Division's 49th Infantry Regiment opened fire on the Soviet gunboats, sinking one, driving a second ashore on a shoal, and forcing the third to retire from the scene. Thirty-seven

Soviet sailors were killed in the attack, including several survivors of the sunken vessel who, while swimming for the northern shore, were machine gunned by Japanese troops on the opposite bank.[29]

News of the Japanese attack reached Moscow quickly and the Soviet government lodged a protest with the Japanese. What is more significant, however, is that there was no immediate Soviet retaliation. In fact, the Litvinov-Shigemitsu talks went on without interruption. Just two days after the sinking, on July 2, Litvinov agreed to a Soviet withdrawal from the disputed island on the understanding that the Japanese forces too would be withdrawn from the immediate vicinity.[30] On July 4 Soviet troops evacuated the island. Moscow seemed anxious to avoid further trouble and let the matter drop, even after Manchukuoan troops occupied Kanchatzu Island on July 6.[31] The issue was settled; Kanchatzu was, de facto, a Manchukuoan possession.

Two historically significant questions arise from this Amur River incident: Why did the USSR act so boldly in blocking the northern channel and occupying the contested island? Why did Moscow then back down so abjectly when the Japanese used force? The islands themselves had no obvious value; the largest of the group, Kanchatzu, had only one permanent inhabitant, a Manchurian lighthouse keeper. However, the principle involved in determining the islands' sovereignty, the principle to which Litvinov referred on June 29, was important to the Soviets. For if Moscow conceded that the natural shift of the main channel there created a new international boundary, that same principle would be applicable elsewhere. And several hundred miles downstream on the Amur, that principle could have had more serious consequences.

Heihsiatzu Island, the most strategically important of the Amur islands, is situated at the juncture of the Amur and Ussuri Rivers and screens Khabarovsk from Manchuria. Here too, the main channel had shifted from south to north of the island.[32] Khabarovsk was the second largest city in the Soviet Far East and the administrative center of the Far Eastern Army. If the channel north and east of Heihsiatzu Island were recognized as the boundary, Japanese naval vessels would be within their rights to steam right up to the city's docks and Japanese artillery on the island would have the ability to fire at point-blank range into the city. This would have been strategically intolerable for the Soviets; hence their insistence on the principle at Kanchatzu. The Japanese, for their part, could claim with some justice that for the Soviets to hold an island on one side of the actual main channel and the mainland on the opposite side of that channel would enable them effectively to dominate navigation of the river, in violation of the spirit and letter of the 1858 and 1860 treaties between Russia and China.[33]

This does not account for the mild Soviet reaction to the sinking of June 30 and the Japanese occupation of Kanchatzu Island on July 6. The Soviet response—or lack of response—to these challenges was probably dictated by two factors. The first was Moscow's sense of military vulnerability, intensified by the purge that had just begun to convulse the leadership of the Red Army. In spite of that, it is unusual for the Kremlin to have allowed such a flagrant and well-publicized challenge to pass without response or retaliation of some sort. The response need not have been immediate. Nearly three weeks elapsed between the "forcing" of the northern channel by the Manchukuoan River Defense Flotilla and the Soviet occupation of Kanchatzu. But on the very next day after the Japanese occupied Kanchatzu, momentous events occurred hundreds of miles away, on the outskirts of Peking (Beijing). There, on July 7, the Marco Polo Bridge incident erupted, which, within a few weeks, was to expand into a full-scale Sino-Japanese war in all but name. But who, on July 8, could be sure what direction those events would take? With its excellent intelligence service, Moscow knew there were powerful elements in both Nanking and Tokyo striving to avert a major Sino-Japanese conflict. And it was perfectly clear that such a conflict would be a veritable godsend to the Soviet Union at that moment. As Deputy Foreign Minister Vladimir Potemkin later told the French ambassador, Alexander Coulondre, "The weakening of Japan," because of its operations in China, had the effect of "reducing the pressure which it exercises on our Manchurian frontier."[34] Thus, after July 7 the importance of the Amur River issue was, for Moscow, eclipsed by the events in Northern China. In July 1937 Stalin was careful to take no action that might distract the Japanese from their pursuits in China and remind them of the Soviet threat and the dangers of a two-front war. So the Amur River incident, overtaken by events in China, was dropped, although not forgotten, by Moscow.

Nor was it forgotten at Kwantung Army headquarters. The more aggressive staff officers vowed that they would never again allow their proud field army to be shackled by central authorities in dealing with border disputes with the Soviets or to be humiliated in exercising command authority over their own subordinate units. When more serious border conflicts arose in 1938 and 1939, Major Tsuji Masanobu, the sole holdover from the Amur River incident period, but an exceptionally charismatic leader, would instill this truculent spirit in his colleagues.[35]

Many observers, such as the U.S. ambassador to China, concluded from this incident that the Soviets had "lost confidence in their arms" and that the Soviets' ability to undertake significant military operations in the Far East was "to no small extent paralyzed."[36] Kwantung Army showed by its subsequent actions that it too drew this conclusion from the Amur River incident. This was a serious miscalculation, for Japan immediately embarked upon the China War, an event that fundamentally altered the East Asian balance of power. The wonder is that the Japanese, especially Kwantung Army, failed to recognize that when fighting a major war against China, they could no longer afford to deal carelessly or rashly with the USSR. The subsequent Soviet-Japanese crises of 1938 and 1939, which seemed to bring the two countries to the brink of war, can be attributed in no small part to this Japanese failure—or refusal—to recognize the new reality.

From Moscow, the able U.S. diplomat Loy Henderson cabled to Washington the Soviet reaction to these developments: "From remarks made by Soviet officials . . . it would appear that the Kremlin is pleased at seeing Japanese attention directed away from the Soviet-Manchurian and Manchurian-Mongolian frontiers, and the Japanese army becoming more and more involved, and probably weakened, in Central China."[37]

The China War

Japan's plunge into China, which greatly reduced the threat to the Soviet Far East, wrought a predictable change in Soviet policy toward Japan. In Moscow's view, the need to appease Japan was gone. In December 1936 the Soviets had acquiesced to Japanese pressure and extended the disputed fisheries agreement despite the recently announced anti-Comintern pact, and, more significantly, had backed down ingloriously in the Amur River Island incident. But after the outbreak of the China War, Moscow adopted a more truculent attitude toward Tokyo. Soviet military aid to China was one obvious manifestation of this new attitude.

In October 1937 William Bullitt, U.S. ambassador to France, reported a conversation with socialist premier Leon Blum, who headed the popular front government in Paris: "He [Blum] had had many discussions with Litvinov in Geneva recently. Litvinov had talked to him frankly and as an old friend. Litvinov had said that he and the Soviet Union were perfectly delighted that Japan had attacked China. He believed that Japan would be so weakened . . . that the Soviet Union was now completely assured of peace in the Far East for many years to come. Litvinov had added that he hoped that war between China and Japan would continue just as long as possible and would result in an attempt by the Japanese to swallow just as much of China as possible."[38]

Soviet leaders did not sit by idly, merely hoping that the China War would continue "just as long as possible." In August 1937, a month after the Marco Polo Bridge incident, the Soviet Union granted Chiang Kai-shek's government credits of 100 million dollars for the purchase of Soviet war materiel. In December of that year, Moscow extended an additional 200 million dollars in credit. Soon two hundred modern Soviet fighter and bomber planes, accompanied by forty flying instructors and several hundred "volunteer" pilots, arrived in China. By May 1938 five squadrons of Soviet aircraft, manned by Soviet pilots, were operating in China.[39] On August 21, 1937, a nonaggression pact was concluded between the USSR and China. Its precise terms were less important than its timing, which put Tokyo on notice that the Soviet Union was standing by China. The extent to which Moscow was willing to back Chinese resistance to Japan was spelled out by Stalin in a meeting with the Chinese special envoy, Sun Fo (son of Dr. Sun Yat-sen). Stalin assured Sun Fo that he knew "China was fighting Russia's battle as well as her own; that it was the ultimate objective of the Japanese to capture the whole of Siberia as far as Lake Baikal; that China would continue to receive all possible help from Russia in the form of munitions, airplanes and other supplies; that the Soviet Union would not, however, intervene in the war."[40]

Thus Stalin's policy toward the China War came to resemble his policy toward the Spanish Civil War. By supplying the Spanish Loyalists and the Chinese Nationalists with enough war materiel to prevent them from being overwhelmed, the Soviet Union, at relatively little cost to itself, was able to keep the three anti-Comintern powers occupied in combat at the two extremities of Eurasia, far from Soviet borders. This strategy was less effective in the West because Spain absorbed only a small fraction of Germany's war potential, but the concept was the same in both theaters of operation. In the Far East, the results were, from the standpoint of the Kremlin, highly rewarding. When the crucial Soviet-Japanese confrontation arose in mid-1939, twenty-eight of the thirty-six Japanese infantry divisions on the Asian mainland were deployed in China.[41] The China War became an endless quagmire for Japan. So much of its resources of men and materiel were eventually committed to China that large-scale operations against the USSR were out of the question. At the same time, Soviet aid to China and the Japanese divisions tied down in Manchuria by the growing Red Banner Far Eastern Army,[42] helped prevent a swift Japanese victory in China. Caught in a classic vicious circle, the only means of extrication for Japan would have been a settlement of the China War or a rapprochement with the USSR. In the period 1937–39, the Japanese were unable to achieve the first and unwilling to attempt the second.

From September 1937 to June 1941, Russia supplied China with 904 planes, 82 tanks, and 1,140 pieces of artillery, several thousand military specialists, and over 450 pilots. In May 1938 Ambassador Coulondre reported from Moscow that "M. Potemkin calls the situation in China splendid. He is counting on resistance by this country for several years, after which Japan will be too enfeebled to be capable of attacking the U.S.S.R. This opinion appears to be shared by the Soviet leadership."[43]

In the final analysis, the China War and Moscow's role in that conflict exerted a dual and contradictory effect upon Soviet-Japanese relations. On the one hand, it drew the Japanese army away from the Soviet borders and made a major Soviet-Japanese conflict less likely. On the other hand, by stiffening Chinese resistance, it further embittered the Japanese toward the Soviet Union and made many military men—especially in the Kwantung Army, which now languished in the noncombatant backwaters of Manchuria—doubly eager to avenge themselves against the Soviet Union.

As the scope and intensity of the fighting in China grew in the second half of 1937, that struggle soon was enshrined in the pantheon of Comintern causes célèbres, second only to that of Spain. Scarcely a week went by without an article on the events in China appearing in one of the Communist news organs. Chiang Kai-shek, who had been vilified by the Comintern since 1927 as one of the most notorious fiends in history, was now praised as a national hero.

As with Spain, the Western democracies were urged to come to the aid of the embattled Chinese people. The Comintern displayed a remarkable solicitude for European colonialism in this instance, pointing out time and again how the Japanese advance in China threatened the British and French imperial positions in Asia and urging them to defend their empires. A favorite argument, often directed to isolationist America, was that armed intervention was not even necessary; the scarcity of raw materials in Japan was so acute that a Western boycott of the island empire would soon bring Tokyo to her knees. Nor was the Comintern above playing on racial emotions to provoke the West into resisting the new "yellow peril." An *Inprecor* headline of January 15, 1938, warned that, "The Japanese Program of Driving the Whites Out of Asia Is on the Way to Realization Unless Democratic Powers Offer Energetic Resistance." The same source later played up a report of Japanese soldiers undressing and slapping helpless British women in Tientsin.[44]

The Soviet tactics in Spain and China were quite similar. The primary difference was one of emphasis. In Spain, Stalin's main interest was in promoting hostility between the West (particularly France) and the Rome-Berlin Axis, and possibly embroiling those two blocs in war. The diversion of a fraction of the Axis military resources to the remote Iberian Peninsula was a fringe benefit of lesser significance. In China the paramount factor was the tying down of the bulk of the Japanese army in the South. The attempt to further involve Japan in conflict with the West was, in comparison, a secondary goal.

Germany and Japan

On November 25, 1936, Germany and Japan concluded the Anti-Comintern Pact. The pact ostensibly was directed only against the Communist International, which was perceived as an arch enemy by the governments in Berlin and Tokyo.

The pact provided for the coordination of German and Japanese efforts to thwart the activities of the Comintern, which Moscow had always insisted bore no official connection with the Soviet government. A secret protocol, however, bound the anti-Comintern partners "to take no measures which would tend to ease the situation of the U.S.S.R." if the other party should become the object of an unprovoked attack or threat of attack. In a further secret article the two states agreed to "conclude no political treaties with the U.S.S.R. contrary to the spirit of this agreement without mutual consent."[45]

In explaining the rationale for the Anti-Comintern Pact to the Privy Council in Tokyo, Foreign Minister Arita Hachiro made clear its strategic implications against the USSR, stating that "Soviet Russia must realize now that she has to face Germany and Japan."[46]

Beyond their mutual hostility to Soviet Russia, the two signatories shared broader world views. Each, for somewhat different reasons, perceived itself to be a "have-not" nation, unjustly discriminated against by the dominant Versailles powers, the Western democracies. Each sought a fundamental revision of the international status quo. Each professed contempt for the decadence of Western bourgeois democracy and extolled the virtues of Teutonic/samurai military discipline and power. A year later, Mussolini brought Italy into this alliance, forging the Rome-Berlin-Tokyo Axis.

Sir Robert Vansittart, undersecretary of the British Foreign Office, was quick to perceive the menace of the Axis. In a memo he wrote in December 1936 appraising the recently concluded Anti-Comintern Pact, Vansittart observed that "at present the *appearance* is that of cooperation against communism; but the appearance convinces no one. . . . What the agreement clearly does do, however . . . is to introduce Japan into the orbit of European affairs at a particularly delicate and dangerous phase, and to increase the probability that, in given circumstances, Germany and Japan would now act together" (emphasis in the original).[47]

The shadow of this threat had a numbing and sometimes paralyzing effect on British foreign policy makers and contributed to the climate of opinion in which the policies of appeasement grew.

The Western Democracies' Relations with Japan, Germany, and the Soviet Union

Japan's expansion on the Asian mainland in the 1930s aroused growing enmity from the Western democracies.[48] This was inevitable, since Japanese expansion required alteration of the international status quo that the Western powers had created in the nineteenth century. Great Britain, the preeminent colonial power in Asia, naturally had the greatest stake in maintaining the status quo. There was a firm conviction in government circles in London that Britain's status as a great power depended on the maintenance of her imperial position not only in Africa, the Middle East, and India, but in East Asia as well. Britain may have been overextended around the world, but her government had little desire to pull back.

With the outbreak of the China War in 1937, the feeling grew in London that if Japan triumphed in China, it might be emboldened to attack the British empire in Asia. Britain, therefore, came to view Chiang Kai-shek as the empire's first line of defense. The Foreign Office officials concerned with East Asian affairs at that time did not advocate a policy of appeasement toward Japan. As Sir John Brenan of the Foreign Office's Far Eastern Department frankly noted:

> The truth of the matter is that we acquired our dominant position in China as the result of our wars with that country in the nineteenth century and we can now only keep it by the same or similar methods. We must either use force, or otherwise bring sufficient pressure to bear on the Japanese authorities to compel them to relinquish in our favour what they regard as the spoils of victory.... It is futile to expect that we shall get what we want for the mere asking, or by protests about the infringement of our "rights," or by a more friendly attitude.[49]

Britain faced a daunting strategic dilemma. While the threat of the Rome-Berlin-Tokyo axis grew, the conventional wisdom in London was that for reasons of fiscal integrity, Britain simply could not afford to undertake a major rearmament program without risking bankruptcy and total collapse. In the autumn of 1937, a special cabinet-level study of defense spending concluded that expenditures on rearmament must not be allowed to exceed 1.5 billion pounds for the entire five-year period 1937–41. The report declared that, "in the long run the provision of adequate defences within the means at our disposal will only be achieved when our long-term foreign policy has succeeded in changing the . . . number of our potential enemies." This procrustean logic was approved by Prime Minister Neville Chamberlain—himself a former secretary of the Exchequer—and endorsed by the cabinet on December 22, 1937,[50] only ten days after the unprovoked Japanese attacks against HMS *Ladybird* and USS *Panay* on the Yangtze River.

At the same time (October–December 1937), the Air Ministry warned the cabinet that Hong Kong would be virtually indefensible against a determined Japanese air attack. The Admiralty provided even sorrier news. Three of the Royal Navy's fifteen capital ships would be dry docked for approximately eighteen months, undergoing modernization. Of the remaining twelve, nine had been built before the Battle of Jutland and only one of them had yet been modernized. Thus, if Britain suddenly were forced to send a fleet to the Western Pacific adequate to match the

Imperial Japanese Navy, she would have virtually no modern capital ships remaining in her home waters to deal with the Italian and German fleets, which were composed of comparatively new ships. Furthermore, it was reported that the new naval base at Singapore, the supposed cornerstone of imperial defense in East Asia, though formally opened in February 1938, would not be capable of performing large-scale repairs and other essential wartime functions until 1940 and that its air defenses too were hopelessly inadequate.[51] It is not without cause that British diplomacy in the late 1930s proceeded from a sense of strategic vulnerability.

Japan's leaders were fully aware of Britain's strategic difficulties and were determined to intensify their pressure on the British position in China. The British, however, did not yield very much. There was a growing belief (hope?) in London that Japan was stuck in an exhausting war in China and that Britain might be able to outlast her. While the Chamberlain government pursued appeasement in Europe, London sought ways to inhibit Japanese expansion and to assist China. Yet Britain's military weakness, her entanglement in the deepening European crisis, and her inability to rely upon American support, prevented her from taking too vigorous a stand against Japan. The resulting British policy toward Japan brought antagonism without deterrence.

U.S. policy toward Japan in the late 1930s was similarly flawed. Although the constraints on U.S. action regarding the China War derived more from domestic politics and public opinion (i.e., isolationism) than from a sense of military or strategic paralysis, the resulting policy resembled that of Great Britain. President Franklin D. Roosevelt's vague words of warning and U.S. Secretary of State Cordell Hull's stern and righteous lectures on international law and morality, without the backing of force or the credible threat of force, also antagonized Japan without effectively deterring her.

Many of Japan's leaders, for their part, sincerely hoped that the strained relations between their country and the Western powers would be relieved once the prime irritant, the China War, was brought to a satisfactory conclusion. However, that outcome, Japan's conquest of China, was precisely what London and Washington were determined to prevent. Unless one side or the other altered its policy objectives, there was little possibility of reconciliation and increasing likelihood of conflict.

In the decades between the world wars, Germany, perhaps even more than Italy and Japan, perceived itself as the victim of an unjust international order, symbolized by the hated Treaty of Versailles. The "good German" and Nobel Peace Prize laureate, Gustav Stressemann, shared with Adolf Hitler a desire to revise fundamentally, if not to nullify, the Versailles diktat. By the mid-1930s, many reasonable and influential men among the victorious Versailles powers had come to feel that there were some injustices in the treaty that warranted revision. On this issue, Hitler, despite his gangsterism, was capable of persuasiveness and, if it suited his purposes, even charm, when discussing Germany's legitimate grievances.

Hitler had another theme he used to great effect when dealing with the Versailles powers, and that was his much-touted anti-Bolshevism. Many foreign political leaders who otherwise would have found Hitler and Nazism utterly repugnant, were impressed with this feature of the Third Reich. Winston Churchill admitted that until 1937 even he was able to find some virtue in Hitler as a useful counterforce against the Soviet Union. Furthermore, in Britain and France, the horrors of 1914–18 on the Western Front were remembered all too well. Leaders in both nations were determined to avoid repetition of that catastrophe at almost any cost, a policy that enjoyed strong popular support. The British chiefs of staffs added to the sense of alarm with their report on imperial defense, occasioned by Italy's adherence to the Anti-Comintern Pact in November 1937: "The outstanding feature of the present situation is the increasing probability that a war started in any one of these three areas [Europe, the Mediterranean, or East Asia] may extend to one or both of the other two. Without overlooking the assistance which we should hope to attain from France, and possibly other allies, *we cannot foresee the time when our defence forces will be strong enough to safeguard our territory, trade and vital interests against Germany, Italy and Japan simultaneously*" (italics added).[52]

At the same time, France, the dominant military power in Western Europe for most of the interwar period, experienced a crisis of national confidence and will. Even the electoral victory of the French Popular Front in May 1936 did not reverse this drift. Many observers expected that the new Popular Front government led by Leon Blum, himself a socialist and a Jew, would take the lead in opposing fascism and Nazism in Europe. Such was not the case.

France already had suffered a major strategic and psychological defeat in March 1936, when an ineffectual caretaker government in Paris allowed Hitler to remilitarize the Rhineland. This direct violation of the Treaty of Versailles seemed to bar easy access into Germany by the French army, an access guaranteed to France at Versailles by the permanent demilitarization of the Rhineland. Deprived of that assurance of German vulnerability, France lost most of whatever confidence it had in its ability to deal militarily with Germany. A few months later, the brand new Popular Front government was confronted with the challenge of Italian and German intervention in the Spanish Civil War. Blum's initial reaction was to aid his Popular Front colleagues in Madrid, but because of the Catholic Church's support of the Nationalist cause and the violent anticlericalism of the Republicans, this threatened to reopen the schism that had split French society since 1789. Furthermore, the Tory government in London, which was suspicious of the leftist coalition in Madrid, put tremendous pressure on Paris to remain neutral in the

Spanish struggle. Beset by these and other problems, Blum and his successors virtually abandoned conducting an independent foreign policy and, in effect, made themselves wards of the British Foreign Office. They then entrenched their still first-rate army behind the Maginot Line and dispiritedly awaited the deluge.

Thus, with the United States seemingly off on some other planet, as far as European diplomacy was concerned, and with French interests in a kind of diplomatic receivership in London, the Chamberlain government, haunted by its sense of weakness and vulnerability, faced the Axis powers. Chamberlain turned a conciliatory face to Hitler, to Mussolini, then back to Hitler again, hoping thereby to convert at least one of them into a "good European." "The dictators," Chamberlain confided to his foreign secretary, Lord Halifax, "were ... men of moods. Catch them in the right mood and they will give you anything you ask for."[53] But with this attitude, it was Chamberlain, of course, who did most of the giving.

The British government showed no sign of challenging Hitler over the question of Anschluss with Austria, and after the German army marched into Vienna in March 1938, London heaved a veritable sigh of relief. At least the Austrian question had been settled peacefully, albeit unilaterally, and war had been avoided. European attention immediately turned to Czechoslovakia, where Nazi propaganda on behalf of the Sudeten-German minority was turning bellicose. The Chamberlain government wanted to avoid war, if possible. The situation was complicated, however, because both France and the Soviet Union were pledged by formal treaty commitments to the defense of Czechoslovakia, and the Czech government, unlike Austria, showed every intention of defending itself. With the specter of a general European war looming over their deliberations in the latter part of March, the government in London sought to find the course that would involve the smallest risk of war. The chiefs of staff contributed their melancholy military assessment on March 21, noting that Britain and France lacked the means to prevent Germany from overrunning Czechoslovakia, and that if Britain became involved in war with Germany, Italy and Japan would probably seize the opportunity to drive her out of the Middle East and East Asia. The next day the cabinet concluded that Britain should offer no guarantee to either France or Czechoslovakia in the event of a German attack, and that the government in Prague should be pressed to compromise with Hitler.[54] Thus, six months before the Munich Conference, Chamberlain's course was already set.

Since British and French leaders believed that their own resources were inadequate to check Axis aggression, without powerful allies their global strategic dilemma appeared insoluble. However, as powerful allies, the United States seemed inaccessible and the Soviet Union undesirable. British and Russian foreign policy had been fundamentally antithetical since the fall of Napoleon, except for the brief episodes when fear of Germany's colossal power drove them reluctantly into each other's arms. With the temporary elimination of the German threat in 1918 and the replacement of the tsars by commissars, the longstanding Anglo-Russian geopolitical rivalry was compounded by ideological antagonism. London perceived Bolshevism as a deadly threat to everything Britain and the empire represented and took the lead in armed intervention in the Russian Civil War to overthrow the red menace. Moscow saw Britain as the archetypal capitalist imperialist power, the nemesis of the international proletarian revolutionary movement. These deepseated perceptions may have been stereotyped and overdrawn, but neither was without substantial validity; Soviet and British interests remained essentially antithetical through the 1920s and early 1930s. The profound suspicion and antagonism between the two powers could not be dispelled readily by Moscow's foreign policy shift of 1935. The appeal for a united front against fascist aggression received a cool reception in London.

Paris seemed less hostile to the Soviet demarche, as attested to by the Franco-Soviet Mutual Defense Pact of May 1935. However, the cunning French premier, Pierre Laval, had his own reasons for this move, which had more to do with French politics than with national security.[55] The French Chamber of Deputies took nearly a year to ratify the treaty, which was never consummated by joint military staff consultations or by any other meaningful joint strategic understanding. The treaty was, in fact, a dead letter in all but name. Nor did the inauguration of Blum's Popular Front government bring any real warmth to Franco-Soviet relations. As France bound herself ever more closely to British foreign policy, London's attitude toward Moscow prevailed. Thus, despite the great show of Soviet diplomatic activity in the mid-1930s—establishing relations with Washington, entering the League of Nations, concluding defense pacts with France and Czechoslovakia, furnishing aid to Republican Spain and Nationalist China, and so forth—in a deeper sense the USSR remained diplomatically isolated.

Moscow's isolation in this period of deepening international crisis was a source of danger and instability. The danger to the Soviet Union is readily apparent. However, the danger was not only to the Soviet Union. Western diplomats had long realized, in theory, that a desperate Soviet Russia might attempt a rapprochement with either Japan or Germany as a means of avoiding a potentially disastrous two-front war. However, the real-life possibility of such a development often was dismissed rather casually. In the words of Sir Victor Wellesley, British deputy secretary of state for foreign affairs, "At present there is fortunately no chance of the Russians and Germans coming together . . . which would be the most formidable thing [Europe] has as yet had to encounter. We have reason to bless both Hitler's blindness and bolshevism which makes this impossible at present. Long may they both live!"[56] Comments such as these can be found scattered throughout the foreign ministry archives of numerous Western states. Yet precious little was done to forestall the dreaded development. Even after Britain's global predicament vis-à-vis the Axis powers had become ruefully apparent in London, the Foreign Office continued to maintain that cooperation with the Soviets would be reprehensible and counterproductive, a step to be taken only as a last resort. From this perspective, the USSR was seen as part of Britain's international problem rather than as part of a solution to that problem.

Stalin contributed to Soviet isolation at this time. The general suspicion with which the Soviet Union was regarded in the West was compounded in 1937–38 by the bizarre reports of the purge of Soviet political and military leaders. Although the vast extent of the purge was scarcely realized in Western capitals, the fate of prominent political figures and top military brass was followed closely. The almost unanimous evaluation by foreign military intelligence experts was that the purge had crippled, perhaps irreparably, the morale and fighting effectiveness of the Red Army, thereby undermining still further the usefulness or desirability of the Soviet Union as an ally. Even the outrageous allegations that the Stalin regime hurled at its victims came back to damage the USSR. If the Red Army really were riddled from top to bottom with treasonous wreckers and spies who regularly betrayed all manner of secret information to enemy agents—as was loudly proclaimed by the Soviet judicial system and the state's news organs—all the more reason for Western governments to be leery of alliance with the USSR. Might not their own military secrets be fatally compromised thereby?[57]

Of course, as seen from Moscow, the diplomacy of the 1930s was dominated by a single, all-important factor, stated succinctly in the opening paragraph of a book by the Soviet historian Leonid Kutakov: "The formation of the German-Japanese military-political alliance, which hastened the outbreak of the Second World War, was facilitated by the anti-Soviet policy of the United States, Great Britain and France, which were loath to accept the Soviet proposals for collective security, and hoped that Germany and Japan might be turned against the USSR."[58]

As we shall see, in the final analysis this Soviet accusation, though one-sided and incomplete, has some validity.

Madrid and Munich: Failure of the United Front Policy in the West

As the depressing sequence of international developments in 1938 dragged the powers inexorably toward war, the isolation of and danger to the USSR grew more acute. This was symbolized by the military collapse of the Communist-supported forces in Spain and by the Munich Conference.

Although in the long-run Stalin was well served by the results of his aid to the Spanish Republic, he must have been disappointed that the maximum objective of his Spanish gambit—the promotion of conflict between the bourgeois democratic capitalists and the fascist capitalists—did not materialize. After all, it was a logical idea. Leon Blum's Popular Front government, for reasons both ideological and strategic, should have roused itself to aid the Popular Front government in Madrid. France and Great Britain should have been alarmed by the fascist military activities in the Western Mediterranean. Yet, despite the tug of political sympathy and strategic self-interest, Paris stuck by the policy of nonintervention dictated by London, where the Conservative government displayed a predisposition for the Nationalist forces of General Franco. In effect this nonintervention policy meant that France and Britain would refrain from "intervening," that is, refrain from furnishing assistance to the democratically elected, internationally recognized Republican government. No effective means were found to prevent the actual intervention by Italy, Germany, and the Soviet Union.

By mid-1938, Stalin decided to pull out of Spain. Although few recognized it as such at the time, the Soviet withdrawal from Spain signaled Stalin's acknowledgment of the failure of his united front/popular front policy.

As the Spanish tragedy dragged on toward its foreseeable conclusion, the Czech crisis grew more intense. Even though Czechoslovakia was tied to France and the USSR with mutual defense treaties and possessed a modern, well-equipped army of its own, in the face of the German threat, Britain was the key to the entire situation. France had bound herself hand and foot to British diplomacy. The Soviet-Czech treaty did not oblige Moscow to act on behalf of Prague unless Paris did so first. Furthermore, the strategic position of Czechoslovakia had been undermined by the Austro-German Anschluss, incorporating Austria into the Third Reich and allowing the German army to outflank the Czech western defense wall, exposing southern Czechoslovakia to German invasion.

Moscow did what it could to stiffen anti-German resistance in Prague, Paris, and London. The Soviet government and the Comintern criticized the earlier weak-kneed diplomacy of the Western powers, and in contrast trumpeted reports of the "powerful rebuff" just dealt to the "Japanese aggressors" in a battle at Changkufeng on the Soviet-Korean border (described in detail in the next chapter). To quell any doubts about Moscow's willingness or ability to meet its military commitments in the West in light of the Soviet-Japanese conflict, the Soviet ambassador in Prague assured Czechoslovak president Eduard Benes on August 4 (at the height of the Changkufeng Battle) that the Soviet Union would stand by its military obligation to Czechoslovakia in the event of a German attack, regardless of the Far Eastern situation.[59] Similar representations were made by Soviet diplomats in London and Paris, to no avail. Britain and France had seriously overestimated Russian military potential on the eve of the First World War and were intent upon not repeating that mistake. Throughout the crises preceding the Second World War, they consistently underestimated Soviet Russian strength and acted—or failed to act—accordingly. In the Czech crisis there was another complicating factor. The governments of Poland and Romania, whose territory completely separated Czechoslovakia from the USSR, refused to allow transit rights to the Red Army. This rendered even more problematic the efficacy of Soviet military assistance to Czechoslovakia.[60]

In any case, Chamberlain was not seeking a Russian ally beside which to fight, but was seeking to avoid a fight. Therefore, he agreed with Hitler and Mussolini to exclude Stalin from the climactic Munich Conference, on the outcome of which hung the issue of peace or war, because the prime minister knew full well that Soviet diplomacy would strive to prevent the consummation of appeasement. So the Soviets were excluded, as were the Czechs themselves, from the conference at Munich that determined the fate of the Sudetenland, and of so much more.

The dismemberment of Czechoslovakia at Munich was not the crucial turning point in European diplomacy that it is often made out to be. Munich was the logical culmination of the policy of appeasement that the West had practiced since 1935. Nor did the Munich Conference result in a fundamental reorientation of Soviet policies. The outcome must have heightened Moscow's alarm over the immediacy of the German menace. And Chamberlain's conduct at Munich probably reinforced Stalin's suspicion that London and Paris meant to channel Hitler's future aggression eastward. Dismaying as this may have been, it can hardly have shocked Stalin very much. Playing enemies off one against the other was a favorite tactic of Stalin's. It had also been a prominent feature of Soviet foreign policy for years. Still, the events of mid-1938 marked an intensification of Moscow's diplomatic isolation and of the German danger, and although the Japanese had been dealt with firmly at Changkufeng, the situation in the West seemed critical.

Stalin's Desperate Six Months

By mid-1938, Stalin had been forced to reevaluate the European situation. Whereas in the mid-1930s the greatest danger to the Soviet Union seemed to be the possible victory of fascism on the continent and the formation of a four-power pact (Germany, Italy, France, and England) against the USSR, it must have become clear by 1938 that Germany alone—or with the benevolent neutrality of the West[61]—posed a serious military threat. Thus, while the possibility of a four-power pact still had to be guarded against, now thought had to be given to the threat of a German attack.

To deal with the Nazi menace that loomed ever larger and closer on his western frontier, Stalin had two options: to turn Hitler's thrust westward, away from the Soviet Union, or to find allies in the West against the possibility of a German attack. Stalin pursued both options. The first alternative was the more desirable. This because of the threats—real or imagined—that a major war posed to Stalin's rule, and also because a great war in the West promised the exhaustion of the capitalist powers, leaving the Soviet Union as the arbiter of Europe.

However, this does not mean that Stalin did not consider seriously the second option. He was not clairvoyant and could not see ahead to the events of 1939. He could not be certain that Poland would resist Hitler, that the Western democracies would undertake to guarantee Poland without a Soviet commitment, and that the West would remain faithful to such a guarantee. Nor could he be certain that Hitler, under any circumstances, would conclude an agreement with the USSR. For these reasons—or until these uncertainties were resolved—Stalin had to consider the alternative of an alliance with the West against Hitler. Soviet dealings with the West in these years may have been two-faced, but they were more than a mere charade.

Munich, however, did produce a change in Soviet tactics. From 1935 to 1938, the USSR had called upon the West, openly and continuously, to join it in a "peace bloc" against fascist aggression. Litvinov's oratorical efforts were directed most often toward this goal. However, the Soviets' repeated requests for an antifascist alliance—requests that at times resembled anxious pleas[62]—ended abruptly after the Munich Conference. Stalin did not lose interest in the project. To the contrary, at least the appearance of cooperation with the Western democracies was absolutely necessary for Stalin, even and especially if he sought an agreement with Hitler. For Stalin could achieve a satisfactory deal with Hitler only if he held some high cards in his hand. And the highest card of all would be the possibility of a military alliance between the USSR and the West. To achieve this goal, Stalin now, in effect, would attempt to play hard to get. By muting his previously too-eager solicitation of an alliance with the West, he hoped to awaken the desire for just such an alliance in Paris and London. The new line from Moscow stated that the strength of the Red Army made the Soviet Union virtually invulnerable. Berlin, Rome, and Tokyo, it was asserted, preferred easier prey. Therefore, the British and French were in grave danger. This theme was elaborated upon in the highly publicized speeches given in Red Square on November 7, 1938, and at the Eighteenth Party Congress in March of the next year. It was neatly capsulated for Western readers in Comintern news organs: "The day that the democracies of the West cut themselves off irrevocably from the great Socialist country in the East is the day that Hitler opens his offensive against the West."[63] This theme, with variations, was repeated many times by Litvinov and his subordinates in conversations with Western diplomats during the winter of 1938–39.[64] While Soviet diplomacy pretended coolness and aloofness bordering on disinterest, Communist propaganda directed toward the British and French public told a very different story.

The Comintern news weekly *World News and Views* accurately reflected Soviet apprehensions and anxiety during the period of political isolation. The dominant theme in the propaganda campaign was that the West (and Poland) faced grave peril at the hands of Germany, Italy, and Japan. This was hardly a new idea for the Comintern, but the frequency and intensity with which it now was stressed far surpassed that of earlier periods. Here are a few examples:[65]

> The plan of Hitler and the fascist alliance is completely to destroy the influence of Britain and France throughout the world. . . . All is not yet lost. But it is only the dogged and united resistance of the masses that can now halt the march towards destruction.

> Mussolini's "minimum colonial demands" were said to be: cession of Tunisia to Italy; complete demilitarization of Corsica; recognition of Balearic Islands as Italian territory; and "internationalization" of the Suez Canal, with four zones of supervision, one to each of the Munich signatories.

> Germany intends to make Britain and France pay for her rearmament by demanding restitution of the reparation sums paid to them after the Great War.

> The German and Italian fascists, having gained possession of the Great Mediterranean port of Barcelona, have no longer hesitated in revealing their real intentions: to encircle France in order to be better able to attack it!

> The Japanese, now Masters of Shanghai, Prepare for Attack on Indochina.

The obvious conclusion from these dire warnings was that London and Paris had better move quickly in concert with Moscow to resist the aggressors and avert disaster. But that is precisely what Moscow and the Comintern had been urging for more than three years without success. Something new had to be added. Immediately after the Munich Conference a scathing campaign against the appeasers, particularly Chamberlain, was begun. The argument was that Chamberlain did not merely surrender to Hitler at Munich, nor was he duped by the German dictator, but that he actively and knowingly conspired with Hitler to destroy Czechoslovakia. Chamberlain and Daladier were denounced as "emissaries of Hitler" who must be removed from power so that a united front could oppose the fascists. One headline shouted "Daladier Working for Hitler Against the French Nation"; another that "Chamberlain Wants a Mediterranean Munich."[66] Another Communist propaganda gambit was to try to split France from Britain by charging that Chamberlain, on behalf of the London capitalists, was betraying France to the fascists. A favorite statement of this ploy was reference to the "Chamberlain-Hitler-Mussolini plan" to repartition the French empire.[67]

Despite the hysterical tone of many of these charges, even the more bizarre accusations enjoyed some credibility from their association with the general popular front line, part of which had proven correct in its early warnings about the dangers of fascism. This propaganda was effective among the growing number of people who were becoming disenchanted with the policy of appeasement and were prepared to believe the worst about Chamberlain and Daladier. The prime target of this invective, however, remained unmoved. Chamberlain wrote on January 8, 1939, that he had been urged to make a grand alliance with the USSR against Germany. "In other words, abandon my policy and adopt Winston's! Fortunately my nature is, as Lloyd G[eorge] says, extremely 'obstinate,' and I refuse to change."[68]

While Moscow was pressing the West to alter its course and swing eastward, it also instituted some seemingly minor alterations in its relations with Poland and Germany.

Soviet-Polish relations hardly ever had been friendly, but in 1938 they became particularly strained. During the height of the Czech crisis, Poland extorted the district of Teschen from Czechoslovakia, temporarily giving Poland's foreign minister, Colonel Josef Beck, the appearance of a junior partner of Hitler and Mussolini. A month later, however, Beck was alarmed to discover that the next item on Hitler's agenda was Poland. Germany demanded the incorporation of the Polish port of Danzig into the Reich and the creation of an extraterritorial German corridor across the Polish corridor, to link East Prussia with the rest of Germany.[69] This signaled the failure of Beck's entire foreign policy, which had been predicated on friendly relations with Germany. Beck tried to keep the German pressure secret while he set out to mend fences with Soviet Russia and the West, but Moscow was not deceived.[70]

A series of seemingly casual conversations between Litvinov and the Polish ambassador in Moscow resulted in a joint statement on November 26, 1938, in which both countries reaffirmed their 1932 Nonaggression Pact and friendly resolution of any problems that might arise between them.[71] This clutching at straws by Beck was important to Stalin, whose security depended on Polish resistance to Hitler. For if Warsaw, like Budapest, decided that circumstances compelled it to become a vassal of Germany, then the Nazi wolf would be at the Kremlin door.

The winter of 1938 was too early for Stalin to propose a deal to Hitler, although that idea was probably already on his mind. But the Soviet leader's hand was too weak; he had nothing substantial to offer Hitler and would not have unless the prospects of a Soviet alliance with the West improved dramatically. In the meantime, some innocuous groundwork was laid. In October Litvinov reached an oral agreement with the German ambassador in Moscow whereby the press and radio of each country would restrain their previously virulent attacks upon the other country and its leaders. Tentative German feelers for an expansion of German-Soviet trade were well-received in Moscow, and on January 10, 1939, Soviet ambassador Aleksey Merekalov in Berlin informed the German Foreign Office that the Soviet government wanted the commercial negotiations to be resumed immediately and in Moscow.[72]

This outward easing of German-Soviet tension primarily served not as a stepping stone toward an alliance with Hitler but as a hint to the West that such an alliance was possible. This supplemented Comintern propaganda aimed at getting London and Paris to cease their appeasement of Hitler. One of the most explicit public statements of this theme came in Stalin's now-famous address to the Eighteenth Communist Party Congress on March 10, 1939, in which he declared, "The tasks of the Party in the sphere of foreign policy are: 1) To continue the policy of peace and of strengthening business relations with *all* countries; and 2) To be cautious and not to allow our country to be drawn into conflicts by warmongers who are accustomed to have others pull the chestnuts out of the fire for them" (italics added).[73]

Strangely enough, only five days after Stalin spoke these words, the change in Western policy that he so fervently desired was set in motion—and Moscow had very little to do with it.

The Watershed

On March 15, 1939, the German army marched into truncated Czechoslovakia. Shorn of its western defense lines, its allies, and its will to resist, as a result of the Munich Conference, Czechoslovakia succumbed without a struggle. Hitler flew to Prague that very night, where, from the Hradschin Castle, the ancient Palace of Bohemia's kings, he wrote the words, "Czechoslovakia has ceased to exist." Another great bloodless victory for Nazi expansion, a testament to Hitler's consummate skill and timing; it would be his last such triumph.

The German occupation of post-Munich Czechoslovakia was more than just another treaty violation. It was incontrovertible evidence even Chamberlain could not disregard that Hitler's appetite grew with eating, that it was whetted rather than satiated by appeasement. Chamberlain was outraged and apparently genuinely shocked by this blatant violation of the pledge Hitler had made at Munich that the Sudetenland was Germany's last territorial grievance. Adding to Chamberlain's indignation was that he had staked his political reputation on the policy of appeasement, proclaiming "peace in our time," and now had been made to look a fool.

Under mounting pressure from the Labour opposition as well as from his own Conservative Party in Parliament, Chamberlain reacted to Hitler's seizure of Czechoslovakia by reversing his previous foreign policy. Further German aggression would be opposed, by force if necessary. On March 18 the British Foreign Office asked Litvinov what the Soviet attitude would be in the event of future German aggression. The commissar for foreign affairs suggested a six-power conference—Britain, France, the USSR, Romania, Poland, and Turkey—to consider the problem. London immediately countered with a proposal for four-power talks aimed at a mutual assistance pact among Britain, France, the USSR, and Poland.[74] London immediately was embarrassed by the refusal of the Polish government to take part in such negotiations.[75] Then on March 23 the urgency of the situation was heightened by Hitler's extortion of the territory of Memel from Lithuania. Chamberlain was provoked into action. Abandoning traditional British circumspection in such matters, and without any Soviet commitment, the prime minister went before the House of Commons on March 31 and announced his historic unilateral guarantee of Polish independence. It is difficult to know who was more encouraged by the events of this momentous fortnight: Beck, who knew that Poland was the next item on Hitler's agenda, or Stalin, who knew that a sure consequence of the British pledge to Poland would be an Anglo-French effort to draw closer to the USSR.

These events signaled that the long and perilous period of Soviet diplomatic isolation was at an end. Stalin's patience had been rewarded. But this striking development was not primarily the result of Stalin's efforts. Soviet diplomacy and Comintern propaganda had had little effect on the obstinate Chamberlain, who wrote on March 26, 1939, "I must confess the most profound distrust of Russia. I have no belief whatever in her ability to maintain an effective offensive, *even if she wanted to*. And I distrust her motives, which seem to me to have little connection with our ideas of liberty, and to be concerned only with getting every one else by the ears. Moreover she is both hated and suspected by many of the smaller states, notably by Poland, Roumania and Finland" (italics added).[76] The greatest single factor responsible for the volte-face of Anglo-French policy (France, pilotless in the storm, continued to follow in Britain's wake) was Hitler's demonstration of rapaciousness in March. Thus, the success of Stalin's diplomacy up to this point was not primarily the result of his actions. In the next few months, however, Stalin made the most of the opportunity given him.

The British prime minister either was slow to realize or reluctant to admit that his guarantee of Poland required actual cooperation with the USSR. This anti-Soviet aversion was shared by many members of his cabinet. As they discussed the prospects of building an effective anti-German coalition, they reviewed all of their reasons for excluding the USSR: Poland, Romania, and Finland would refuse to cooperate with the USSR; Catholic opinion in Spain, Portugal, and elsewhere resented any "flirtation with the Bolsheviks"; Italy or Japan, or both, would be "driven into Hitler's arms"; Soviet military potential vis-à-vis Germany was "negligible"; and furthermore, they simply did not trust Stalin.[77]

Immediately after Chamberlain announced the guarantee to Poland in the House of Commons, he was called to a private meeting with David Lloyd George, the former wartime prime minister and outspoken critic of appeasement. Lloyd George wanted to know the specific circumstances under which Chamberlain had risked involving Britain in war with Germany. Chamberlain replied that he was confident Germany would not risk fighting a two-front war. Lloyd George then asked "where the second front might be," to which Chamberlain answered: "Poland." The aged Lloyd George burst into sarcastic laughter, warning Chamberlain that such a policy was "an irresponsible game of chance which can end up very badly."[78]

In succeeding weeks the point of Lloyd George's criticism became increasingly evident at the Foreign Office and in cabinet discussions. Strategically, the Soviet Union was indispensable both as a deterrent to German aggression and as an ally in case Germany were not deterred. Yet Britain's old reluctance to associate too closely with Bolshevism still was strong, particularly with Chamberlain, who now professed to believe that the announcement of an Anglo-Soviet alliance "might be expected to sting Germany into aggressive action. That was an unnecessary provocation to offer to Germany, and one which ought to be avoided."[79] London sought in vain for an acceptable formula whereby Moscow could be committed to act in defense of Poland and Romania without seeming to create an Anglo-Soviet alliance. The Soviets would have none of that and insisted upon the necessity of a formal, concrete political-military alliance not unlike the Triple Entente of 1914.[80]

An atmosphere of anxiety, mistrust, and fear of betrayal overhung the negotiations between London and Moscow. Each side suspected the other of trying to maneuver them into becoming the lightning rod for German aggression. It now appears that the suspicions on both sides may have been justified. Declassified British documents bear witness to the validity of Soviet ambassador Ivan Maisky's view, which he cabled from London to his government on May 20, that "the British Government is avoiding a three-power [Anglo-Franco-Soviet] pact purely from a desire not to burn its bridges to Hitler and Mussolini." Indeed, Chamberlain clung to the belief, after most others in his government had been disillusioned, that in the end Hitler might be dissuaded from plunging Europe into war. He saw an alliance with Stalin as a provocative step toward war rather than as a sobering deterrent.

However, the threat of an Anglo-Soviet alliance might be helpful in "taming" Hitler, and so the continuation of the talks with Moscow served that purpose, as well as quieting the parliamentary opposition to his government's foreign policy. Chamberlain's foreign minister, Lord Halifax, explained on April 25 that it was his policy "not to estrange Russia, but always to keep her in play." A bit later he put it more bluntly in a cabinet meeting, when he acknowledged that "*our main object* in the negotiations was to prevent Russia from engaging herself with Germany" (italics in the original).[81] If Britain sought to use the USSR as a "bogeyman" with which to frighten Hitler, then Soviet fears were not groundless that in the event of war, the bogeyman might become the fall guy.

Conversely, British fears of Soviet duplicity were also amply justified. On May 17 Georgie Astakhov, the Soviet chargé d'affaires in Berlin, met with a senior German diplomat, who filed this report of the conversation: "Astakhov stated in detail that there were no conflicts in foreign policy between Germany and the Soviet Union and that therefore there was no reason for any enmity between the two countries.... He commented on the Anglo-Soviet negotiations to the effect that under the present circumstances, the result desired by England could hardly be achieved."[82]

Joachim von Ribbentrop and Hitler could not fail to note the purport of Astakhov's words, but they offered no direct or immediate reply. They, no less than Chamberlain and Halifax, were intensely suspicious of Stalin's motives.

If British leaders at that time are to be criticized for wishing not to "burn their bridges" to Germany, Soviet policy is no less culpable for its covert efforts at bridge building with Germany. However, since Hitler did not respond to the initial Soviet overture, Stalin had good cause to continue the Anglo-Soviet negotiations, because Stalin knew that the threat of a triple alliance, of a repetition of Germany's great error of 1914, would bring Hitler around—if anything would. And if that gambit failed, the talks with Britain were all the more vital for Stalin in order to assure himself of allies in the event of war.

Toward a German-Japanese Military Alliance?

One reason why the diplomatic seeds that Stalin was sowing in Berlin did not bear fruit promptly was the German fear that it was a tainted offering, meant to bring forth an apple of discord among the anti-Comintern allies.[83]

While the Anglo-Soviet talks limped on, and before the furtive Soviet-German dealing had even begun, serious negotiations aimed at converting the Anti-Comintern Pact into a full military alliance had been under way since mid-1938. The negotiations were protracted because Germany and Japan were pursuing divergent and, as events were to prove, irreconcilable objectives. Nonetheless, those talks require more than a mere footnote in history; they must be brought into the picture in order to show the background against which subsequent German-Soviet relations developed.

The two biggest problems that Japan faced in early 1939 seemed to be her inability to bring China to its knees, and the threat of war with the USSR. Since many Japanese leaders blamed Soviet aid to Chiang for the prolongation of the China War, and the bitter memory of the fighting at Changkufeng was still fresh in their minds, Soviet Russia appeared to many in Tokyo to be at the crux of Japan's problems. In the negotiations that Japan began with Germany immediately after the Changkufeng conflict (August 1938), Tokyo sought a military pact directed explicitly against the Soviet Union. Japanese army leaders were especially eager for such an alliance.

In Berlin, meanwhile, the diplomatic situation was developing along different lines. As early as April 1938, Foreign Minister Ribbentrop, after consultation with Hitler, informed Ernst von Weizsacker, state secretary for foreign affairs, that Germany's new foreign policy would have to take English opposition into account, and that while Soviet Russia still might officially be designated as the primary enemy, in reality Germany's plans were directed against Great Britain.[84] Hitler and Ribbentrop wanted a military alliance with Japan, but they sought a pact that would apply to any potential enemy. The Germans hoped thereby to forestall British and French opposition in Europe by heightening the Japanese threat to their vulnerable Asian empires.

This did not sit well with the Japanese Foreign Ministry, which had no intention of becoming a German cat's-paw. The Japanese navy at that time also opposed any agreement that might bring it up against the combined naval strength of Britain and the United States. Therefore, in spite of the army's willingness to accept the proposed German alliance, the Japanese government held out for reservations and qualifications that would direct the pact against Japan's nemesis, the USSR.[85]

Hitler's policies, however, were moving Germany steadily further away from the Japanese position. Chamberlain's opposition to further German expansion after March 1939 was driven home in Berlin by his guarantee to Poland, his intensification of rearmament, and finally, his unprecedented request for peacetime conscription. The significance of these measures was underlined still further in Berlin by Poland's rejection of German demands on the status of Danzig and the Polish Corridor. In dealing with Poland, therefore, Hitler realized that he might encounter more than mere verbal opposition. He still hoped to overawe Britain and France and force them to back down, but if it came to war over Poland, he correctly reckoned that his Wehrmacht was ready. However, the mistake of 1914 was to be avoided at all costs; Hitler did not wish to fight Britain, France, and Russia simultaneously. If he acquiesced in the Japanese desire for a military pact against the USSR, the effect might be to drive Stalin into alliance with the Anglo-French powers. Therefore, German diplomats steadfastly resisted Tokyo's efforts to turn the projected military alliance against Moscow. Their resistance was stiffened further by the tantalizing statements of Astakhov in Berlin. Ribbentrop instructed his ambassador in Tokyo, General Eugene Ott, that, in regard to the proposed military alliance, "it is quite out of the question that an anti-Russian tendency should be allowed to appear in any of the articles of the pact."[86] This, of course, would rob the pact of its primary value to Japan. The Japanese government, conversely, while claiming to accept the principle of a general military alliance, sought German acceptance of a secret written understanding that would relieve Japan for the time being of any obligation to go to war with the Western democracies and would allow her to covertly inform London, Paris, and Washington that the new Rome-Berlin-Tokyo alliance was directed exclusively against the USSR.[87] Naturally this was unacceptable to Berlin.

In view of the divergent interests of Tokyo and Berlin, it is not surprising that the negotiators could not draft a military pact satisfactory to both governments. The talks, however, continued into August 1939. Furthermore, through the efforts of Richard Sorge, the Soviet master spy in Tokyo, Moscow was kept abreast of the secret negotiations, and of Japan's determination to make the pact an anti-Soviet military alliance.[88] This too is part of the background against which the German-Soviet rapprochement developed.

Before considering the end game in this web of cross-cutting diplomatic and geostrategic relationships—namely, the conclusion of the German-Soviet Nonaggression Pact—it is necessary to bring one more critical and often-overlooked factor into focus. That factor is the eruption of large-scale Soviet-Japanese military conflicts in the summers of 1938 and 1939.

CHAPTER 3

CHANGKUFENG

I n the year following the Amur River incident of June 1937, enmity between Japan and the USSR increased. This was mostly related to the China War. Japan's deepening involvement in its war in China emboldened Moscow to take a tougher stance toward Tokyo. Soviet aid to China infuriated the Japanese and Soviet penetration of the northwestern Chinese province of Sinkiang aroused anxiety and animosity in Tokyo. The atmosphere of Soviet-Japanese enmity also encouraged and was fueled by an increasing number of border violations and armed border clashes. These reached a new peak in July–August 1938 when a border dispute at the juncture of the USSR, Manchukuo, and Korea exploded into a major pitched battle, raising the specter of a second Russo-Japanese War.

This crisis, referred to by the Japanese as the Changkufeng incident and by the Soviets as the battle of Lake Khasan, took place in strategic circumstances very different from the Amur River incident. By mid-1938, Japan was deeply committed to subduing China. July of that year found the greater part of the Japanese army embarked on a massive operation to capture the triple cities of Wuchang, Hanyang, and Hankow in central China, known collectively as Wuhan. Situated at the junction of two major north-south railway lines and the Yangtse River flowing west-east, Wuhan was a vital communications hub for both sides in the China War. Chiang Kai-shek had moved his capital to Hankow after being driven out of Nanking in December 1937. Imperial General Headquarters (IGHQ) in Tokyo already had been forced to draw heavily upon Kwantung Army's anti-Soviet reserve, and by July 1938 only six divisions remained in Manchukuo, plus one in Korea, to cope with possible trouble from the north. The Soviet Red Banner Far Eastern Army by that time was estimated to have reached a strength of approximately twenty divisions.[1] These figures bespeak a dramatic shift in the balance of power in Northeast Asia. However, this was not widely appreciated or accepted by the Japanese military establishment, which held a very low opinion of the fighting effectiveness of the Red Army. This impression was reinforced by the spectacle of self-destruction as Stalin's purge swept through the Soviet High Command like a manically wielded sickle. The purge of the armed forces that began in earnest in the spring of 1937 reached its zenith in the summer of 1938 and tapered off by that autumn, but not before it had swept up one-quarter to one-third of the entire officer corps, including 80 percent of the staff of the Red Banner Far Eastern Army.[2] Thus, with the bulk of the Japanese army ready to plunge into central China, the Red Army writhing in a dance of death at home, and the Czech crisis holding the center of the international stage, a series of obscure and seemingly insignificant events began to unfold in the vicinity of Changkufeng Hill.

Opening Phases

At a tripoint on the Tyumen River about ten miles inland from the Sea of Japan and seventy-five miles southwest of Vladivostok, the borders of what were then Korea, Manchukuo, and the USSR met. For a distance of twenty-five miles northwest of that meeting point the Soviet and Korean frontiers ran near one another, separated by a narrow, tapering finger of Manchurian territory. The Tyumen River provides the boundary between this strip of Manchurian territory and Korea. The boundary between that part of Manchukuo and the USSR, as established by the Russo-Chinese border pacts of 1861 and 1885, was less precise, following a series of ridges from Lake Hanka to the point on the Tyumen River where Korea, Manchuria, and the USSR met. On the southern extremity of this ridgeline, between the villages of Yangkuanping and Podgornaya, three miles north of the point where the three boundaries merge, humpbacked Changkufeng Hill rises some 450 feet high and dominates that end of the tapering ridgeline. Dotted occasionally with short scrub pine and shrubs, the clearly defined, nearly bald, reddish hill is flanked on the west by the Tyumen River and on the east by Lake Khasan. Between Changkufeng Hill and the Tyumen River, the Manchurian salient is only one mile wide.

Changkufeng Hill, unlike Kanchatzu Island, was strategically significant. The high ground commanded the immediate vicinity for miles in all directions. To the west, within easy sight—and artillery range—was the Rashin-Hsinking railroad, which ran alongside the Tyumen River and was one of the major arteries between Manchukuo and Northern China. A few miles further to the south lay Poset Bay, where the Soviets were busily constructing a submarine base. Only sixty miles up the coast from Poset Bay is Vladivostok.

The dispute arose in this sensitive area over conflicting interpretations of the Hunchun Protocol of 1886, which fixed the boundary between the Russian Maritime Province, Manchuria, and Korea. The Soviets relied upon the Russian text and the Japanese upon the Chinese text, both of which were considered official, but which were not identical in defining the boundary. This situation was

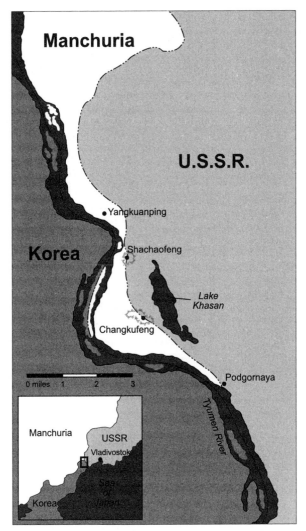

Map 2. Locale of Changkufeng Incident, July–August 1938

further confused by a number of additional factors. The strip of Manchukuoan territory was inhabited largely by people of Korean extraction. Furthermore, the salient belonged to Manchukuo in 1938, and the responsibility for the defense of Manchukuoan territory had been assigned specifically to the Kwantung Army by an Imperial Order of 1932. The peculiarities of local geography and logistics, however, prompted military authorities to assign defense of the Manchukuoan salient to the Army of Korea, which, like Kwantung Army, was a territorially defined, wholly Japanese force. Both Japanese and Soviet border garrison units had been stationed in this area since the Japanese seizure of Manchuria and tacitly had arranged themselves so that they occupied alternate points of high ground along the ridgeline boundary. If the crest of the ridgeline was an international boundary, as the Soviet side maintained, the practice of having key high points occupied in alternating sequence by the troops of either side was of dubious wisdom and legality, because the troops and their fortifications would inevitably spill over onto both sides of the crest line, thereby constituting a technical border violation. This situation invited conflict. Indeed, at Shuiliufeng Hill, some miles north of Changkufeng and occupied by Japanese troops, a minor conflict arose between small Japanese and Soviet border patrols in October 1937, but the Soviet forces soon withdrew and the area reverted to uncontested Japanese control. Changkufeng itself, however, lay at the extreme end of the ridge and apparently had been overlooked by both sides.[3]

This oversight ended abruptly on June 16, 1938. On that day, General Genrikh Lyushkov, commander of NKVD (the main Soviet internal security service, predecessor of the KGB) forces in the Soviet Far East, defected to the Japanese, walking across an unguarded stretch of the frontier in the vicinity of Changkufeng.[4] Lyushkov's name, like that of so many other high-ranking officials, had just found its way onto one of the innumerable lists of future purge victims. But this particular general, all too familiar with the ways of the NKVD and the purge, discovered he was a marked man and defected to the enemy rather than be devoured by the apparatus he had helped to operate.

Lyushkov, one of the highest-ranking Soviet officers ever to defect, was a tremendous prize for the Japanese, who publicly announced his presence in Tokyo on July 3, hailing it as a major intelligence coup. And so it was. Lyushkov, recipient of the Order of Lenin, member of the USSR Supreme Soviet (elected in 1937), and commander of twenty to thirty thousand NKVD troops, brought with him a wealth of information about Soviet troop dispositions and border security. NKVD troops, not regular Red Army troops, were responsible for border security throughout the Soviet Union. He also had some insight into the workings of the highest levels of Soviet power. He had received detailed instructions in a long meeting with Josef Stalin, Premier Vyacheslav Molotov, NKVD chief Nikolai Yezhov, Army chief of staff Kliment Voroshilov, and others in June 1937 before assuming his post as Far East NKVD commander. He even knew of the dark cloud hanging over the head of the Marshal Vasily Blyukher, the renowned commander of the Soviet Red Banner Far Eastern Army, but now believed by Stalin to be "unreliable," and soon to be arrested.[5] Lyushkov revealed this and more to his Japanese captors/protectors.

One can imagine the consternation and anxiety the news of Lyushkov's defection caused in Khabarovsk, where purges and liquidations had been conducted for months on the flimsiest of pretexts. Now, with a real case of treason and conspiracy with the enemy at their doorstep, heads surely would roll. Not only was the local border garrison commander removed, fate unknown, but a brand-new border garrison unit was assigned to tighten security in the Changkufeng sector. In the flurry of activity surrounding the reshuffle of the local security forces, the new Soviet officer in charge of the Lyushkov defection area sent a radio message on July 6 to his commander, Lieutenant General V. D. Sokolov, in Khabarovsk. This message, intercepted by Kwantung Army intelligence, sought permission to occupy Changkufeng.[6] That same day Japanese border guards observed three Soviet horsemen briefly on Changkufeng Hill. On July 9 the local Soviet commander reported that thirty of his troops had occupied Changkufeng and dug trenches along the crest with the intent of "preventing the Japanese from taking this hill-top, advantageous as it is for the continual surveillance of our territory. There was no breach of the frontier," he added.[7]

The Japanese troops responsible for the defense of the frontier in that region were elements of the 76th Infantry Regiment, 19th Division, Chosen (Korean) Army. The 19th Division commander, Lieutenant General Suetaka Kamezo, took no immediate action other than to inform the Chosen Army commander, Lieutenant General Koiso Kuniaki, who promptly notified IGHQ in Tokyo. General Koiso recommended that even in the face of an obvious Soviet border violation, on the eve of the Wuhan offensive, vital operations in China should not be jeopardized by minor diversions in the north; therefore, he would try through local diplomatic means to persuade the Soviets to withdraw and would consider resorting to force only if negotiations failed.[8]

The Japanese chargé d'affaires in Moscow met with Deputy Foreign Minister Boris Stomonyakov and requested an immediate Soviet withdrawal from Changkufeng. Stomonyakov replied that the hill was within Soviet territory and their troops would not withdraw. Ambassador Shigemitsu Mamoru hastily returned to his Moscow embassy and took up the issue with Foreign Minister Maksim Litvinov. While the diplomats bandied arguments and maps, their negotiations were overtaken by events.

At Kwantung Army Headquarters, news of the Soviet occupation of Changkufeng Hill triggered a quick response. Operations Section staff officer, Major Tsuji Masanobu (a man who will figure prominently in these pages) and a fellow officer were dispatched to Changkufeng to ascertain the situation. Their report, coupled with the moderate policy of the Chosen Army commander, confirmed the worst suspicions of the belligerently anti-Soviet staff officers at Kwantung Army

Headquarters: a blatant Soviet violation of the territory of Manchukuo (Kwantung Army's unique responsibility) was going unchallenged because of the "weak-willed" policy of Chosen Army.[9]

These officers, who savored Kwantung Army's reputation as an elite force, remembered bitterly the AGS attempt to block their firm action against the Soviets on the Amur River a year earlier. The younger officers, especially, also burned with frustration over their sedentary role in Manchukuo while the China Expeditionary Army won fame and glory for themselves and the emperor in the growing war in the south. Kwantung Army sent a series of strongly worded telegrams to IGHQ and Chosen Army Headquarters, urging and then demanding the use of force at Changkufeng. They warned that if Chosen Army did not act forcefully and soon, Kwantung Army would itself expel the invaders. Kwantung Army began to concentrate troops in eastern Manchukuo to effect such a policy. This raised hackles at Chosen Army Headquarters, where General Koiso was in the process of being replaced by Lieutenant General Nakamura Kotaro in a prescheduled command rotation.

While this verbal struggle flared between Kwantung Army "firebrands" and the "moderates" of Chosen Army and IGHQ, a similar struggle was taking shape quietly within IGHQ, where some younger staff officers were questioning the wisdom of relying on diplomacy to resolve the problem at Changkufeng. The leader of these "activists" was Colonel Inada Masazumi, chief of the Operations Section of IGHQ. Inada proposed using the Changkufeng incident as a probe or reconnaissance-in-force to test Soviet intentions. He warned that Moscow might be planning to take advantage of Japan's deepening involvement in the China war to attack Manchukuo. Therefore, before committing massive forces to the Wuhan operation, Japan should probe Soviet intentions with a controlled military challenge at Changkufeng. If the Soviets backed down, as they had a year earlier on the Amur River, or responded only locally to the probe at Changkufeng, Inada argued, Japan could continue its operations in China without anxiety and the USSR probably would be dissuaded from further border violations. If, however, the Soviets responded to the probe at Changkufeng by launching a major attack against Manchukuo, then the Wuhan operation must be canceled and combat in China minimized while Japan marshaled its main strength to deal a crushing blow to the Soviet Union.[10]

Inada succeeded in rallying powerful support for his proposal; but not all those who backed the plan shared Inada's motives. The deputy chief of AGS, General Tada Hayao, for one, had been arguing for some time that the China War be terminated so that the army could turn north and deal decisively with the USSR. He and other like-minded officers supported Inada's proposal. Some in IGHQ who believed that the Soviets would continue their vexatious border violations unless dealt a sharp blow, and others who were stung by the taunting barbs from Kwantung Army, joined the group advocating action at Changkufeng.[11] In a few days, Inada recalls, most of the key figures in AGS and the Army Ministry had been won over with surprising ease. The Navy General Staff in IGHQ was opposed at first, but navy opposition soon was overridden. On July 19 Inada's plan was approved by a three to two vote at a five ministers' conference, the main decision-making body in Premier Konoye Fumimaro's cabinet. Prince Konoye and the army and finance ministers overrode the objections of Foreign Minister Ugaki Kazushige and Navy Minister Yonai Mitsumasa.[12] However, as we will see, Ugaki, himself a full general and former army minister and governor general of Korea, and Admiral Yonai, a future premier, would not submit silently.

As a preparatory move on July 16, IGHQ ordered General Suetaka to concentrate his 19th Division near Changkufeng, but to take no further action without specific orders. When news of this Japanese troop concentration reached Khabarovsk, Marshal Blyukher put his 40th Infantry Division near Poset Bay on combat alert and ordered two of its regiments to the threatened area. This force was commanded by Colonel V. K. Bazarov.[13]

While Litvinov and Shigemitsu continued their talks unproductively in Moscow, AGS in Tokyo prepared to launch a probing attack at Changkufeng. Anticipating prompt Imperial approval of the plan, on July 19 AGS brought in General Nakamura, who had not yet left Tokyo for his new command in Korea, and gave him a detailed briefing. Nakamura was told that the 19th Division was to seize and hold Changkufeng; but important restrictions were imposed. It was hoped that the Red Army would not make a determined counterattack. If the Soviets did counterattack, the 19th Division was to hold Changkufeng with the minimum requisite force. Under no circumstances was Chosen Army to expand the scope of operations beyond the immediate vicinity of Changkufeng Hill. If the Soviets broadened the field of battle, authorities in Tokyo would take appropriate steps. To further avoid the danger of escalation, no Japanese aircraft were to be allowed near the combat zone, even if the Soviet side brought air force units into the action. Finally, to ensure that Chosen Army would clearly understand and faithfully implement all orders from Tokyo, AGS would assign several staff officers as liaison with Chosen Army Headquarters in Seoul and 19th Division. These instructions were communicated to General Suetaka, who rushed preparations for his 19th Division to launch a night attack against Changkufeng on July 21. But before the attack could begin, an unforeseen obstacle arose that seemed to cancel the entire operation.

On Friday morning, July 20, Army Minister Itagaki Seishiro went to the Imperial Palace in central Tokyo to obtain permission from the emperor to use force at Changkufeng. This was considered a purely formal, almost ritualistic procedure, for although the supreme command of Japan's armed forces rested ultimately with the emperor, it was a prerogative that the throne rarely exercised in modern times. However, unknown to the army leaders, Foreign Minister Ugaki and Navy Minister Yonai had already conveyed to the emperor their strong opposition to the proposed Changkufeng operation. The emperor told his aide-de-camp to advise the army chief of staff and army minister that the emperor "unofficially" had decided not to approve the operation, so they need not approach the throne on that matter. Accounts differ as to where and how communications broke down, but all agree that General Itagaki, unaware of the changed situation, was eventually granted an Imperial audience in which he requested permission to mobilize troops for the Changkufeng operation. The emperor, annoyed at his army minister's persistence in a matter on which the throne had already indicated a negative attitude, pointedly asked Itagaki about the opinions of the Navy Ministry and Foreign Ministry. The general replied that both ministries had been consulted and had agreed to the use of force at Changkufeng. The emperor, feeling that Itagaki intentionally was deceiving him, began to upbraid his army minister in a most vehement and uncharacteristic manner. The Imperial ire was perhaps intensified by the fact that Itagaki had been one of the two chief conspirators behind the Mukden incident of September 18, 1931, that archetypical example of *gekokujo* that launched Japan's seizure of Manchuria. The emperor branded as "abominable" the Mukden incident of 1931 and the Marco Polo Bridge incident of 1937, and warned, "Nothing like that must happen this time." The general retreated from the Imperial presence with this admonition ringing in his ears: "Hereafter you may not move a single soldier without my command."[14]

Itagaki was awed and mortified by this almost unprecedented display of Imperial anger. It took several days before he was fully convinced by knowledgeable court circles that the Imperial tongue-lashing did not require him to resign as army minister. One fact that was crystal clear to the chastened army minister was that General Suetaka's attack, due to begin the following night, would have to be stopped. Orders swiftly were passed down the chain of command to Suetaka's headquarters near Changkufeng countermanding the scheduled attack.

The 19th Division Headquarters and its commanding general burned with disappointment and frustration. General Suetaka was a professional soldier, a warrior who viewed his calling not as a necessary evil but as a noble and honorable pursuit. Suetaka was personally austere and a rigid disciplinarian. Those who served under him used such terms as "bullish," "short-tempered," and "unbending" to describe him.[15] Up to that time, the 19th Division had never tasted combat. At a division commanders' conference in Tokyo in late 1937, Suetaka had pleaded not to have his division left behind in Korea, but to be allowed to participate in the "real war" in China. He was frustrated by his continued assignment to the quiescent post in Korea. Suddenly, it appeared that the 19th Division might get a chance at "real war" at Changkufeng. This was what Suetaka had spent a lifetime preparing for; he desperately wanted to seize the opportunity. But then, orders from Tokyo indicated that the emperor himself had set his face against it.

General Suetaka's frustration was shared by Colonel Inada and the activists at IGHQ. Despite the unmistakable negative tone of the Imperial audience of July 20th, the Operations Section of IGHQ sent a series of messages to Generals Nakamura and Suetaka stressing the "temporary" character of the postponement of the Changkufeng operation.[16] Internal IGHQ documents show that some officers, frustrated by the Imperial Order, were "covertly" hoping that the local commander would attack "on his own initiative," thereby relieving IGHQ of responsibility in the matter.[17] Major Arao Okikatsu, IGHQ's special liaison officer at 19th Division Headquarters, recalled, "I did not interpret the fact that Imperial sanction could not be obtained for the use of force at Changkufeng to mean the same as an Imperial Order *forbidding* the use of force. As far as I was concerned, I emphasized the importance of judging how best to deal with matters, given the *suspension* of the use of force" (italics in the original).[18]

General Suetaka came to share this view. In retrospect, some Japanese scholars have criticized IGHQ for failing clearly to convey the intention of the emperor to Chosen Army. They identify this sort of "communication by mental telepathy" as a prime cause for the outbreak of fighting at Changkufeng.[19]

The ambiguous signals that Chosen Army and 19th Division were receiving from Tokyo began to show effects immediately. On July 21 Suetaka radioed Chosen Army Headquarters for permission forcibly to evict the Soviet invaders "for the purposes of non-aggravation." Nakamura rejected this proposal. That same day, Suetaka ordered the occupation of Chiangchunfeng, a smaller hillock some eight hundred yards west of Changkufeng. Nakamura, fearing that fighting might "spontaneously" erupt with the opposing troops so close, instructed Suetaka to withdraw from the hillock, which the 19th Division commander declined to do. After a day or two of wrangling over this issue, the new Chosen Army commander relented, issuing ex post facto permission for the occupation of Chiangchunfeng. These developments spurred Major Arao on July 23 to notify his superiors at IGHQ that Suetaka still was preparing to attack at Changkufeng. This brought forth a new Imperial Order on July 26, directing immediate withdrawal and suspension of offensive plans for Changkufeng. Suetaka obeyed this order. By July 28 the main body of the 19th Division was back to its normal peacetime positions. Suetaka left two infantry battalions on the west bank of the Tyumen River with instructions to keep the Soviets under observation—to wait and see.[20]

What these troops saw on the morning of July 29 was most disturbing. Soviet border troops, apparently concluding that the danger had passed with the withdrawal of the main body of the 19th Division, began digging in on Shachaofeng, a lesser hill on the same boundary ridgeline, about a mile and a half north of Changkufeng. It is not clear at what level of the Soviet command this decision was made. General Suetaka, who personally had remained in the troubled area despite the withdrawal of his division headquarters, decided that his mission demanded the expulsion of the Soviets from Shachaofeng. Without consulting higher authority, he ordered an attack by part of his residual force. At 2:30 that afternoon, a two-prong Japanese assault routed the Soviet infantry squad on Shachaofeng Hill. The first blood had been drawn; all ten soldiers in Lieutenant Aleksey Makhalin's squad on Shachaofeng were killed or wounded.[21]

The Soviet forces on nearby Changkufeng responded quickly. That same afternoon, they brought up reinforcements, shrouded by rain and heavy fog. At 5:00 p.m. two companies of Colonel V. K. Bazarov's 119th Infantry Regiment, supported by several tanks, drove the Japanese assault force from Shachaofeng.[22]

That night, General Suetaka reported the outbreak of the "Shachaofeng incident" to Chosen Army Headquarters and requested permission to reconcentrate the 19th Division in the threatened area. By labeling these actions the Shachaofeng incident, Suetaka hoped to have it classified as an entirely new event, thereby circumventing the orders forbidding the use of force at Changkufeng.

Chosen Army Headquarters tentatively agreed to treat the affair separately from the Changkufeng incident but continued to try to restrain Suetaka, instructing him that "enemy forces attacking our troops . . . will be defeated. However, you should be satisfied with just driving them back across the border." Nakamura's final injunction to Suetaka was to "take great care not to enlarge this conflict." As the 19th Division redeployed near the Tyumen River, IGHQ sent a cautionary telegram, stating that "the Shachaofeng incident should be handled by adhering to the policy of non-aggravation."[23]

The next day, General Suetaka made the decision for which the activists at IGHQ had been covertly hoping (and hinting) for ten days. On July 30 he ordered his most dependable line officer, Colonel Sato Kotoku, commander of the 75th Infantry Regiment, to launch an attack that night against the intruding Soviet troops.

Suetaka's divisional chief of staff and most of the staff officers, attuned to Chosen Army's stated policy of "nonexpansion" of the incident, argued against their commander's decision. The general insisted, however, arguing that "the offensive which was suspended by Imperial Order, and this particular situation, are completely different matters. If we do not seize an opportunity such as this to hit the Russians and thus show the power of the Imperial Army, then the Soviet-Manchukuo border will hereafter be dominated by Soviet forces, and that will only leave roots for trouble in the future."[24]

Suetaka forbade any of his officers to report this decision to Chosen Army Headquarters or to Tokyo, lest his attack plans be canceled again by higher authorities. Even liaison officers from Tokyo respected the general's wish. Suetaka had decided to "act on his own initiative."

The hollowness of Suetaka's claim that he was now dealing with a new situation, completely different from the Changkufeng incident, is demonstrated by Colonel Sato's decision, which Suetaka approved, that "in order to sweep the enemy out of the heights southwest of Shachaofeng, the foe on Changkufeng must be ejected also." Only one infantry company was assigned to take Shachaofeng; the main body of the 75th Regiment prepared to assault the Soviets on Changkufeng.[25]

From the record of the divisional staff conference cited above, it seems clear that Suetaka's primary motive was to "teach the Russians a lesson" and uphold the honor and prestige of the Imperial Army. This was quite different from Colonel Inada's concept of a calculated reconnaissance-in-force. Inada was well aware of Suetaka's attitude and sympathized with it to a certain extent. But he counted on Suetaka's iron self-discipline to keep the situation under control when the fighting actually started. Inada later wrote that Suetaka's decision was in "complete accordance" with IGHQ wishes at that time, in "arbitrarily" launching an offensive that IGHQ could not authorize formally because of the emperor's prohibition.[26]

Thus, General Suetaka placed himself and the 12,000 men under his command in a position to be used in Colonel Inada's probe. The cost of this operation, exacted on the slopes of Changkufeng Hill, would be higher than either officer anticipated, the results more questionable and controversial.

The Battle

This was to be the first real test between the Imperial Army and the new Red Army. Colonel Sato selected his finest battalions for the assault. The attack, at Inada's suggestion, would be launched during the hours of greatest darkness, ensuring maximum tactical surprise and minimizing the effectiveness of Soviet tanks and artillery.[27] Approximately 1,600 men would take part in the actual assault, relying on stealth as well as ferocity in the enshrined Japanese battle doctrine of the "human bullet." The assault force began to deploy across the Tyumen River at 2:15 a.m. on July 31. Visibility extended only ten to fifteen yards.

The Soviet troops on the heights failed to detect the 75th Regiment crossing the river and were taken completely by surprise by the first wave of Japanese attackers sweeping up the slopes. The Soviet frontline troops called for artillery support, and while furious close combat raged along the high ground, Red Army gunners sent up illuminating flares and commenced artillery fire. But the attackers already had penetrated the defensive positions, and the issue was decided by the infantry, often in hand-to-hand combat, with the Japanese enjoying the advantages of surprise and superior numbers. By 5:15 a.m. Colonel Sato's troops controlled the crest of Changkufeng, and by 6:00 the last Soviet defenders had been driven from the heights. A Russian NCO who took part in the action reported that nearly all the defenders were either killed or wounded, and those who could swim plunged into the frigid waters of Lake Khasan to save themselves. As the sun rose higher over the battlefield, it was greeted by the *Hi no Maru*, Japan's own "Rising Sun," fluttering triumphantly from a flagpole at the summit of Changkufeng.[28]

By modern standards the action was a small one, but it was a hard-fought and relatively prolonged affair conducted at close quarters. The defenders gave a good account of themselves before being driven from the heights, as shown by the number of Japanese casualties: 45 killed and 133 wounded out of 1,600 attackers, approximately one in nine. Soviet accounts admit to 13 killed and 55 wounded on their side, plus one tank and one field gun destroyed. This almost certainly understates their losses.[29]

Within minutes of securing the crest of Changkufeng, General Suetaka notified Chosen Army Headquarters. Then and in many subsequent communications, Suetaka justified his actions by characterizing them as a counterattack against Soviet offensive action at Shachaofeng.[30] This misleading information, along with the results of the night attack, were quickly passed along to the authorities in Tokyo.

That General Suetaka and Colonel Sato were aware of having violated at least the spirit, if not the letter, of an Imperial Order, is shown by this entry in the 75th Regiment Combat Diary: "It was a truly awe-inspiring thing, since we have heard that, in accordance with the Imperial Will, it was decided not to use force against Changkufeng." Sometime later, after the true circumstances surrounding the night attack were more widely and accurately known, a revised version of the justification was circulated. This version held that while there had been no Soviet attack on July 30 or 31, "Colonel Sato judged that the enemy had an attack in mind . . . and therefore he decided to stage a preventive night assault against the enemy facing him."[31]

News of Suetaka's night attack stirred mixed reactions that morning in Tokyo. The Army High Command acknowledged that Suetaka's action implemented their intentions and broke open the impasse. But there was the problem of the emperor's admonition against the use of force at Changkufeng. Colonel Inada felt a heavy sense of responsibility for Suetaka's seeming violation of an Imperial Order and wanted to intercede on the general's behalf at the palace. However, staff colonels were rarely granted Imperial audiences and it fell to General Tada, deputy chief of AGS, to inform the emperor. Tada, a supporter of the use of force at Changkufeng, approached this task with apprehension.

That same afternoon, July 31, at the Imperial villa at Hayama, General Tada nervously explained to the emperor what had transpired. Tada took great pains to emphasize that the 19th Division had acted to keep within the guidelines of the "nonexpansion" policy by refraining strictly from crossing the boundary line into the USSR in pursuit of the enemy. Based on Tada's somewhat misleading report, the emperor expressed his satisfaction that the frontline troops had acted with restraint under trying circumstances, and, noting that what had been done could not be undone anyway, gave his sanction for the night attack. Tada, immensely relieved, withdrew from the Imperial Presence and returned to Tokyo with "face beaming." Such was the emotional importance attached to the emperor's judgments that, according to the diary of Colonel Saito, 19th Division chief of staff, when word of the emperor's approval of the night attack reached General Suetaka, "tears glistened in the eyes of the division commander, and he quickly retired to his room. I too could not control my tears and sobbed, despite the fact that other people were present."[32]

And so, to the immense relief of the officers at IGHQ, Chosen Army Headquarters, and 19th Division, there was no reprimand or chastisement from the emperor. The retribution that followed came from an entirely different quarter.

Later in the afternoon of July 31, Suetaka requested permission from General Nakamura to transfer the bulk of his division across the Tyumen River and onto the heights in case of a Soviet counterattack. The request was denied. Nakamura considered the border rectified and the incident closed. The Soviet command did not share that view.

On that same eventful July 31, in Khabarovsk, General Grigori Shtern was appointed commander of the 39th Corps of the Red Banner Far Eastern Army. This corps was strengthened to include the 32nd, 39th, and 40th Infantry Divisions and the 2nd Mechanized Brigade. The next day, Marshal Blyukher received orders from Marshal Voroshilov, Red Army chief of staff, in Moscow: "Destroy those who have intruded within the limits of our boundaries." That responsibility fell to General Shtern. The new commander of the 39th Corps, a veteran of the Spanish Civil War, had just stepped into the shoes of a recently purged comrade. Scarcely acquainted with his new command, threatened by the Japanese before him and the NKVD at his back, Shtern must have regarded the impending test at Changkufeng with apprehension. This may help explain his clumsy handling of the tactical situation.[33]

Shtern reported that he would be unable to concentrate all his units at the front until August 5. Instead of waiting until then to mount a powerful offensive, he frittered away much of his strength by throwing his units piecemeal against the heights as they arrived off the march. This began on August 1, when three thousand men of the 40th Division were hurled in a frontal assault along the ridge and were driven back with heavy losses.[34]

After this first Soviet counterattack, General Nakamura recognized the incorrectness of his earlier view and allowed Suetaka to deploy the entire 19th Division in the Changkufeng area. August 2 and 3 brought repeated and costly frontal assaults against the Japanese-held heights as more units of Shtern's 39th Corps reached the area. Colonel Sato's 75th Regiment distinguished itself in repelling these Soviet attacks but suffered heavy losses itself.

Shtern was also able to bring Soviet air force attacks and heavy artillery bombardments to bear on the 19th Division. Although the rain and fog that persisted in the area through the early phases of the battle hampered the effectiveness of Soviet aircraft and artillery, their employment in large numbers posed a serious threat to the Japanese defensive positions, because the 19th Division's organic artillery was far outgunned by the Soviet 39th Corps and Japanese air force units had been forbidden categorically to enter the combat zone, an order they obeyed.

The mounting Soviet counterattacks convinced General Suetaka and his staff that a static defense of the Shachaofeng-Changkufeng ridgeline was tactically unsound, because it tied the 19th Division to the high ground, exposed to air and artillery bombardment against which they had no effective defense or reply. Even more ominous was the threat of envelopment by the rapidly growing Soviet forces, a move that could easily be effected if the Soviets expanded the combat zone in the north or south. To forestall this threat and to relieve some of the pressure on his embattled troops, on August 2 Suetaka proposed a flanking attack of his own in which his 76th Regiment would attack the Soviet forces north and east of Lake Khasan, that is, several miles inside the USSR. Chosen Army Headquarters approved this tactically sound maneuver, but IGHQ in Tokyo immediately rejected the plan on the grounds that such a move would expand the scope of the incident, a tendency that was to be avoided at all costs.[35] The unequivocal orders from IGHQ were for Suetaka to continue holding the heights and adhere to the policy of "nonexpansion," staying exclusively on the defensive. The 19th Division was specifically forbidden to expand the combat zone, attempt flanking maneuvers, call upon air support, receive strategic reinforcements, or retreat from the hills—despite increasingly powerful attacks launched by a superior enemy force. This unenviable situation was implicit in Colonel Inada's concept of a probe of Soviet intentions. The probe had been placed; it was now for the Soviets to demonstrate their intentions.

As Shtern's attacks continued and the fighting began to turn against the Japanese defenders, Kwantung Army drew up plans for a diversionary attack against the Soviet flank to relieve the pressure at Changkufeng. This too was prohibited by central authorities in Tokyo. Behind this Japanese restraint were decisions reached by IGHQ and confirmed by the cabinet, that the incident was to be settled diplomatically. In the meantime, expansion of the conflict was to be avoided by having the forces on the spot maintain the status quo. But the leaders in Tokyo and on the ground at Changkufeng found that with the Soviets holding the whip hand, even those limited objectives might be difficult to achieve.

Meanwhile, within some parts of AGS and the Army Ministry, the idea was beginning to gain ground that Japanese troops should be withdrawn unilaterally from Changkufeng because the honor of the 19th Division had been satisfied by the night attack of July 31 and the continued fighting was threatening the Wuhan operation.

In the Army Ministry, in particular, nearly all important figures, including Vice Minister Tojo Hideki, began to urge withdrawal. The deputy chief of AGS, General Tada, weakened and began drawing up orders for the withdrawal of the 19th Division at the first appropriate opportunity. However, Colonel Inada's influential Operations Section objected, arguing that a unilateral withdrawal of the Japanese forces under such circumstances would "wreck the proud traditions of the Imperial Army" and would "exert unfortunate effects upon Soviet-Japanese relations in the future." These conflicting views could not be resolved, and indecision prevailed in Tokyo.[36]

On August 4, while Shtern continued to mass his forces and hammer at the Japanese entrenched on the high ground, Ambassador Shigemitsu again met with Litvinov in Moscow. The Japanese envoy proposed that both sides immediately suspend hostilities and refer the dispute to a joint commission to establish a clear and mutually satisfactory boundary. He supplemented this proposal with a series of "on-the-spot" photographs that the Japanese army had fabricated, purporting to show Soviet fortifications and corpses some fifty yards inside Japanese territory. Litvinov was unmoved, replying that the fighting would end only after the Japanese army ceased its attacks and withdrew all its forces from Soviet territory. He declared firmly that there would be no alteration of the boundary, as understood by the Soviet Union.[37] Litvinov and Stalin seemed confident that unless the Japanese were willing and able to terminate the war in China, they would have to bow to the Soviets at Changkufeng.[38]

Shigemitsu's report of the uncompromising Soviet diplomatic position reached Tokyo at the same time as grim news from the fighting front. From August 4 to 5, Shtern relied primarily on intensive artillery and air bombardment of the Japanese positions while he continued to build up his frontline troops and prepare for a renewed assault. Colonel Sato likened the rate of Soviet artillery fire to that of machine guns, and Japanese artillery to lightly falling raindrops. The ratio of Soviet to Japanese artillery fire may have reached 100:1 according to Japanese estimates, an incredible disparity attributable in part to differing tactical concepts and to Japan's lack of experience with massed artillery fire—a lesson the European armies had learned in the First World War. Meanwhile, the 19th Division dug in and awaited the expected onslaught. On August 6 Shtern renewed his ground assaults.

Suetaka's position would have been altogether hopeless except for the terrain, which favored the defenders of the heights. Colonel Inada of IGHQ had taken that into account in proposing his probe at that point on the frontier. If the Soviets meant to keep the hostilities localized, they would have to attack with the lake close at their back, leaving little room for deployment and maneuver. Japanese artillery on the high ground commanded all approaches to the hills. Moreover, the southeastern and northeastern approaches to the hills—which the Soviets would have to traverse unless they were willing to expand the combat zone by crossing the Tyumen River—were flat marshland with little protective cover, most ill suited for the deployment of large formations of men and tanks.[39] Yet it was precisely through these murderous fire lanes that the Soviet infantry and tank attacks of August 6–10 were channeled. This suggests that Shtern, as well as Suetaka, was under restraint from higher authorities to keep the fighting localized. Within the context of this strategic constraint, however, the Soviets spared no effort to achieve their goal of driving the Japanese from Changkufeng.

The renewed Soviet attacks were pressed relentlessly, heedless of their heavy losses of men and machines. Official Japanese military records report that on August 6 "Japanese positions appeared to be on the verge of collapse. The defenders managed to hold on, however, with the aid of steadily received reinforcements from the 19th Division." The next day brought even stronger Soviet assaults. Losses were extremely heavy on both sides. "Again the Japanese defenses appeared to be crumbling, but the units still clung to the heights."[40]

This was not the only pressure the Soviets applied. The Soviet press abandoned its earlier restraint, and in August *Pravda* and *Izvestia* headlines clamored for a "Savage Rebuff to the Brazen Aggressors." An American journalist was encouraged by the Soviet news censor at the Foreign Ministry to emphasize strongly in his reports the possibility of war between the Soviet Union and Japan unless Japan ceased its aggression. The journalist was authorized to ascribe this view to "the Soviet circles here."[41] Such press campaigns by totalitarian governments often are used to prepare the populace for an impending crisis. The Japanese press, in contrast, gave Changkufeng low-key treatment, leading the U.S. embassy in Tokyo to conclude correctly that Japan was trying to play down the fighting and terminate the incident.[42]

By the end of the first week of August, military and civilian authorities in Tokyo were growing alarmed. The specter of simultaneous wars against China and the USSR was beginning to take shape, a grim prospect that even the activists at IGHQ dreaded. Against this was weighed the restraint shown by the Red Army in two respects: restricting the fighting to the immediate vicinity of Changkufeng Hill despite the major tactical disadvantage this imposed on the attacking troops, and not threatening Japan by concentrating offensive forces at other points along the three-thousand-mile frontier.

In view of these factors, IGHQ ordered some "emergency" military measures. The 19th Division's artillery, consisting of 75-mm mountain guns and some smaller ordinance, was beefed up with heavy artillery drawn from North China and from Kwantung Army. The 104th Infantry Division, earmarked for the China Expeditionary Army, was ordered to the Hunchun area in eastern Manchuria, where it took up a threatening position on the flank of Soviet forces in that area. Kwantung Army itself deployed its main forces to eastern Manchuria to exert "silent pressure" on the USSR. In addition, on August 4 the Japanese male population of Harbin and other Manchukuoan cities was ordered to prepare to report for military service with units on the frontier. No such order had ever before been issued.[43]

Despite all these efforts, the Soviet attacks grew still fiercer from August 7 to 10. The casualties grew alarmingly, reaching 51 percent of Colonel Sato's 75th Regiment. Morale among the frontline Japanese troops began to sink after August 7, as the hopelessness of their situation bore in on them. To the Japanese defenders on the ridges, as well as to military authorities in Tokyo, it was becoming increasingly clear that if IGHQ attempted to maintain the current position in the combat zone without committing substantial reinforcements to the battle, the 19th Division faced annihilation.

In absolute terms, the Soviet 39th Corps was taking even heavier casualties in its repeated frontal assaults against the dug-in Japanese defenders. On August 8 Chosen Army intercepted a message from Shtern to Blyukher to the effect that Soviet losses could be expected to double if the fighting continued.[44] This news, which must have provided some grim satisfaction to Suetaka and his men, is doubly revealing, for in spite of it, the Soviet attacks continued without letup.

As early as August 6 Shigemitsu was informed by Foreign Minister Ugaki that the government was considering serious concessions to the Soviets in order to settle the incident and that, depending on the circumstances, the abandonment of Changkufeng might even be permissible. However, the deadlock within IGHQ persisted, with the staff officers of the Operations Section stubbornly resisting any notion of Japanese withdrawal. Consequently, Shigemitsu was not sent clear instructions and the negotiations continued into the second week of August as the agony of the 19th Division approached the breaking point.

By August 10 Shtern had achieved a 3:1 superiority in manpower and a 4:1 margin in artillery. This pressure on the 19th Division, which had been in continuous action since July 31, was simply too much. That afternoon, Soviet infantry at terrific cost succeeded in wresting control of the southern corner of the crest of Changkufeng. The defenders temporarily stabilized the situation and drew up a new defense perimeter, but the Soviet entrenchment on the high ground signaled that a turning point had been reached. Suetaka could not bring himself openly to admit defeat, but his chief of staff took the remarkable step of signaling to Chosen Army Headquarters requesting the immediate suspension of operations and asking that IGHQ be notified that "appropriate diplomatic measures are immediately necessary."[45] Chosen Army Headquarters was so startled by this unprecedented request that they did not relay it to Tokyo. However, one of IGHQ's own staff officers, Colonel Terada Masao, had just returned to Tokyo on August 10 from a battlefield inspection and argued vigorously for the immediate withdrawal of the 19th Division. The opinion of Colonel Terada, himself a member of Inada's Operations Section, carried substantial weight. That afternoon, in an atmosphere that was "rather gloomy and permeated with a sense of disaster," "appropriate diplomatic measures" finally were authorized. Foreign Minister Ugaki sent the following instructions to his ambassador in Moscow:

1. Settle the matter quickly.
2. Consent to withdraw to the lines as of July 29.
3. Base the settlement on the Hunchun Treaty [as the Soviets insisted].
4. Permissible to withdraw one kilometer from the Changkufeng and Shachaofeng line and agree not to re-enter.[46]

Shigemitsu met with Litvinov that evening and offered to have the Japanese troops withdraw one kilometer westward from the ridgeline if the Soviet side would agree to a cease-fire. Litvinov quickly agreed, and it was decided that the cease-fire would go into effect at noon the following day, August 11. Later that same evening, while the Japanese embassy staff was celebrating the cease-fire with a few drinks, a telephone call came from Litvinov's office advising that it would not be necessary for the Japanese troops unilaterally to withdraw one kilometer. The Soviet government would be satisfied with a cease-fire along the line that both sides were occupying as of midnight, August 10. The Japanese diplomats jumped at the offer, and the authorities in Tokyo were delighted when notified that their forces would not be compelled to withdraw unilaterally.[47]

The Litvinov-Shigemitsu agreement of August 10 established a joint border commission to redemarcate the boundary. This commission never reached a mutually acceptable definition of the boundary in that area, but the real outcome became clear before the border commission's first meeting. On the afternoon of August 11, a few hours after the cease-fire went into effect, General Shtern met with one of the 19th Division's regimental commanders to arrange details for the separation of forces. With the hostilities "honorably" terminated, IGHQ ordered the immediate withdrawal of all Japanese forces to the west bank of the Tyumen River. When the last Japanese soldier crossed the Tyumen on the night of August 13, that river became the de facto border. Soviet troops reoccupied Changkufeng and the other nearby heights—with unforeseen and far-reaching consequences.

The Meanings of Changkufeng

Authoritative Japanese military sources conclude that if the negotiations in Moscow had been prolonged for one more day, the 19th Division most likely would have been driven from Changkufeng and the surrounding heights.[48] No doubt General Shtern's infantry also was greatly relieved that the bloodletting had come to an end. Still, one wonders why Moscow accepted a cease-fire at a moment when its troops were so close to achieving complete victory on the battlefield.

Perhaps the leadership in Moscow concluded that it would be prudent to accept the "three-quarters of a loaf" offered by Shigemitsu rather than try to win it all. After all, there had been threatening Japanese troop mobilizations in eastern Manchuria and the Imperial Army already had established a record of brash and unpredictable action. Furthermore, in the midst of the crisis over Czechoslovakia, Moscow might not have wanted to risk an escalation of hostilities in Asia. Another possibility is that Moscow was incorrectly informed about the actual battlefield situation. Perhaps the news of the seizure by their troops of a small section of the crest of Changkufeng was taken to mean that the entire ridgeline already was, or shortly (i.e., before midnight August 10) would be, in Soviet hands. The surprising telephone call from Litvinov to the Japanese embassy on the night of August 10, trading the one-kilometer Japanese withdrawal for a cease-fire line based on actual frontline positions, suggests that faulty communications between Shtern's headquarters and the Kremlin may have helped save the "face" of many Japanese army men, effecting the removal of the 19th Division from Changkufeng by diplomatic rather than military means.

Both sides sustained heavy casualties. Immediately after the battle, the Japanese press reported 158 Japanese troops killed and 740 wounded. The medical records of the 19th Division show 526 killed and 914 wounded, for a total of 1,440. The actual total may have been somewhat higher, perhaps 1,500–2,000. After the armistice, TASS announced 236 Red Army men killed and 611 wounded. In view of Shtern's tactics, these figures are far too low. The attackers, forced to advance uphill across exposed terrain against an enemy in prepared positions, probably suffered a casualty rate two to three times greater than that of the defenders. This would place Soviet casualties in the neighborhood of 3,000–5,000. That conforms to the findings of a Soviet Military Council inquiry into the conflict (August 31, 1938), which said Soviet casualties were 408 killed and 2,807 wounded. The official Japanese estimate of Soviet casualties is 4,500–7,000.[49]

Not all the casualties fell on the battlefield. Vasily Konstantinovich Blyukher, marshal of the Soviet Union, distinguished soldier and diplomat, one-time warlord of the Soviet Far East, and candidate member of the Central Committee of the CPSU, was recalled to Moscow in August 1938, relieved of his command in September, and, together with his family, arrested in October. He was accused of failing adequately to prepare his forces to meet the Japanese aggressors and, more ominously, of concealing a multitude of "enemies of the people" at all levels in his command. On November 9, 1938, Blyukher died under interrogation, a sanitized way of saying he was tortured to death.[50]

Other victims included several hundred-thousand rice farmers of Korean origin living in the Ussuri region of the USSR. Immediately after the fighting, Soviet authorities deported these hapless peasants to the Soviet Central Asian Republic of Kazakhstan in order to eliminate all Korean hamlets, some of which had been used by Japanese espionage agents.

The Changkufeng incident also exerted an indirect influence on the Japanese army's Wuhan operation. The massive flow of men and material needed for this "climactic" campaign in Japan's futile attempt to force China into submission was interrupted temporarily while fighting flared on the Soviet frontier. Especially missed by the Japanese army advancing on Wuhan was Kwantung Army's 2nd Air Group, which had been earmarked for the Wuhan operation but was held back because of Changkufeng. Chiang Kai-shek's decision to blow up the dikes of the Yellow River, flooding the distant approaches to Wuhan through which the Japanese had to pass, also slowed the Japanese offensive. By the time Japanese forces entered Hankow on October 25, 1938, Chiang Kai-shek had transferred his capital far inland to Chungking. Ironically, the fall of Wuhan, which severed the rail lines from Canton to the interior, increased Chiang's dependence on Soviet aid, which came overland and by air from Soviet Central Asia into western China. The Japanese achieved their immediate goal, but the decisive victory for which they hoped eluded them. Chinese resistance continued, and the one million Japanese troops on the mainland could not be withdrawn from the occupation and "pacification" of China.

To the question, "What is the real meaning of Changkufeng?" there are many answers. For General Suetaka and the men of the 19th Division, it was an experience that would be remembered with bitterness and pride. The general and his officers who hungered for battle had their fill, albeit under circumstances far from their choosing. To many 19th Division veterans, remembering comrades who bled and died on those barren slopes, Changkufeng may have seemed a pointless and tragic waste. Yet they fought bravely under harrowing conditions, holding their position to the bitter end. And the end brought retreat—humiliation—and direct praise from the emperor—elation.[51] A bittersweet legacy.

For the Red Army, the battle was not only the first major test of its mettle, but was an important gauge of the impact of the purge. While General Shtern and the Red Banner Far Eastern Army did not fight brilliantly, they performed creditably under difficult circumstances. The U.S. military attaché in Moscow concluded that "any adverse effects on Red Army efficiency which may have been occasioned by the purge have now been overcome. . . . The recent events around Lake Hassan have shown that the personnel of the Red Army is not only dependable, but that it can be called upon for extraordinary exploits of valor, that the material with which the Red Army is equipped is adequate and serviceable, if, indeed, it is not entitled to higher rating."[52]

The U.S. military attaché in China, Colonel (later General) Joseph Stillwell, reached a similar, if more succinct, conclusion: "the Russian troops appeared to advantage, and those who believe the Red Army is rotten would do well to reconsider their views."[53] A year later, however, on the eve of the outbreak of World War II, no such reconsideration of views had taken place. Most British, French, German, and Japanese military leaders clung to the idea that the Red Army was a "paper tiger."

The top Soviet leadership in any case seemed pleased with the performance of the army. Shtern was given command of the entire TransBaikal Military District—Marshal Blyukher's old job—and was promoted to colonel general in 1940.[54] Medals and decorations were bestowed generously on the "Heroes of Lake Khasan," as they were proclaimed. At the annual celebration of the Bolshevik Revolution in Red Square on November 7, 1938, Marshal Voroshilov delivered a particularly bellicose speech. Referring to the recent fighting at Lake Khasan, he warned that if another such border violation occurred, the Red Army would not confine itself merely to repelling the incursion, noting that "it is more convenient and easier for us to crush the enemy in his own territory."

Perceptions in Tokyo were quite different. Disagreements within and between the army and the government regarding the handling of the Changkufeng incident persisted in divergent evaluations of the episode. Many military men and government officials felt that the honor and prestige of the Imperial Army had suffered a serious blow at Changkufeng. This attitude was especially prevalent in Kwantung Army, which felt doubly mortified because the defeat had occurred on Manchukuoan territory, which was that army's sacred duty to defend.

Colonel Inada, however, denied that it was a defeat at all, arguing that his reconnaissance mission had been executed according to plan and ended with the return of the reconnaissance force to its original position. The probe, he said, accurately revealed Soviet intentions vis-à-vis Japan and the China War: the USSR would defend its frontiers vigorously but showed no intention of launching or preparing to launch a major assault against Japan. Consequently, he concluded, Japan could go ahead with the Wuhan operation without fear of a Soviet "stab in the back."[55]

Many of the activists at IGHQ denied being particularly interested in the reconnaissance aspect of the affair but supported Inada's plan mainly because it proposed attacking the Soviet troops that had occupied Changkufeng. Major General Hashimoto Gun's concurrence in this is particularly significant because he was Inada's boss, chief of the Operations Division. This casts doubt on the accuracy of Inada's interpretation. Even allowing that Inada's concept of a reconnaissance probe may have been the guiding spirit behind General Suetaka's actions on July 29–31, other serious questions remain. The editors of the respected *Gen Dai Shi* (*Modern History Documents*) strongly criticize Inada's idea of a reconnaissance-in-force, arguing that IGHQ failed to draft any plans in the event that the Soviet Union actually did respond massively to the "probe." Preliminaries for the Wuhan operation had begun on June 15. At the time of the Changkufeng fighting, they claim, the Wuhan operation was already in motion.[56] A leading authority on Japanese military history states this view more strongly: "But what if the Soviet Union had dared to intervene in the Sino-Japanese struggle at that particular point? One may suppose that Japan might not have been able to escape the danger of losing both Manchuria and Korea, even if the Japanese forces had stopped the Wuhan operation and headed north. In this respect it can be said that Japan was playing with fire."[57]

Yet the army leaders showed little recognition of having been "burned" at Changkufeng. Misled by the limited scope of the fighting, AGS drew few "lessons learned." The demonstrated superiority, both quantitative and qualitative, of Soviet materiel (artillery, tanks, aircraft, etc.) was almost entirely ignored. The Imperial Army's low opinion of the Red Army's fighting effectiveness was not revised as a result of Changkufeng. The 19th Division had, after all, held its ground against a Soviet force three to four times its size, hadn't it? Also, "the example remained that arbitrary action undertaken by a local unit, even when close to violating an Imperial Order, was accepted without censure."[58] This attitude of disrespect toward the Red Army as well as toward the restraining influence of the government in Tokyo was especially prevalent in Kwantung Army, where it would have grave consequences a year later.

The Kremlin apparently learned an important lesson from Changkufeng. The Japanese army had not behaved as Soviet leaders expected it would. Despite Japan's deepening involvement in China, the Imperial Army had dared to challenge the Red Army at Changkufeng. But for the intervention of the emperor, the fighting might have escalated far beyond the levels actually attained. The Changkufeng incident was a disturbing reminder to Stalin that the Japanese threat to his eastern flank, which was thought to have been neutralized by the China War, was still present. What if the anti-Soviet elements in Tokyo and in the Japanese army forces in the field had prevailed and raised the stakes by committing major ground and air forces and expanding the geographical scope of the battle? In view of the political situation in the USSR and the mounting Czech crisis, in which the Western democracies showed little inclination forcibly to resist German eastward expansion, Moscow might have been compelled to sue for a diplomatic settlement rather than risk war with Japan. Thus, it could be said that Japan was not the only one "playing with fire" at Changkufeng.

In the event, moderation prevailed in Tokyo and the Japanese backed down. But Chosen Army was not Kwantung Army, and the surprisingly firm resistance of Chiang Kai-shek's forces would not indefinitely tie down the main strength of the Japanese army. Furthermore, the Soviet tactical victory at Changkufeng was followed within weeks by the strategic defeat at the Munich Conference, which brought German troops closer to the Soviet borders. The specter of a coordinated German-Japanese attack almost surely lurked in the mind of the paranoid dictator Stalin, although he was at least able to derive satisfaction from the way the conflict at Lake Khasan ended.

On August 11, the day of the cease-fire agreement, Premier Konoye remarked to Baron Harada about the recent fighting, "It's cleared up for the time being, but we must be more careful from now on."[59] But at Kwantung Army Headquarters, a very different conclusion was drawn. Soon after the cease-fire, Kwantung Army began pressing to have the Manchurian salient and the Soviet-occupied Changkufeng Hill removed from Chosen Army responsibility and reassigned officially to Kwantung Army. Authorities in Tokyo concurred, and on October 8, 1938, responsibility for the disputed area was transferred to Kwantung Army. Even the onset of subfreezing weather that autumn did not cool the desire for revenge that smoldered at Kwantung Army Headquarters.

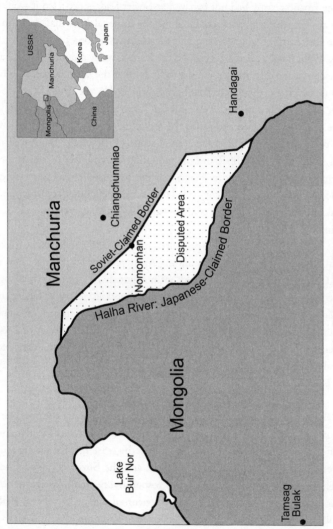

Map 3. Nomonhan Disputed Border

CHAPTER 4

NOMONHAN: PRELIMINARIES

A glance at the map 3 (opposite) shows Manchukuo and the Mongolian People's Republic (MPR) each extending a bulging protrusion into the other's territory. While both of these projections could be viewed as potentially aggressive "thrusts" into hostile territory, each also faced the possibility of being enveloped and absorbed by the empire into whose territory it extended. A northward thrust from western Manchuria through Mongolia would threaten to sever the MPR and the Soviet Far East from the rest of the USSR. Conversely, a pincer attack from Mongolia and the Soviet Maritime Province would threaten to envelop and strangle Manchukuo. This underlines the strategic significance of the MPR-Manchukuo frontier in the 1930s. One of the most sensitive sectors of that troubled frontier was the thick Mongolian salient projecting eastward about 150 miles into west central Manchukuo. There, in mid-1939, the Soviet-Japanese power struggle exploded into large-scale combat. This conflict, called the Nomonhan incident by the Japanese and the Battle of Khalkhin Gol by the Soviets and Mongolians,[1] far exceeded the Changkufeng incident in duration, intensity, and significance. Lasting four months, with thirty to fifty thousand killed or wounded, the Nomonhan conflict was a small undeclared war—the first instance in the modern age of limited war between great powers.

The Setting

The Mongolian salient is a semiarid area of mostly flat, sometimes gently undulating, sandy plains and grassland studded with occasional short scrub pines and low shrubs. The extreme continental climate is harsh. In May the days can be hot, with frigid nights. In July and August, the daytime temperature regularly rises above 100 degrees Fahrenheit, but the nights remain cold. Mosquitoes and enormous horseflies swarm in the summer, making netting imperative. There is little rainfall, but in the summer, especially in August, dense fogs often rise at dawn. After September the temperature falls sharply, serious snows begin in October, and readings of –30 degrees Fahrenheit are common in midwinter. This region, which combines some of the worst points of North Africa and North Dakota, is sparsely populated. The primary indigenous group is composed of two related but distinct Mongol tribes.

The Buriat (Barga) Mongols moved into the Nomonhan area from the northwest in the late seventeenth to early eighteenth centuries, probably as a result of the Russo-Chinese Treaty of Nerchinsk (1689), which ceded to Russia what previously had been their territory. The Buriats, migrating southeastward away from Russian control, were organized and recognized by Manchu emperors in 1732 to 1735. The new Buriat lands lay east of the river they called Khalkhin Gol (*gol* is the Mongolian word for river), in a territory that one day would be called Manchukuo.

The Khalkha Mongols take their name from the Mongol word *khalkha*, which means "barrier" or "shield." The Khalkha tribes traditionally had inhabited the northern frontier of the Mongol empire. They were the gate wardens, the barrier of the north. The Khalkha lands lay west of, but adjacent to, those of the Buriats, in a territory that one day would be called the Mongolian People's Republic. These neighboring Mongol tribes had tended and followed their flocks and herds across the sand, river fords, and desert tracks for centuries, heedless and, for the most part, unaware of any boundary line.

For several hundred years, the line separating the Mongolian salient from western Manchuria had been a vague administrative boundary between components of the Ch'ing empire. Then in the twentieth century, Russia detached Outer Mongolia from China, Japan seized Manchuria, and this vague, ill-defined boundary became the dividing line between two antagonistic empires.

The Nomonhan incident began, not surprisingly, over a disputed borderline. Near the northeastern corner of the Mongolian salient, the river known to the Mongols (and Soviets) as the Khalkhin Gol, and to Manchurians (and Japanese) as the Halha River, flows along a northwesterly course, emptying into Lake Buir Nor. The dispute revolved around whether or not this river was, as the Japanese claimed, the historic and official boundary between Manchukuo and the MPR. The Soviet and MPR governments maintained that the border did not follow the river, but a line roughly parallel to, and some ten to twelve miles east of, the river. Thus, both Manchukuo and the MPR claimed the land lying between the river and the line east of the river.

Over time, Japanese authorities presented no fewer than eighteen different maps of Chinese as well as Japanese origin supporting their claim that the Halha River was the boundary. This claim also had logic and practicality on its side: the river is the only natural boundary in that semiarid wasteland. Nonetheless, Soviet and Mongolian authorities amassed an impressive array of cartographic evidence backing their claim of a borderline east of the Halha River. These include a Chinese postal atlas map of 1919 and maps published by several agencies of the governments of Japan and Manchukuo between 1919 and 1934. Unknown to either side at the time of the conflict, in July 1939 the Chinese military attaché in Moscow gave his American counterpart a detailed Chinese General Staff map (circa 1934) showing a borderline east of the river.[2]

Postwar Japanese research in eighteenth-century Chinese sources confirms that in 1734 the Ch'ing emperor established a boundary line between the Buriat and Khalka Mongols that ran east of the Halha River and through the tiny hamlet of Nomonhan, as the Soviets claimed. However, it appears that Kwantung Army Headquarters (KwAHQ) did not consider that decision binding, because it was not the product of an international agreement but merely an internal administrative decision within the Chinese empire to which Russia was not a party.[3]

A plausible explanation suggested by two former Kwantung Army staff officers is that from 1931 to 1935, when the Soviet Far Eastern Army was relatively weak, Kwantung Army and Manchukuoan authorities enforced the Halha River as the de facto border and MPR authorities acquiesced. In the mid- to late 1930s, as Soviet Far Eastern strength grew, the Japanese did not want to show any signs of weakness by backing away from their earlier position. Mongolian and Soviet authorities, however, no longer accepted the Halha River line, leading to disputes and conflict.[4]

In 1935 Kwantung Army officials altered the boundary line markings on their maps of the Lake Buir Nor–Halha River area, in conformity with their claim of the river as boundary.[5] Beginning in late 1935, this sector of the frontier became the scene of frequent disputes and shooting incidents between Manchukuoan and MPR border patrols and their supporting units.

Until mid-1938, responsibility for frontier security in Northwestern Manchukuo rested primarily with the Eighth Border Garrison Unit (BGU), headquartered near Hailar. The 8th BGU was composed of some seven thousand Manchukuoan troops in widely dispersed units. It had little mobility or field training and, in Kwantung Army's view, low combat effectiveness. In the summer of 1938, a new Japanese infantry division was formed, designated as the 23rd Division, assigned to Kwantung Army, and based at Hailar. The 8th BGU was then subordinated to the 23rd Division commander, Lieutenant General Komatsubara Michitaro.

General Komatsubara, then fifty-two years old, was one of the Imperial Army's leading Russian experts, having served two tours as a military attaché in the Soviet Union and later as head of Kwantung Army's Special Services Agency in Harbin, a Russian-populated city in northern Manchuria. Komatsubara stood five feet, seven inches tall and was solidly built, wore eyeglasses, and sported a small mustache. Personally meticulous, the general kept exhaustively detailed dairies; wrote long, detailed letters; and composed poems. He had no prior combat experience.[6]

In July 1938, before leaving Tokyo to assume his new command, Komatsubara was briefed by Colonel Inada Masazumi, chief of the AGS Operations Section. Inada, who was just then drafting plans for the reconnaissance-in-force at Changkufeng, advised Komatsubara that, in view of the major combat operations in Central China, AGS hoped that his section of the Manchukuo-MPR border would remain quiet. Inada suggested these guidelines: Do not be too concerned about, or overreact to, minor border incidents. Focus on gathering information about Soviet forces East of Lake Baikal. Study plans for military operations against the western sector of the Soviet Far East.[7]

Because of his years as head of the Special Services Agency in Harbin, General Komatsubara was familiar with northwest Manchukuo and with the posture of a low profile. Neither reckless nor excitable by temperament, and cognizant of the AGS guidelines, Komatsubara kept his inexperienced 23rd Division near Hailar and left routine border patrols to the 8th BGU. An episode that autumn illustrates how he interpreted those guidelines.

On the morning of November 1, 1938, an 8th BGU border patrol was attacked by MPR forces. According to the Japanese report, the three-man patrol, led by a young lieutenant, carelessly approached the boundary and was attacked by MPR cavalry while still fifty meters within Manchukuoan territory. The lieutenant managed to escape, leaving behind his two men, who were killed. General Komatsubara dispatched a 23rd Division infantry company to the scene later that day to secure the area, but ordered no retaliation. He left recovery of the two bodies to diplomatic negotiations and filed a protest with local MPR and Soviet authorities. Komatsubara's only other official action was to discipline his officers. The two officers in charge of the local garrison were confined to their quarters for five days each "as punishment for not educating their troops to use more caution." The lieutenant who led the patrol was confined to quarters for thirty days.[8]

Despite Komatsubara's restraint, momentum was building at AGS and at KwAHQ that would plunge the 23rd Division into the cauldron of combat.

Attitude of Kwantung Army

It is normal practice for modern armies to draft operational plans against potential enemies. The existence of such contingency plans does not prove aggressive intent. Nonetheless, changes in Japanese operational planning against the USSR may have contributed to the outbreak of the Nomonhan incident. From 1934 to 1938, Japanese war plans called for a massive surprise attack against the Soviets in the Ussuri River region while fighting a holding action in northwestern Manchuria. However, from mid-1938 to early 1939, proposals for a new operational plan against the USSR were drawn up by a top-secret joint study group from AGS and Kwantung Army's Operations Departments. The new plan called for a holding action in the east and north while launching an all-out offensive from Hailar on a west-northwest axis toward Chita and on to Lake Baikal, cutting off the trans-Baikal Soviet Far East.[9]

This new proposal, known as Plan Eight-B, was endorsed by Kwantung Army in March 1939. A group of General Staff officers, Colonels Hattori Takushiro and Terada Masao and Major Shimanuki Takeharu, who had figured prominently in drafting Plan Eight-B, were then transferred from AGS to KwAHQ to phase in the new operational plan, which envisioned a five-year preparation period prior to execution. Colonel Hattori became Kwantung Army's chief operations staff officer.[10]

A quick glance at the map reveals that one strategic problem with Plan Eight-B was that the Japanese offensive would be exposed to interdiction along its southern flank by a Soviet counterattack launched from the Mongolian salient. It is likely that in the spring of 1939 Kwantung Army began to view the Mongolian salient as a potential strategic problem. However, at the time of the outbreak of hostilities at Nomonhan, KwAHQ had not yet drafted specific operational plans for the Nomonhan area.

At this same time, the Japanese began preparations for constructing a strategic railroad from Harlun Arshan to Hailar. It is not clear if this was specifically in connection with Plan Eight-B, but the proposed railroad was to run very near the Halha River. The vulnerability of the projected rail line also may have drawn Kwantung Army's attention to the Mongolian salient and its disputed eastern border near the Halha River. In early 1939 the 23rd Division stepped up reconnaissance patrols in the vicinity of the Halha River. In mid-March 1939, General Grigori Shtern, the new commander of Soviet Far Eastern forces, publically warned that Japan was preparing to attack the MPR.[11]

At about the same time that Plan Eight-B was being drafted and the Harlun Arshan–Hailar Railway proposed, KwAHQ promulgated an unusually tough and aggressive new set of guidelines for the conduct of its troops on and near the frontiers. These guidelines are widely believed to have played an important part in the outbreak of the Nomonhan incident. Furthermore, they suggest a causal link between the 1937 Amur River incident, the Changkufeng incident of 1938, and the conflict at Nomonhan.

As we have seen, resentment and frustration welled up in KwAHQ because of perceived AGS "interference" in its command prerogatives during the Amur River incident. This was compounded a year later at Changkufeng when, after the mauling suffered there by General Suetaka Kamezo's 19th Division, the disputed territory, Manchukuoan territory, was surrendered de facto to the enemy.

This prompted Kwantung Army to push for taking over responsibility from Chosen Army for the sliver of Manchukuoan territory near Changkufeng. The following month, Major Tsuji Masanobu of Kwantung Army's Operations Section was dispatched on a reconnaissance mission to ascertain the precise situation at Changkufeng. Major Tsuji, a daring and outspoken officer, did not like what he found. Soviet troops controlled all the territory between the previously contested ridgeline and the Tyumen River.

Tsuji conducted a number of additional reconnaissance trips to the area that winter. On his last such mission in March 1939, he led a detachment of forty men to the foot of Changkufeng Hill, where thousands had bled and died seven months earlier. Tsuji had his men sling their rifles across their backs to show nonbelligerent intent and marched them conspicuously up the hill to within two hundred yards of the Soviet defense lines. There he formed them into a single line abreast, whereupon they all undid their trousers and urinated in unison, to the surprised laughter of the Soviet troops. They then moved off a few yards and, forming a circle, sat down to enjoy *obentos* (a kind of Japanese box lunch) and sake. Later, after singing some rousing Japanese army songs, Tsuji and his men departed, leaving behind cans of meat, chocolates, and whiskey for the bemused Soviet onlookers. This burlesque performance was an elaborate diversion staged by Tsuji to mask clandestine photography of the enemy positions, showing Soviet fortifications incontrovertibly on Manchukuoan territory.[12]

Tsuji Masanobu was an extraordinary individual. Despite, or perhaps because of, humble family origins,[13] he sought to personify the samurai warrior spirit transmuted to the requirements of twentieth-century warfare. Tsuji possessed a keen mind entrapped in a sickly and often disease-ridden body, upon which he forced an almost superhuman regimen of daring-do. An innovative and sometime brilliant operational planner, he craved the battlefield as much as the planning room. He delighted in personally conducting clandestine intelligence, political intrigue, aerial reconnaissance, operational planning, and battlefield command, and distinguished himself in all of these activities in a long and checkered career. Yet something was lacking. At times he displayed narrow-minded intolerance. He was a violent racist and was capable of inhuman brutality. Despite the enormous influence he came to exercise, he seemed always to have the instincts of the scheming outsider "on the make." In 1939 Tsuji held the rank of major. The dominant role he played at Nomonhan and after can only be understood in the context of *gekokujo*, the Japanese tradition of rule from below.

Upon returning to Hsinking from his unusual reconnaissance mission at Changkufeng in March 1939, Major Tsuji drafted plans for dealing with Changkufeng. Tsuji proposed negotiations with the Soviets to "rectify" the border;

if negotiations failed, Kwantung Army should attack and drive the invading troops out of Manchukuo.[14] This proposal was adopted by Kwantung Army Command. Major General Yano Otozaburo, Kwantung Army deputy chief of staff, flew to Tokyo armed with Tsuji's photographs to seek approval of the General Staff. At AGS, however, General Yano was told that the Changkufeng incident was a closed case and would remain so and that Kwantung Army should ignore the "technical" border violation there because Tokyo did not seek conflict with the USSR at that time. To Yano's (Tsuji's) argument that such a weak policy at Changkufeng would embolden the Russians to further aggression against Manchukuo, a General Staff officer replied that because of the tense European situation in the spring of 1939, the Soviet Union could not afford to cause trouble with Japan.[15]

General Yano's return to Hsinking brought much gnashing of teeth. Kwantung Army felt that the rejection of their request by AGS prevented their army from fulfilling the sacred mission assigned by the emperor, to defend Manchukuo. It was a frustrating, and for some a mortifying, situation. Resentment ran high throughout KwAHQ, nowhere more than in the Operations Section.

This was the background for the Operations Section's tough new guidelines for troops on the frontiers, drafted by none other than Major Tsuji. The basic premise of the guidelines, entitled "Principles for the Settlement of Soviet-Manchukuoan Border Disputes," declared, "If Soviet troops transgress the Manchukuoan frontiers, Kwantung Army will nip their ambitions in the bud by completely destroying them." Some of the specific guidelines laid down for local commanders were:

> If the enemy crosses the frontiers . . . annihilate him without delay, employing strength carefully built up beforehand. To accomplish our mission, it is permissible to enter Soviet territory, or to trap or lure Soviet troops into Manchukuoan territory and allow them to remain there for some time. . . .
>
> Where boundary lines are not clearly defined, area defense commanders will, upon their own initiative, establish boundaries and indicate them to the forward elements. . . .
>
> In the event of an armed clash, fight until victory is won, regardless of relative strengths or of the location of the boundaries.
>
> If the enemy violates the borders, friendly units must challenge him courageously and endeavor to triumph in their zone of action without concerning themselves about the consequences, which will be the responsibility of higher headquarters.[16]

Tsuji later explained that under the old guidelines, local commanders on the frontier were subject to "contradictory orders," to scrupulously maintain the inviolability of Manchukuoan territory, but to take no action that would provoke conflict. According to Tsuji, those orders sometimes inhibited local command-ers from dealing firmly with border violations for fear of provoking a larger inci-dent. The new guidelines, he claimed, were designed "to remove this anxiety from the local commanders, so that they could act more firmly without fear of personal responsibility for the consequences."[17]

In reality, however, Tsuji's "Principles for the Settlement of Soviet-Manchukuoan Border Disputes" were better suited to provoking than to set-tling disputes. Such innovations as having local commanders unilaterally establish boundaries in areas not clearly demarcated, ordering them to enforce their deci-sions on a "shoot first, ask questions later" basis, authorizing invading enemy ter-ritory, and encouraging luring enemy troops across the border, all these things not only ignored government policy but also were wholly incompatible with official army doctrine.[18]

Tsuji's proposed principles for settling border disputes were discussed heat-edly in Kwantung Army's Operations Section. The section chief, Colonel Hattori, and his colleague, Colonel Terada, both outranked Major Tsuji. However, those two officers, together with Major Shimanuki, had been transferred from AGS to Kwantung Army only a month earlier. Tsuji had served in the Operations Section since November 1937 and had been at KwAHQ since April 1936. In terms of length of service and experience in that post, Tsuji was the "senior" operations staff officer. Hattori and Terada were reluctant to overrule their outspoken colleague. In an interview in 1960, Major Shimanuki stated that Tsuji had enjoyed a very high reputation at KwAHQ because of his intelligence, persuasiveness, forcefulness, and knowledge of Kwantung Army and Manchuria. He had "very positive" views, and he usually spoke up first in staff discussions, advocating his views and carrying the rest of the operations staff with him.[19] So it was with the new guidelines for settling border disputes.

The Operations Section, united in support of Tsuji's proposals, presented them to Kwantung Army Command for approval. The army commander, Lieutenant General Ueda Kenkichi, consulted with his chief of staff and vice chief of staff, Generals Isogai Rensuke and Yano. These three men, sober, experienced, and responsible senior officers, should have recognized the inflammatory nature of the proposed new guidelines. But they were blinded by the resentment and frustration growing out of the friction between their command and AGS. Generals Ueda and Isogai and Major Tsuji were the only three Kwantung Army staff officers in 1939 who had been serving at KwAHQ at the time of the fighting on the Amur River and at Changkufeng. Nor was that the only bond they shared. In 1932 Tsuji, then a thirty-year-old captain, commanded a company in the 7th Regiment of the 9th Infantry Division stationed in China. Tsuji, who already had distinguished himself as an outstanding leader, was the standard-bearer for the 7th Regiment, which was commanded by Isogai, then a colonel. Yano was a 7th Regiment staff officer. The 9th Division was commanded by General Ueda when, in 1932, it saw action in the Shanghai incident, in which Tsuji was wounded.[20]

Tsuji has written of the intense comradely, almost fraternal relationship between himself and Ueda, Isogai, and Yano, in which Hattori, Terada, and Shimanuki came to share. According to General Isogai, Tsuji was "extremely influential" in this "clique," although he and General Ueda always took responsibility for the consequences.[21] After some initial hesitation on the part of General Isogai, who usually was the most moderate of the group, the proposed guidelines were approved. General Ueda promulgated the guidelines as Kwantung Army Operations Order 1488 on April 25, 1939, at a division commanders conference convened at KwAHQ for that purpose.

A copy of Order 1488 was sent routinely to AGS in Tokyo, which received the report but sent no official response. The General Staff was focused on the China War and negotiations for a military alliance with Germany and may not have been paying much attention to Manchukuoan border security. Colonel Inada, head of the Operations Section at AGS, recalls that the General Staff "basically accepted" Order 1488 but expected Kwantung Army to consult with them before taking any action in response to a specific border violation. This opinion was communicated unofficially to Hattori and Terada, who had served under Inada at AGS until the previous month. This unofficial opinion was rejected at KwAHQ, where it was interpreted as yet another attempt by central authorities to interfere in their legitimate command prerogatives.[22]

Some authoritative Japanese sources have argued that if AGS had issued a firm and unambiguous repudiation of Order 1488, the disaster at Nomonhan might have been averted.[23] That may be so, but taming Kwantung Army at that point probably would have required the forced transfer of much of the KwAHQ staff. No one in authority at AGS wanted to rock the boat so abruptly at that time. Tsuji argues that if AGS had allowed Kwantung Army "to act forcefully at Changkufeng, the Nomonhan incident would not have happened."[24] Besides confirming the link between Changkufeng and Nomonhan, Tsuji's protest ultimately may come down to questioning the site of the 1939 conflict at Nomonhan rather than at Changkufeng.

There is no doubt that the promulgation of Kwantung Army's Operations Order 1488 on April 25 was an important factor leading to the outbreak of the Nomonhan incident three weeks later. Japanese records show that Khalkha Mongols and MPR border patrols regularly crossed the Halha River, which in the Mongolian government's view lay some ten miles within their territory. Such river crossings—border violations in the view of Manchukuo and Japan—occurred without incident as late as March and April 1939. When this activity recurred after the promulgation of Order 1488, General Komatsubara, 23rd Division commander, took action.

The Opening of Hostilities

On May 11–12, 1939, a border clash occurred that escalated into major conflict at Nomonhan. There are more than a dozen "authoritative" versions of the initial clash, differing in perspective, emphasis, and detail.[25] After sifting through the mass of purported evidence and checking one account against another, the following reconstruction of events emerges. On the night of May 10–11, a twenty-man MPR border patrol crossed the Halha River moving eastward. Approximately ten miles east of the river, on a sandy hill 150 feet high, stood the tiny hamlet of Nomonhan, a few rough huts, the dwelling places of a handful of Mongols. Just south of Nomonhan is the Holsten River, a stream that flows west below Nomonhan and spills into the broader Halha River. On the morning of May 11, the MPR border patrol was discovered by Manchukuoan forces north of the Holsten River and just west of Nomonhan. In the MPR/Soviet view, the hill on which the hamlet of Nomonhan is located was (and is) on the Mongolia-Manchuria border. In the Manchukuoan/Japanese view, Nomonhan, ten miles east of the Halha River, was ten miles inside Manchukuo.

A Manchukuoan cavalry force of about forty men drove the Mongolian border patrol back across the Halha River. The MPR patrol leader reported the Manchukuoan force that evicted him to be two hundred men. Some casualties were sustained by both sides, but the Manchukuoans had drawn first blood. On the next day, an MPR border troop force of some sixty men, commanded by Major P. Chogdan, pushed the Manchukuoan cavalry out of the disputed area and reestablish their position between the Halha River and Nomonhan. The Manchukuoan cavalry unit reported the MPR force to be seven hundred men.[26] Sporadic and indecisive fighting and jockeying for position continued throughout the week. On May 13, however, two days after the initial clash, the local Manchukuoan commander notified General Komatsubara's 23rd Division Headquarters in Hailar of the situation. At about the same time, MPR Major Chogdan reported the fighting to Soviet military headquarters in Ulaanbaatar, Mongolia's capital. A Mongolian-Manchukuoan border skirmish was about to become a Soviet-Japanese confrontation.

The question of which side was responsible for the border violation on May 10–11 depends on whose interpretation of the border one accepts, since both sides claimed the territory between the Halha River and Nomonhan. However, nearly all the accounts agree that the actual fighting was initiated by the Manchukuoan forces. After May 13, the day on which the two client states notified their respective great-power patrons of the clash, the historical record is less ambiguous.

At midday on May 13, General Komatsubara was presiding over a conference he had convened specifically to discuss with his staff officers and regimental commanders the implications of the recently received Kwantung Army Operations Order 1488. Ironically, the first report of fighting at Nomonhan reached Komatsubara at the very moment he was discussing Major Tsuji's new border principles. According to officers who were present, the general, "decided in a minute to destroy the invading Outer Mongolian forces," in conformity with Order 1488.[27]

Komatsubara notified KwAHQ that afternoon of the incident at Nomonhan and of his intention to wipe out the intruders, requesting air support and trucks to facilitate his countermeasures. The prompt reply from Kwantung Army commander, General Ueda, approved of Komatsubara's "positive attitude" and dispatched to the 23rd Division an air wing consisting of six scout planes, forty fighters, and ten light bombers as well as two antiaircraft batteries and two motorized transport companies. Ueda cautioned, however, "to take the most extreme caution not to let the matter become enlarged."[28] It is illustrative of the overheated atmosphere at KwAHQ that authorities there could recommend the destruction of a Mongolian army unit on territory claimed by the MPR while at the same time urging "extreme caution" lest the matter become enlarged. Apparently these were not seen as contradictory objectives.

On the same day, General Ueda sent a summary of Komatsubara's initial report, together with Kwantung Army's response, to AGS in Tokyo. The deputy chief of staff immediately radioed his reply that "it is expected that appropriate measures will be taken by Kwantung Army." Thus, in spite of its reputation for rash action, Kwantung Army was left to its own initiative in the matter. Perhaps authorities in Tokyo felt that the strategic situation in the north, where Kwantung Army's eight divisions faced approximately thirty Soviet divisions from Lake Baikal to Vladivostok, would compel the local forces to act "appropriately," that is, with discretion. If so, their confidence was misplaced.

On May 14 Major Tsuji flew from KwAHQ and personally conducted an air reconnaissance flight over the Nomonhan area. He sighted about twenty horses but saw no enemy troops. However, upon landing he discovered what appeared to be a fresh bullet hole in the fuselage of the light scout plane. He correctly concluded that some MPR troops probably were still east of the Halha River and so informed the 23rd Division staff before returning to KwAHQ, where he reported to General Ueda that the Nomonhan incident seemed to be a small and unimportant one.[29]

Meanwhile, in accordance with the letter as well as the spirit of Kwantung Army's new "Principles for the Settlement of Border Disputes," General Komatsubara dispatched a force to expel the intruders. This force, led by Lieutenant Colonel Azuma Yaozo, consisted of an armored car reconnaissance company, two infantry companies, and a cavalry troop. The Azuma detachment reached Nomonhan on May 15 to learn that the bulk of the Outer Mongolian forces had withdrawn to the left bank of the Halha on the previous night, that very small elements still remained on the right bank, and that even they appeared about to withdraw. Nonetheless, Azuma began pursuit operations that afternoon. His advance from Nomonhan to the Halha made almost no contact with the enemy, which had retired across the river. A flight of Japanese light bombers, however, sighted a small enemy troop concentration on the left (west) bank of the Halha River and attacked. The target was MPR Border Outpost Number 7, which reported two men killed and fifteen wounded in the air raid. The Japanese flyers reported killing thirty to forty enemy troops. All accounts agree that the air attack was directed against troops west of the Halha River, indisputably within the territory of the Mongolian People's Republic.[30]

When news of the events of May 15 reached General Komatsubara, he concluded that the Outer Mongolian intruders had been chastised appropriately and that the mission was completed. The Azuma detachment returned to Hailar on May 16. KwAHQ also considered the incident closed. Soviet authorities, however, took a different view.

The events in mid-May prompted Soviet action on behalf of the MPR. A Red Army force designated as the 57th Corps had been stationed in Mongolia for several years in accordance with the Soviet-MPR Mutual Defense Pact of 1936. At the time of the initial clashes, Corps commander Nikolai Feklenko and his chief of staff, A. M. Kushchev, were both away from headquarters, Feklenko on a hunting trip in the hinterland and Kushchev with his ailing wife in the Soviet city of Ulan Ude, north of the Soviet-MPR border. The Soviet High Command first learned of the clashes from international newspaper accounts based on Japanese/Manchukuoan press releases. Red Army chief of staff Boris Shaposhnikov's angry call to 57th Corps demanding information caused a minor panic. Feklenko and Kushchev hurried back to Ulaanbaatar. They dispatched a mixed force—one battalion from 149th Infantry Regiment (36th Infantry Division) plus light armor and motorized artillery from the 11th Tank Brigade—to Tamsag Bulak, a staging area about eighty miles west of the Halha River. This force, commanded by Major A. E. Bykov, was ordered to support the Mongolian 6th Cavalry Division in securing the border. Bykov and the MPR cavalry commander, Colonel Shoaaiibuu, drove to the site of the clashes on May 15 and found that the Azuma detachment had left. The cavalry division was dispatched to the combat zone that day and arrived two days later, supported by Bykov's force, which was ordered to stay west of the river and, if possible, to avoid being drawn into the skirmishing. Some MPR troops recrossed the Halha and took up positions between the river and Nomonhan, in the disputed territory. Combat resumed between MPR and Manchukuoan cavalry and gradually grew in intensity.[31]

When notified of the renewed hostilities, Komatsubara became angered by what he took as defiance by the enemy and a direct challenge to him as the area commander. Spurred on by Order 1488, the general resolved not merely to chase the intruders back across the river again.[32] This time, by employing greater stealth and strength, he would encircle and destroy them. The incident was about to become enlarged.

The May 28 Battle

Although Kwantung Army considered itself an elite component of the Imperial Army, the 23rd Division, less than one year old, was a green unit that had not yet reached the level of training and élan characteristic of Kwantung Army. The 23rd Division staff officers, from the commander on down, shared a universal lack of significant combat experience. The division intelligence officer, Major Suzuki Yoshiyasu, a cavalryman, had no intelligence experience prior to joining the division. The senior line officers (regimental commanders) were experienced men, graduates of the military academy, but most company and platoon leaders were recently called-up reservists or youngsters one or two years out of the academy. When the brand-new division arrived in Manchukuo in August 1938, its base at Hailar had not been completed. Only half the division could be billeted there. Other division components were scattered in different locations. The division was not assembled in Hailar until November, by which time the onset of severe winter weather hampered large-scale training exercises. Unit commanders had not had enough time to get to know one another very well. This overall lack of experience, training, and cohesion would weigh heavily against the 23rd Division in the coming test at Nomonhan.[33]

From 1930 to 1937, the size of the Imperial Army had been fixed at seventeen divisions. But with the growing conflict in China, seven new divisions were created in 1938 and nine more in 1939. The demands of the China theater prevented properly equipping all these new units simultaneously. The 23rd Division, assigned to what was believed to be a quiescent backwater, was near the end of the queue. Until the late 1930s, Japanese army divisions were "rectangular," with a core of four infantry regiments. The 23rd Division was of the new "triangular" configuration, with three infantry regiments (64th, 71st, and 72nd). There were materiel deficiencies as well.

The 23rd Division's area of operations was almost entirely flat, open country—tank country. The division had a transport regiment equipped with trucks. The reconnaissance regiment included a company of light tracked armored vehicles, "tankettes" with thin armor skin and a machine gun as its main armament. But overall, the division lacked the mobility and weaponry appropriate to the region. When the division deployed from Hailar to the Nomonhan area, the infantry marched the last fifty miles. Most of the artillery was horse drawn. Twenty-four of the division's sixty artillery pieces were Type 38 short-range 75-mm guns. Dating from 1907, they were the oldest in the Imperial Army, in use in no other division. Each infantry regiment was allotted a battery of four rapid-fire 37-mm guns and four 75-mm mountain guns (circa 1908). The artillery regiment, in addition to the ancient Type 38s, had twelve 120-mm howitzers. The mountain guns and howitzers were high-angle, short-range weapons. The division had no high-velocity, low-trajectory guns appropriate to the terrain—and vital against tanks. The lack of antitank weapons was a critical weakness in a region so suited to armored warfare. Besides its rapid-fire guns, the division's main antitank weapons were demolition charges and incendiary fire bombs (gasoline-filled bottles) that, in open country, required "human bullet" (i.e., suicidal) tactics to employ effectively.

The 23rd Division's most valuable asset was its men, drawn mainly from Kyushu, the southernmost of Japan's four main islands. For centuries Kyushu had been renowned for producing strong and resilient fighting men. The personnel of the 23rd Division were no exception. Deficiencies in training and equipment were partially offset by personal hardiness, fortitude, courage, and a strong sense of loyalty and honor. Moreover, the scope and intensity of the fighting at Nomonhan developed gradually, and Japanese-Manchukuoan forces in the early stages enjoyed numerical superiority over their Soviet-Mongolian adversaries.

The Soviet position was hampered by a major logistical problem. The nearest Soviet rail line was at Borzya, some four hundred miles west of the Halha River. From Borzya, supplies had to be transported by truck over dirt roads or no roads at all, through flat, open territory vulnerable to air attack. In contrast, the major northern Manchurian center of Hailar was two hundred miles from Nomonhan, while the Japanese railhead at Handagai was only fifty miles from the battle zone. Hailar and Handagai were connected to the Nomonhan area by three unpaved roads. Perhaps these facts, plus the rapidly developing Polish crisis, helped convince AGS and Kwantung Army officials that the Soviet Union would not risk a serious test at Nomonhan. In any case, General Komatsubara, with the approval of KwAHQ, decided on a policy of force to settle the bothersome Nomonhan incident.

When on May 20 Japanese reconnaissance discovered the Soviet infantry battalion and armor near Tamsag Bulak, Komatsubara decided to "nip the incident in the bud." He formed a new, more-powerful strike force for this purpose, led by Colonel Yamagata Takemitsu, commander of the 64th Infantry Regiment. This new unit, the Yamagata detachment, was built around the four companies of the 3rd Battalion, 64th Regiment (approximately eight hundred men), a regimental gun company (three 75-mm mountain guns and four rapid-fire 37-mm guns), three truck companies, and Lieutenant Colonel Azuma's reconnaissance group, composed of mounted cavalry and light motorized elements (220 men, a tankette, 2 sedans, and 12 trucks). Yamagata was also supported by some four hundred and fifty Manchukuoan troops in the area. With a total strength of approximately two thousand men, Colonel Yamagata was ordered to destroy all enemy forces east of the Halha River. The attack was scheduled for May 22–23.[34]

No sooner had General Komatsubara made this disposition then he received the following message from KwAHQ:

> In settling the affair Kwantung Army has definite plans, as follows:
>
> For the time being Manchukuoan Army troops will keep an eye on the Outer Mongolians operating near Nomonhan and will try to lure them onto Manchukuoan territory. Japanese forces at Hailar [23rd Division] will maintain surveillance over the situation. Upon verification of a border violation *by the bulk of the Outer Mongolian forces*, Kwantung Army will dispatch troops, contact the enemy, and annihilate him within friendly territory. According to this outlook it can be expected that enemy units will occupy border regions for a considerable period; but this is permissible from the overall strategic point of view (italics added).[35]

At this point, KwAHQ was urging tactical restraint in order to achieve an ultimately more decisive result. However, Komatsubara already had issued preliminary orders for Yamagata to launch his attack. Komatsubara radioed Hsinking that it would be "undignified" for him to cancel his order, meaning that he resented KwAHQ interference in his local command prerogatives no less than KwAHQ resented interference from AGS. However, Komatsubara added that, "out of deference to Kwantung Army's feelings," he would postpone the attack for a few days. The date was pushed back to May 27–28.[36]

Soviet air force units attached to the 57th Corps made several unsuccessful forays over the Halha River from May 17 to 21. Inexperienced Soviet pilots, flying obsolescent I-15 biplanes, fared poorly. At least nine and perhaps as many as seventeen Soviet fighters and scout planes were shot down. Defense Commissar Kliment Voroshilov ordered air operations suspended. This contributed to the tactical surprise achieved by the Japanese.[37]

Colonel Yamagata concentrated his force at the town of Kanchuerhmiao, situated roughly forty miles north of Nomonhan, and from there dispatched reconnaissance patrols to the Nomonhan area. His reconnaissance units soon reported that the enemy had constructed a bridge across the Halha River just above its junction with the smaller Holsten River. Two mixed groups of MPR and Soviet troops, about two hundred men each, were identified east of the Halha, on either side of the Holsten, as well as a small MPR position less than a mile west of Nomonhan. Yamagata decided to trap these enemy troops east of the Halha and destroy them there. His plan was to have the Azuma unit drive south along the east bank of the Halha River directly toward the bridge, cutting off the enemy's escape route. The four infantry companies and the Manchukuoan troops, with artillery support, would attack individually from the west along different axes toward identified pockets of MPR troops, driving the enemy toward the river and the waiting Azuma unit. The enemy would be trapped between the Japanese forces east of the river, where they would be destroyed. Yamagata further ordered that after enemy forces east of the Halha had been destroyed, any remaining enemy elements on the west shore near the river—indisputably MPR territory—should be mopped up as quickly as possible.[38] This complex battle plan would have been more than adequate to deal with the Outer Mongolian forces that had been engaged in the first few days of fighting. However, with striking lack of foresight, neither Komatsubara nor Yamagata took into account the possibility of encountering any of the Soviet army units that their reconnaissance had discovered at Tamsag Bulak on May 20.

In the predawn hours of May 28, the Yamagata detachment left Kanchuerhmiao for Nomonhan. The 220-man Azuma unit separated from the main body and began its southward thrust toward the bridge near the confluence of the Halha and Holsten Rivers to block the enemy's presumed route of retreat. Unknown to Lieutenant Colonel Azuma, the bridge was defended not only by Mongolian light cavalry, but also by a Soviet infantry company, combat engineers, armored cars, and a battery of self-propelled 76-mm artillery. Before daybreak, the Soviet-MPR forces detected the approaching Azuma unit but remained ignorant of the disposition of the main body of the Yamagata detachment. The element of surprise would cut both ways in the coming action.

The core of Soviet-MPR forces near Nomonhan was Major Bykov's infantry battalion, consisting of three motorized infantry companies, a company of sixteen BA-6 armored cars, a battery of four 76-mm self-propelled guns, a combat engineer company, and a reconnaissance platoon with five more armored cars (total about 1,000 men). The 6th MPR Cavalry Division (about 1,250 men) comprised two small cavalry regiments, an artillery unit (four 76-mm guns), an armored car unit, and a training company. Major Bykov deployed his forces on a north-south axis

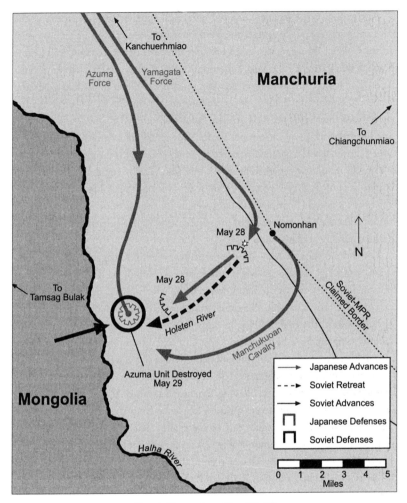

Map 4. Nomonhan, May 28–29

with two of his infantry companies holding the northern and southern flanks and the Mongolian cavalry in the center—an odd configuration, since cavalry typically was positioned on the flanks rather than the center. These forces were strung out along a ten-mile front roughly parallel to the Halha River but well east of it, only a mile west of Nomonhan. Bykov held one infantry company, his combat engineers, and artillery in reserve near the bridge but on the west side of the Halha. Colonel Shoaaiibuu's four 76-mm guns were also held west of the river to keep them from being bogged down in the sandy terrain on the east side.[39]

At the outset, the Japanese enjoyed numerical superiority and surprise at the point of attack, especially against the Mongolian cavalry. This was offset by several factors. Colonel Yamagata dispersed his force into at least five separate units, none of which was particularly strong. His complex attack plan required careful coordination, but radio communication between units broke down immediately because of chronic equipment failures. Most important was the Soviet advantage in fire power from their self-propelled artillery (plus the four MPR guns) and armored cars. The BA-6 armored car was not some 1930s version of a Brinks or Wells Fargo money carrier. It was a genuine armored fighting vehicle with the same turret as the T-26 tank, mounting a high-velocity 45-mm gun. Tracks could be installed over the two sets of dual rear wheels, giving it the off-road capability of a half-track. However, its speed (27 mph) and light weight (five tons) came at the expense of armor protection (9-mm, one-third of an inch) which could be penetrated by heavy machine gun fire at close range.

On the morning of May 28, the battle began with Yamagata's infantry companies attacking the Soviet-MPR units near Nomonhan. The lightly armed Mongolian cavalry was routed and driven back, which forced the Soviet infantry companies to retreat as well, abandoning their positions near Nomonhan and falling back toward the Halha River. In desperation, Colonel Shoaaiibuu shifted his training company from his command post area to the front lines. Japanese infantry overran his command post and the colonel and most of his staff were killed.

As the fighting gradually moved closer to the river, however, Soviet artillery and armored cars came into action, slowing Yamagata's advance. At that point, Yamagata decided to shift his main forces' primary objective from the juncture of the two rivers to a low hill several miles east of the Halha, where Soviet forces were dug in. Unaccountably—and unforgivably—Azuma was not informed of Yamagata's change of plans.[40] Bykov was able to regroup his forces 1–2 miles east of the junction of the Halha and Holsten Rivers and hold there. By late morning, Yamagata's attacks stalled and his men began to dig in for protection against Soviet shelling and counterattacks.[41]

Meanwhile, Azuma, who had been out of communication with Yamagata from the outset because of faulty radio equipment, found himself in an even worse situation. His force was intended to be the anvil against which Yamagata's hammer blows would crush the enemy. If the hammer lacked power, the anvil was even weaker. When Lieutenant Colonel Azuma approached his objective on the morning of May 28, he was startled to find the bridge held by a Soviet infantry company and combat engineers with armored car and artillery support.

The commander of the Soviet artillery, Lieutenant Yu. Vakhtin, quickly recognized the Japanese intent and on his own initiative shifted his battery of self-propelled 76-mm guns to the east bank of the Halha to prevent a Japanese seizure of the bridge. The Azuma unit had no artillery or other antitank weapons and was wholly incapable of dislodging the Soviet force. When Yamagata's attack bogged down, Azuma found himself trapped between two superior enemy forces. The would-be encirclers had become encircled. Unable to contact Yamagata by radio, Azuma sent several runners to report his plight. By the time they reached Yamagata, his main force was dispersed into four separate groups and their offensive energy spent. Even though most of these units were only a few miles apart, radio communication between them and Yamagata's command post rarely worked and runners had to brave a gauntlet of enemy fire. Yamagata could neither reassemble his main force nor break through Bykov's position to relieve Azuma.[42]

By noon Azuma was surrounded and under increasingly heavy pressure from enemy infantry and cavalry pressing in from the east (away from Yamagata) and under continuous bombardment from artillery, armor, and mortars to the west, on both sides of the Halha. His cavalry had to fight dismounted, and they all struggled under fire to dig defensive positions in the sand. Azuma could probably have broken out of the encirclement at that point, but he understood his mission to be to hold the bridgehead east of the Halha and block enemy retreat while awaiting the arrival of Yamagata's main force. He refused to abandon his position without orders and determined to hold on there as long as possible, in hope of relief or reinforcement from Yamagata—ignorant of the latter's change of plans.

As the day wore on, the pressure on the Azuma unit intensified. The rest of the Soviet 149th Infantry Regiment, with its organic artillery support, joined the fight. This unit, commanded by Major I. M. Remizov, which had only recently been sent to Tamsag Bulak as a precautionary measure, was transported to the combat zone by truck and immediately thrown into battle at the bridgehead, increasing the odds against the beleaguered Azuma. Yamagata's infantry remained pinned down several miles to the east, unable to relieve Azuma. Several attempts to resupply Azuma with ammunition failed, with the resupply units destroyed.

The pressure on Azuma slackened somewhat after dark. A major attached to the reconnaissance unit tried to persuade Lieutenant Colonel Azuma to withdraw toward Yamagata, but again he refused, insisting that his mission was to hold the area near the confluence of the rivers. This refusal to retreat on one's own initiative in the face of a hopeless tactical situation, preferring instead to fight to the last man, was typical of the Japanese army. The word "retreat" literally was not in the army's vocabulary; instead there were euphemisms such as "advance in a different direction." But such a step was deemed shameful, and for a combat commander to do so without specific orders was a criminal offense punishable by death.

At dawn on May 29th, Soviet artillery—122-mm howitzers, field guns, mortars, and armored cars—unleashed even more intense fire against the Azuma unit than the day before, caving in Japanese trenches in the sandy soil. An incendiary shell ignited the gas tank of Azuma's sedan. The resulting fire engulfed the remaining trucks, including those containing wounded soldiers and the unit's dwindling ammunition stocks.

By late afternoon, Soviet troops had advanced to within fifty yards of Azuma's lines on three fronts and several armored cars had penetrated from the rear. The remaining Japanese fought on desperately. Finally, between 6:00 and 7:00 p.m., Azuma led the fewer than two dozen of his men still standing in a "banzai charge." He was immediately cut down by machine gun fire. Most of his men fell nearby. The sole surviving officer, a wounded medical lieutenant, ordered any other survivors to try to rejoin the main force. Four men managed to escape that night; the rest were killed or captured.[43]

When notified of the seriousness of the situation, General Komatsubara belatedly reinforced Yamagata with more artillery and antitank guns and several fresh infantry companies on May 29. Several Japanese sources assert that Major Tsuji showed up at Yamagata's command post and berated the colonel for his inactivity on Azuma's behalf. Tsuji reportedly then cajoled Yamagata into a mission that night to recover corpses. Over the next three nights, the Yamagata detachment managed to recover nearly two hundred bodies of their fallen comrades from the Azuma unit, including its commander. That done, and apparently still unable to dislodge the Soviet-MPR forces from their bridgehead near the junction of the two rivers, Yamagata was ordered to withdraw from the combat zone and redeploy near Kanchuerhmiao.[44] Ironically, Major Remizov mistook the headlights of Japanese trucks prowling the battlefield in search of their dead for signs of a renewed Japanese offensive. He temporarily withdrew most of the 149th regiment to the safety of the west side of the Halha. Only on June 3 did Remizov discover that Yamagata had departed, whereupon Soviet-MPR forces redeployed in the disputed territory.

In evaluating this battle, the Japanese attributed the destruction of the Azuma unit to (1) poor planning and reconnaissance by General Komatsubara and Colonel Yamagata, (2) very poor communications between Azuma and Yamagata, and (3) the Azuma unit's lack of heavy weapons. In addition to the nearly 200 men lost in the Azuma unit, Yamagata suffered an additional 159 killed, 119 wounded, and 12 missing from his main force. Total Japanese casualties in the battle of May 28 were nearly five hundred, close to 25 percent of the Yamagata detachment.[45]

Soviet sources single out Lieutenant Vakhtin for special praise. He and his self-propelled artillery battery are credited with a major role in thwarting the Japanese pincers movement and in destroying the Azuma unit. Soviet sources claimed that

Major Bykov's units suffered sixty to seventy casualties. According to TASS, total Soviet/MPR casualties on May 28–29 were forty killed and seventy wounded.[46] A recent Russian account, however, puts Soviet losses at 138 killed and 198 wounded.[47] Mongolian cavalry suffered substantial casualties, not only from the initial Japanese attack but, as they were pushed toward the river, from "friendly fire" from Soviet and MPR artillery as well.

Although the Soviet-MPR forces acquitted themselves creditably on May 28, neither the Soviet press nor their other propaganda instruments made any mention of the battle at that time. The first official Soviet news release regarding the fighting near the Khalkhin Gol did not appear until June 26. KwAHQ also clamped a tight security lid on the events of May 28. This apparently extended as far as misinforming Tokyo about the setback on the Halha River.[48] On May 30 General Isogai, Kwantung Army chief of staff, sent an optimistic report to AGS in which he assured the authorities in Tokyo that Kwantung Army planned to avoid a protracted conflict by inflicting heavy losses upon the enemy whenever he violated the frontier. Isogai predicted that the Russians would not be able to deploy large ground forces in the Nomonhan area and that the incident definitely was not expected to expand into a large-scale conflict. Nevertheless, he concluded his report with the following request:"At this time, it is imperative that the [Kwantung] Army be supplied immediately with river-crossing materials—the weakest aspect of the Army's operational preparations. It is [also] desired that various types of river-crossing craft be provided."[49]

This last request should have alerted AGS that despite General Isogai's assurances, KwAHQ was contemplating a large-scale crossing of the Halha River. Even according to the Japanese interpretation of the border, this would constitute an invasion of the MPR. Nevertheless, General Hashimoto Gun, who headed the Operations Division at AGS, replied to Isogai the following day, affirming his confidence in Kwantung Army's intention and ability to keep the incident localized: "The Soviet side will continue to do vexing things, and one must handle them adequately; but looking at various estimates of the situation, we find it hard to believe that any great problem is in the offing in the Nomonhan area. It ought to be rather easy to achieve the objective of chastisement."[50]

Colonel Inada's AGS Operations Section secretly made the following assessment of the situation on May 31:

1. The USSR probably does not wish to expand the incident.
2. The General Staff will trust Kwantung Army to keep the incident limited and localized.

3. The General Staff will intervene if Kwantung Army plans any action which might provoke the USSR or expand the incident, such as air attacks deep inside Outer Mongolia.[51]

Thus ended the first phase of the Nomonhan incident. Kwantung Army described the outcome as, "one victory for each side, one defeat for each side," but that was hardly accurate. The Azuma unit had been destroyed, other heavy losses sustained, and according to the army's official history, "remorse ate at the heart of General Komatsubara."[52]

CHAPTER 5

NOMONHAN: A LESSON IN LIMITED WAR

On June 1, 1939, an urgent telephone call from Moscow summoned the young deputy commander of the Byelorussian Military District from his headquarters in Minsk to a meeting with Marshal Kliment Voroshilov, the commissar for defense. Catching the first Moscow-bound train, the deputy commander betrayed no outward sign of apprehension about the abrupt summons that came while the deadly purge of the army was still winding down. But the rising young cavalry and tank commander was not destined to meet a bullet in an NKVD execution cellar. His name was Georgy Konstantinovich Zhukov, future Hero of the Soviet Union, who would command the defense of Moscow in 1941 and lead the Red Army through Stalingrad and Kursk, all the way to Berlin.

Zhukov was born in 1896 into a poor Russian family. His father was a cobbler. He was drafted into the Imperial Army in 1915 and served in the cavalry. Of average height but with a solid build, Zhukov possessed unusual physical strength and stamina and became an excellent horseman. In 1916 he received the Cross of St. George and was promoted to NCO for bravery in battle. After the October Revolution, he joined the Red Army and the Bolshevik Party and fought in the Civil War from 1918 to 1921. With his working-class origin, military acumen, and driving ambition, Zhukov rose rapidly through the ranks. By 1923 he commanded a cavalry regiment and, in 1931, a division. He became an early proponent of tank warfare, survived the purge unscathed, and continued to rise in prominence despite a reputation for bluntness and sometimes crude and overbearing behavior toward subordinates. More important, he impressed his superiors as a man who could get things done, which was why he was tapped to deal with the problem on the Mongolia-Manchuria border.

In Voroshilov's office on the morning of June 2, Zhukov was briefed on the recent fighting. He was instructed to fly there immediately, assess the situation, and if he deemed it necessary, to take command of Soviet forces in Mongolia. A few hours later, Zhukov met with an old acquaintance, Ivan Smorodinov, who recently had been promoted to acting deputy chief of the General Staff. After reviewing the military situation, Smorodinov added, "Please, the moment you arrive, see what's going on out there and report to us, without pulling any punches."[1] The growing conflict with Japan was causing concern in Moscow, and apparently in the Kremlin, as war clouds gathered over Europe. A few hours after meetings with Voroshilov and Smorodinov, Zhukov and a small staff were airborne, heading east.

In the early morning of June 5, Zhukov's party arrived at Tamsag Bulak, which had become headquarters for the Soviet 57th Corps. Zhukov promptly called a meeting with the corps' headquarters staff and concluded that corps commander Nikolai Feklenko and most of his staff were completely out of touch with the situation. Only one of the senior officers, regimental commissar M. S. Nikishev, had visited the combat area. That afternoon, Nikishev accompanied Zhukov on an inspection tour of the combat zone near the Halha River. Nikishev impressed Zhukov with his thorough knowledge of the situation. By the end of the day they had completed their inspection and Zhukov reported to Moscow, as directed, without pulling any punches. The gist of Zhukov's report was that the fighting near the Halha River did not appear to be a mere border clash, the Japanese were likely to escalate their aggression, and the 57th Corps did not seem adequate to stop the Japanese. Zhukov recommended a temporary holding action to safeguard the bridgehead on the east bank of the Halha River until major reinforcements could be brought up for a counteroffensive. He also gave an unflattering evaluation of corps commander Feklenko.[2]

One day later came the reply from Moscow, which in both its promptness and its content bespoke the esteem in which Zhukov was held by the High Command. Feklenko was relieved of his command and Zhukov named to replace him. Reinforcements were allocated to strengthen Zhukov's new command: the 36th Mechanized Infantry Division; 7th, 8th, and 9th Mechanized Brigades; 11th Tank Brigade; and 8th (MPR) Cavalry Division; a heavy artillery regiment; and a tactical air wing of more than one hundred planes, including a group of twenty-one pilots who had won combat citations as Heroes of the Soviet Union while fighting in Spain. This enlarged force was soon given a new designation: First Army Group.[3]

Throughout June, as these new forces were pouring into Tamsag Bulak, eighty miles west of the Halha River, Komatsubara's 23rd Division and KwAHQ remained largely ignorant of the scope of the Soviet buildup and of the change in command. This was an intelligence failure similar to that of the previous month that had contributed to the destruction of the Azuma unit. It owed as much to Japanese carelessness and overconfidence as to Soviet stealth, and like the earlier intelligence blunder, it would have grave consequences on the battlefield.

The first half of June passed without major incident in the Nomonhan area. The Soviet-MPR forces expanded the perimeter of their bridgehead, in accordance with Zhukov's recommendations, but they still hugged fairly close to the east bank of the river. There was no significant response from Manchukuoan or Japanese forces. The Kwantung Army commander, General Ueda, hoping that the affair was closed, left Hsinking on May 31 for an inspection tour of the newly formed Fourth Army in Northern Manchukuo. Ueda returned to headquarters on June 18. On the following day, the relative calm on the frontier was shattered.

On June 19 General Komatsubara reported to KwAHQ that two Soviet air attacks had struck inside Manchukuo. According to his initial report, "Fifteen Soviet planes attacked Arshan, causing some casualties among men and horses. Thirty Soviet planes attacked near Kanchuerhmiao, setting fire to one hundred barrels of petroleum."[4] These air raids were not quite as inflammatory as Komatsubara's report suggested.

The market town of Kanchuerhmiao—population three thousand, situated some forty miles northwest of Nomonhan—was not attacked. Actually, it was an area south of Kanchuerhmiao and only twelve miles from the frontier, where Manchukuoan forces had been stockpiling military supplies, which received the larger of the two air raids. Komatsubara's report of an air raid at Arshan was interpreted at KwAHQ to mean Harlun Arshan, a railhead and population center of some significance, nearly one hundred miles southeast of Nomonhan. Instead, the smaller air attack struck Arshanmiao, a small village near Kanchuerhmiao and very near the border, which was being used by Manchukuoan cavalry as a bivouac area and supply depot. Also, it appears that the Soviet air raids were strafing rather than bombing attacks.[5]

These Soviet air attacks may have been belated retaliation for the Japanese air raid of May 15 that struck MPR Border Outpost Number 7, killing two and wounding fifteen Mongolian border troops. They may have been staged in connection with Zhukov's expansion of the bridgehead across the Halha. Although the attacks were authorized by Defense Commissar Voroshilov, the rationale behind them is unclear.[6] For whatever reason they were launched, the Soviet air raids caused a sensation at KwAHQ. The Japanese army, which had used its air power ruthlessly and with impunity in the conquest of Manchuria, during the Shanghai incident of 1932 and throughout the China War, simply was not accustomed to being subjected to air attacks. Psychologically, it was as if the North Vietnamese Air Force in 1973 had attacked U.S. air bases in Thailand. It could not have been called "unprovoked," but the effect was startling. KwAHQ was enraged.

The Operations Staff met at midday to discuss the Soviet air raids. Major Tsuji Masanobu spoke up first, as usual, urging swift retaliation. Colonel Terada Masao initially disagreed, calling for restraint at least temporarily. He argued that Japan's confrontation with Great Britain over Tientsin was reaching a crucial stage (a Japanese blockade of the British Concession at Tientsin, near Peking, had just begun) and the central authorities in Tokyo ought not to be distracted by an expansion of the Nomonhan incident at that time. Tsuji replied that especially for that reason, Japan must act firmly at Nomonhan to impress the British with their determination. Furthermore, he argued, if Japan offered no firm response to these provocative air raids, the Soviets would be emboldened to bomb further into Manchukuo, and perhaps even attempt an invasion. Tsuji's arguments won over the Operations Section chief, Colonel Hattori Takushiro, and after further discussion, the entire Operations Staff, including Terada, united around Tsuji's position.[7]

The Operations Section immediately drafted a position paper that they circulated among the other departments at KwAHQ: "The situation at Nomonhan has become so grave that it is now impossible for us to remain passive. . . . If we undertake no counteraction, the Soviet Army will attack and invade [Manchukuo] with much larger forces, taking advantage of our passiveness. This in turn will only lead the British to doubt our real military strength and will aggravate their attitude toward Japan."[8]

After joint consultations lasting only two hours, most of the headquarters staff adopted this basic policy of strong action against the enemy at Nomonhan. That same afternoon the hyperactive Major Tsuji drew up plans for a large-scale attack across the Halha River to trap and destroy the Soviet-MPR forces there once and for all.

Colonels Hattori and Terada then brought Tsuji's plan to General Isogai Rensuke, Kwantung Army chief of staff, for his approval. Isogai was somewhat embarrassed by the situation. Despite his position as chief of staff, his area of expertise was Manchukuoan internal affairs. He felt out of his depth with major combat operations, responsibility for which he regularly delegated to his deputy chief of staff, General Yano Otozaburo. However, Yano was still at Fourth Army Headquarters in the north. General Isogai suggested to his operations officers that they await Yano's return before reaching a final decision. They countered stressing the urgency of the situation. Isogai observed that their plans would require approval from AGS in Tokyo anyway, which probably would take several days. To this, Hattori and Terada objected vigorously. The two colonels, who had been transferred from AGS to Kwantung Army only three months earlier, took the position that this was a local matter within the legitimate jurisdiction of Kwantung Army. They then cited the 1937 Amur River incident in which AGS canceled a Kwantung Army attack order. If notified, AGS "surely would object" to this attack also, they argued. Kwantung Army's traditions of élan and independence evidently had been assimilated quickly by Hattori and Terada, under Tsuji's influence. The operations officers continued to press Isogai on the grounds that the situation was too critical for delay and that it was both unnecessary and unwise to seek AGS approval. The chief of staff finally yielded and gave his assent to the plan, contingent upon the approval of the commander, General Ueda.[9]

Having persuaded—or subdued—the chief of staff, Hattori and Terada brought the attack plan to Kwantung Army's commanding general for final approval. Unlike Isogai, General Ueda expressed no objection to the basic idea of the offensive. However, he insisted that the primary responsibility be given to General Komatsubara Michitaro's 23rd Division, rather than to the 7th Division, as proposed in Tsuji's operational plan. Colonel Hattori replied that the 7th Division was Kwantung Army's finest, while the 23rd Division was only one year old and had demonstrated "unreliable combat effectiveness" in May. The 7th also was a "square" division with four infantry regiments, compared to the 23rd Division's three. Ueda agreed with his staff officers' assessment but reminded them that the Nomonhan area was the direct responsibility of the 23rd Division. He declared that "to assign another division commander to handle the incident . . . would imply a loss of confidence in the 23rd Division Commander. If I were in Komatsubara's place, I would commit suicide."[10] Hattori and Terada could not get around this argument, and on that basis the plan won final approval. The entire sequence of events from the report of the Soviet air strikes to General Ueda's final approval of the attack plan transpired in one day, June 19. This was *gekokujo* in action.

The attack plan as finally approved called for reinforcing Komatsubara's 23rd Division with powerful additional forces. Most notable among these were the 2nd Air Group, with 180 planes under the command of Lieutenant General Gigi Tetsuji, and the Yasuoka Detachment, a powerful strike force commanded by Lieutenant General Yasuoka Masaomi, built around two regiments of medium and light tanks (Japan's only operational independent tank brigade at that time), a motorized artillery regiment, and the 7th Division's excellent 26th Infantry Regiment. The total attack force consisted of approximately 15,000 men, 120 artillery and antitank guns, 70 tanks, and 180 aircraft.[11] Kwantung Army's estimate of enemy strength in the Nomonhan area at that time was approximately 1,000 infantry, 10 pieces of field artillery, and about a dozen armored vehicles. KwAHQ was confident that their designated attack force would strike the enemy, "like a butcher's cleaver dismembering a chicken." So great was their confidence that the most frequently voiced concern was that they might inadvertently tip off the enemy to the impending attack. Consequently, they curtailed air reconnaissance west of the Halha River so as not to alert or alarm the enemy.[12] This overconfidence was both a result and a cause of inadequate Japanese intelligence work, and helps explain Kwantung Army's consistent underestimation of Soviet strength.

Not everyone in the 23rd Division shared headquarters staff's confidence. The division's ordnance chief, a full colonel, committed suicide on the eve of the offensive, appalled by the "awful equipment," especially artillery, that he was powerless to improve.[13] Toward the end of June, the Japanese military attaché in Moscow, Colonel Doi Akio, stopping briefly at KwAHQ on his way to Tokyo, advised the Operations and Intelligence Sections that Soviet strength in Outer Mongolia had been increased by as much as two divisions in recent weeks and that Kwantung Army's attack plans were altogether inadequate. The Operations Staff was annoyed by this report and told Doi not to express such pessimistic thoughts when offensive operations were imminent. Kwantung Army's own Intelligence Section was concerned about Doi's report and other evidence of Soviet strength, but the Operations Section brushed aside these misgivings.[14] Zhukov's actual strength at that time consisted of approximately 12,500 men, 109 artillery and antitank guns, 186 tanks, 266 armored cars, and more than 100 aircraft.[15] The modest quantitative edge the Japanese enjoyed in some categories was offset by the more than 6:1 Soviet advantage in armor.

The operational plan that Major Tsuji drafted and that, in modified form, had been approved by General Ueda was essentially a more ambitious version of the ill-fated battle plan Colonel Yamagata Takemitsu had employed on May 28. It called for the main body of the 23rd Division to approach the Halha River and seize a group of hills called the Fui Heights near the east bank of the river, some eleven miles north of the confluence of the Halha and Holsten. This force would then cross the Halha on a pontoon bridge built secretly at night and strike southward along the western bank of the river toward the Soviet bridge. Simultaneously, elements of the Yasuoka Detachment, concentrated near Fui Heights, would push southward on different attack axes east of the Halha against Soviet and MPR units identified there. Komatsubara and Yasuoka would trap the Soviet-MPR forces between them in the vicinity of the Soviet-built bridge near the junction of the two rivers and there destroy them.

On June 20 Tsuji flew to Hailar and communicated the attack plans to General Komatsubara and his divisional staff. On his own initiative, Tsuji related to Komatsubara the gist of the discussion between Ueda and Hattori regarding the roles of the 7th and 23rd Divisions in the attack. Komatsubara was moved to tears by Ueda's confidence in him and by the opportunity given him to erase the shame of the May 28 defeat.[16]

Kwantung Army possessed only a limited amount of pontoon bridge-building materiel. Their bridge would not be strong enough to support the weight of armored vehicles, and if the pontoon bridge were destroyed, there was not enough materiel to build another. The Operations Staff was concerned about the vulnerability of the bridge, and of the men and supplies that must cross it, to Soviet air attack. Consequently, Tsuji took off from Hailar on an aerial reconnaissance mission toward Tamsag Bulak, where he discovered the growing Soviet air strength. He returned to KwAHQ that night with the conviction that the success of their operation depended upon a preemptive air strike to neutralize Soviet air power in the vicinity. This proposal was adopted quickly by the Kwantung Army Command.[17]

KwAHQ transmitted to Tokyo a vague outline of the planned offensive, highlighting the provocative Soviet air raids and the need for firm countermeasures, without going into much detail regarding their operational plans. They made no mention whatever of the proposed air strike against the Soviet air base at Tamsag Bulak. Even this intentionally incomplete notification caused some concern at Army Headquarters in Tokyo. Opinions differed within both AGS and the Army Ministry regarding the wisdom of Kwantung Army's proposed retaliation. At a special liaison meeting of senior AGS and Army Ministry personnel on the evening of June 21, army minister Itagaki Seishiro spoke for the majority when he observed that despite the unfortunate timing of the incident, Kwantung Army should be allowed to go ahead with its planned attack out of respect for the dignity of Kwantung Army commander Ueda, who already had approved the plan. Besides, concluded Itagaki, "There is no need for us to be nervous about the operations of a force of only one division's strength." On that note they decided to concur in Kwantung Army's proposal, ignorant of its scope and of the planned air strike into Mongolia.[18]

KwAHQ feared that if Tokyo got wind of their intention to attack a Soviet air base nearly one hundred miles inside the MPR, the attack would be prohibited. They took care to guard the secrecy of the attack not only from the Soviets but from Tokyo. The air strike was scheduled for one or two days before the beginning of the ground offensive on July 1. Orders were sent to Kwantung Army's 2nd Air Group only by courier, for maximum security. Nonetheless, on June 24, word of the planned air strike leaked to the General Staff in Tokyo.[19] An extraordinary exchange of communications ensued between Tokyo and Hsinking, illustrating the spirit of *gekokujo* that pervaded the Japanese military, especially Kwantung Army.

Immediately after learning of Kwantung Army's intention to bomb Tamsag Bulak, General Nakajima Tetsuzo, deputy chief of AGS, sent the following telegram to KwAHQ:

1. The policy of the Army General Staff is to prevent the border conflict from spreading. In the course of operations to repel enemy forces invading Manchukuoan territory from the west, it is essential that maximum efforts be made to avoid any fighting on other border fronts, and that *no air attacks be*

mounted against Outer Mongolian territory to the west. It is believed that this policy accords with that of Kwantung Army.

2. *In particular, the bombing of Outer Mongolian territory is considered improper in our opinion,* as it will lead to the gradual extension of bombing assaults by both sides behind the opposing frontiers, thus prolonging the incident.

3. For operational liaison purposes, Lt. Colonel Arisue is being flown to Kwantung Army Headquarters on 25 June (italics added).[20]

After receiving this telegram, there can have been no doubt about the attitude of AGS toward the planned air raid. Nakajima, however, took care to express the General Staff's negative views in the form of a subjective opinion rather than as a direct order prohibiting the air raid. This was in keeping with formal Japanese usage, in which direct and explicit statements, requests, orders, even questions, between parties of roughly equal status, are considered curt and impolite, to be avoided when possible in favor of subtle circumlocutions that convey their meaning implicitly rather than directly. AGS regularly adopted this polite and indirect manner in its communications with Kwantung Army out of respect for the latter's tradition as an elite and independent-minded organization. In this case, middle-echelon Kwantung Army staff officers took advantage of the General Staff's polite and respectful form of address to thwart Tokyo's will.

Despite the unmistakable intent of General Nakajima's telegram, Kwantung Army's Operations Section chose to interpret it merely as a suggestion, rather than as an explicit cancellation order. Knowing that more specific orders were being carried from Tokyo to Hsinking by Lieutenant Colonel Arisue Yadoru, the Operations Section decided to act quickly. Tsuji convinced his colleagues in the Operations Section not to reveal the contents of the AGS telegram to Generals Ueda, Isogai, or Yano at that time. Instead, they would advance the date of the air strike against Tamsag Bulak so that it could be accomplished before the arrival of Lieutenant Colonel Arisue from Tokyo. The date for the air attack was advanced secretly from June 29–30 to June 27.[21] Meanwhile, Arisue's flight from Tokyo was delayed by bad weather and did not reach Hsinking until June 27. The restrictive orders that Arisue brought from AGS reached KwAHQ a few hours after the 2nd Air Group hit Soviet air bases at Tamsag Bulak and at Bain Tumen (present day Choibalsan, capital of Dornod Province, even deeper inside Mongolian territory).

The Japanese air raid was highly successful. The attacking force, approximately 120 planes, achieved complete tactical surprise, catching the newly arrived Soviet squadrons on the ground. The initial Japanese bombing run forced the Soviet fighters to scramble to avoid being destroyed on the ground, but they came up in ones and twos and were overwhelmed by the Japanese fighter squadrons, which had the advantages of surprise, numbers, and altitude. The dauntless Major Tsuji, flying in one of the bombers, counted twenty-five enemy planes destroyed on the ground and nearly a hundred more shot down by Japanese fighters as they tried to take off. The 2nd Air Group's official report claimed ninety-eight Soviet planes destroyed and fifty-one damaged. An additional fifty to sixty military and civilian personnel were killed on the ground at Bain Tumen.

Japanese losses were slight: a bomber, two fighters, and a scout plane shot down, seven flyers killed. A second Japanese bomber made a forced landing in Mongolian territory, but its crew was rescued by an accompanying aircraft that landed on the open grassland and plucked the endangered airmen from approaching enemy armored cars. Even allowing for exaggeration and duplicate claims by excited Japanese flyers, they had achieved a major tactical victory that gave them mastery of the air over the Halha at the start of Kwantung Army's July offensive.[22]

Moscow was furious about the losses inflicted by the Japanese air raid, attributed in part to the failure of the early warning system to provide any warning of the approaching Japanese squadrons. In the atmosphere of Josef Stalin's purges, the deadly questions were: Who was to blame? Was it "merely" incompetence, or treason? In either case, heads would roll. Zhukov and his staff were on the spot. It was found—or claimed—that the telephone lines on which the primitive early warning system relied had been cut. Luvsandonoi, deputy commander of the Mongolian army, and A. M. Kushchev, the former deputy commander of the 57th Corps, were denounced as Japanese agents and saboteurs—perhaps by Zhukov himself—arrested, and bundled off to Moscow. Luvsandonoi was shot. Kushchev, imprisoned for four years, somehow not only survived but was recalled to service in 1943, ending the war as a major general and Hero of the Soviet Union.[23]

News of the successful air strike generated tremendous excitement at KwAHQ. In the Operations Section, which had planned the attack and taken responsibility for launching it against the wishes of AGS, emotions ran high. Their nervousness was replaced by exultation as Major Tsuji eagerly recounted details of the attack and the extent of their victory. The Operations Staff went en masse to the communications room and clustered around the radio as Colonel Terada notified AGS of their action. There was silence in the communications room as they waited tensely for Colonel Inada Masazumi, head of the AGS Operations Section, to be summoned to the radio at General Staff Headquarters in Tokyo. Inada was known to be one of the more hawkish officers at AGS. Terada was chosen to convey the news because he was a personal friend and former military academy classmate of Inada. Terada made his report, masking his emotion as best he could. After a pause, Inada's voice came crackling over the radio's speaker—"You damned idiot! What do you think will be the real meaning of this little success of yours?!" He went on to vehemently upbraid his listeners for their indiscipline and bad judgment.[24]

Terada and his colleagues were stunned by this rebuke, which they considered altogether unjustified both in form and substance. They were stunned but not remorseful. A short time later a formal reprimand reached KwAHQ from Tokyo:

> Report was received today regarding bombing of Outer Mongolian territory by your air units. . . . Since this action is in fundamental disagreement with policy which we understood your army was taking to settle incident, it is extremely regretted that advance notice of your intent was not received. Needless to say, this matter is attended with such far-reaching consequences that it can by no means be left to your unilateral decision. Hereafter, existing policy will be definitely and strictly observed. It is requested that air attack program be discontinued immediately.
>
> By Order of the Chief of Staff[25]

By this time, the Kwantung Army staff officers were in high dudgeon. Tsuji later wrote that "tremendous combat results were achieved by carrying out dangerous operations at the risk of our lives. It is perfectly clear that we were carrying out an act of retaliation. What kind of General Staff ignores the psychology of the front lines and tramples on their feelings?"[26]

Tsuji drafted a caustic reply, which they shot back to Tokyo, apparently without the knowledge of Kwantung Army commander Ueda or other senior officers at KwAHQ: "There appear to be certain differences between Army General Staff and this Army in evaluating the battlefield situation and measures to be adopted. It is requested that the handling of trivial matters in border areas be entrusted to this Army."[27]

This sarcastic message from KwAHQ made a deep impression at AGS, where it was felt that something had to be done to restore discipline and order. When General Nakajima informed the Throne about the air raid, the emperor rebuked the general and asked who would assume responsibility for the unauthorized attack. Nakajima replied that military operations were still under way, but that appropriate measures would be taken when this phase had ended. Inada sent Terada a telegram implying that the Kwantung Army staff officers responsible would be sacked in due course. Inada tried to have Tsuji ousted from Kwantung Army immediately, but personnel matters went through the Army Ministry, and General Itagaki, the army minister, knew Tsuji personally and defended him.[28]

The men in Tokyo realized that this was a tricky situation in which Kwantung Army's position was not altogether groundless. Since 1932 that army had been operating under an Imperial Order to "defend Manchukuo." This was a very broad mandate. Opinions differed in AGS about how best to limit or restrict Kwantung Army's operational prerogatives. One idea was to secure Imperial sanction for a new directive limiting the scope of combat operations that Kwantung Army could undertake on its own initiative to no more than one regiment. There were other plans as well. In the meantime Kwantung Army had to be brought under tighter rein.

On June 29, AGS sent firm instructions to KwAHQ

Directives:

a) It is the responsibility of Kwantung Army to localize matters in the settlement of border disputes.

b) Areas in which the border is disputed, or in which defense is tactically unfeasible, need not be defended.

Orders:

c) Ground combat will be limited to the border region between Manchukuo and Outer Mongolia east of Lake Buir Nor.

d) Enemy bases will not be attacked from the air.[29]

With this heated exchange of messages, relations between Kwantung Army and AGS reached a critical stage. Tsuji called it the "breaking point" between Hsinking and Tokyo. According to Colonel Inada, after this "air raid squabble" *gekokujo* became much more pronounced in Hsinking, especially in Kwantung Army's Operations Section, which "ceased making meaningful reports" to the AGS Operations Section, which he headed.[30] At KwAHQ this controversy and the attendant perception of AGS "interference" in local affairs cemented the resolve of wavering staff officers concerning the necessity of moving decisively against the USSR. Thereafter, Kwantung Army officers as a group rejected the General Staff's policy of moderation in the Nomonhan incident. Tsuji characterized the conflict between Kwantung Army and the General Staff as typical of the antagonism between combat officers and "desk jockeys." In his view, AGS was advocating a policy of "not invading enemy territory even if one's own territory was invaded," while Kwantung Army's policy was "not to allow invasion." In explaining Kwantung Army's (and his own) attitude toward the USSR in this border dispute, Tsuji cited the samurai warrior's traditional warning when encroached upon: "Do not step any closer or I *shall be forced* to cut you down."

Tsuji claimed that Kwantung Army had to act firmly at Nomonhan to avoid the necessity of a larger war later. Tsuji also stressed the importance felt by him and his colleagues of Kwantung Army's maintaining its dignity, which was threatened by the actions both of the enemy and of the Army General Staff.[31] In this emotionally charged atmosphere, Kwantung Army launched its July offensive.

Kwantung Army's July Offensive

The success of the 2nd Air Group's attack against the Tamsag Bulak air base added still further to the already excessive confidence at KwAHQ about their upcoming offensive. Although Japanese aerial reconnaissance intentionally had been limited so as not to alarm or forewarn the enemy, some reconnaissance missions were flown. The scout planes reported seeing numerous tank emplacements being prepared, although most spotted few tanks. The one report of large numbers of tanks was played down at headquarters. What attracted a great deal of attention at KwAHQ, however, were reports of large numbers of trucks leaving the front daily, streaming westward into the Mongolian interior. This was interpreted as evidence of a Soviet pullback from their forward positions. Perhaps the enemy had gotten wind of the imminent attack. Orders were issued to speed final preparations for the assault before all Soviet forces could be withdrawn from the area where the Japanese "meat cleaver" soon was to dismember them.[32]

What the Japanese scout planes actually had seen was not a truck-borne Soviet withdrawal, but part of a massive truck shuttle that General Grigori Shtern, now commander of Soviet Forces in the Far East, had organized in support of Zhukov. Each night, the roads from the distant MPR railway depots to Tamsag Bulak and the combat zone were jammed with Soviet trucks, their lights dimmed, carrying tons of supplies and reinforcements eastward. During the day, the trucks returned westward for fresh loads.[33] It was these returning trucks, mostly empty, that the Japanese scout planes had sighted. The interpretation Kwantung Army put on this mass of west-bound Soviet traffic was a serious error, albeit an understandable one. But the Soviet side was also largely ignorant of the Japanese preparations, partly because the Japanese air raid of June 27 had thrown Soviet air operations, including reconnaissance, into disarray.

In late June the 23rd Division and Yasuoka's tank force deployed from Hailar and Chiangchunmiao toward Nomonhan. All manner of military and civilian vehicles were pressed into service, but still there was not enough motorized transport to move all the troops and equipment at once. Most of the infantry marched 120 miles to the combat zone, under a hot sun, carrying eighty-pound packs. They arrived after four to six days of marching, tired and thirsty, with little time to recover before the scheduled assault.

With Komatsubara's combined force of 15,000 men, 120 guns, and 70 tanks poised to attack, Kwantung Army estimated Soviet-MPR strength in the immediate vicinity of Nomonhan and the Halha River at about one thousand men, with perhaps ten antiaircraft guns, ten artillery pieces, and several dozen tanks. In fact, Japanese air activity, particularly the big raid of June 27, had put the Soviets on the alert. Zhukov suspected that a Japanese ground attack might be forthcoming, although nothing as audacious as a large-scale crossing of the Halha River was foreseen. During the night of July 1, Zhukov moved his 11th Tank Brigade, 7th Mechanized Brigade, and 24th Mechanized Infantry Regiment (36th Division) from their staging area near Tamsag Bulak to a position just west of the Halha River.[34] Powerful forces were being marshaled by each side in ignorance of their enemy's disposition.

At 4:00 a.m. on July 1, 15,000 heavily laden Japanese troops began marching eighteen to twenty miles to their final assembly and jump-off points. Just ten

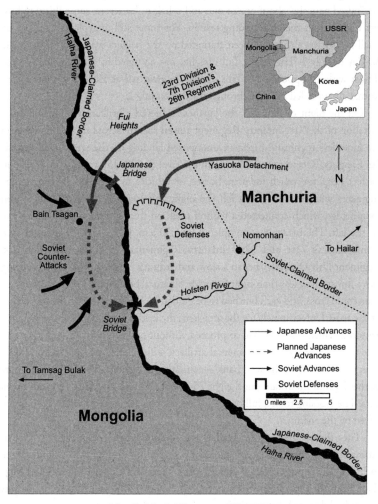

Map 5. July 1–3 Japanese Offensive

days after the summer solstice, the sun rose there at 4:00 a.m. and set at 9:00 p.m. Nevertheless, the Japanese advance went undetected by Soviet/MPR commanders, partly because the Japanese air raid of June 27 had temporarily swept Soviet reconnaissance planes from the skies.

On the night of July 1, as Soviet reinforcements were being brought up, Komatsubara began the first phase of his attack. His 23rd Division, together with the Yasuoka Detachment, converged on Fui Heights, just east of the Halha River, some eleven miles north of its confluence with the Holsten. The designation "heights" in this case is misleading. A Japanese infantry colonel described Fui as a "raised pancake" about one to one-and-a-half miles across, some thirty to forty feet higher than the surrounding terrain. For some still-unexplained reason, the small Soviet force that had been stationed on the heights was withdrawn during the day on July 1. That night, Fui Heights was occupied by Komatsubara's forces almost without opposition.[35] This caused no great stir at Zhukov's headquarters. Komatsubara bided his time through the day on July 2.

On the night of July 2–3, the Japanese achieved a brilliant tactical success. A battalion of the 71st Infantry Regiment rowed silently across the Halha River on the moonless night and made an unopposed landing on the west bank opposite Fui Heights. Recent rains had swollen the river to 100–150 yards wide and about six feet deep, too much for men, horses, or vehicles to ford. As planned, combat engineers worked swiftly through the night and spanned the river with a pontoon bridge, which connected a natural track on the right shore with a dirt road on the left. The bridge was completed by 6:30 a.m. July 3 and the main body of Komatsubara's 71st and 72nd Infantry Regiments (23rd Division) and 26th Regiment (7th Division), began a slow and arduous crossing. The pontoon bridge was a flimsy affair less than eight feet wide, a natural bottleneck. Only one truck at a time could cross, and each one had to be guided carefully because of the narrowness of the span. Unfortunately for the attackers, the bridge could not bear the weight of armored vehicles, so they had to proceed without tank support. At least they were able to carry across their regimental artillery—dismantled and packed on horses, then reassembled on the west bank—consisting of eighteen 37-mm antitank guns, twelve 75-mm mountain guns, eight 75-mm field guns, and four 120-mm howitzers. The crossing took a full day. They were fortunate indeed to have been unmolested by the enemy.

The thrust across the Halha was commanded personally by General Komatsubara, who was accompanied by several Kwantung Army staff officers, including the deputy chief of staff, General Yano, and Colonel Hattori and Major Tsuji from the Operations Section. Still no Soviet/MPR scouts or reconnaissance planes had detected the crossing.

Even though the big Japanese air raid had put Zhukov on his guard, the initial Japanese moves of July 1–3 achieved complete tactical surprise and found the Soviet-MPR forces in a vulnerable position. This was due, in no small part, to the boldness of Tsuji's operational plan. The first indication the Soviets had that a major Japanese offensive had begun came in the predawn hours of July 3, when General Yasuoka's tanks attacked. Yasuoka thought he detected evidence of Soviet troops south of him attempting to retreat across the Halha River to the relative security of its west bank. Fearing that his prey might escape the trap before it was sprung, Yasuoka ordered his tanks to attack immediately. His infantry was not yet in position and so the tanks rumbled into the night without them—unheard of tactics for Japanese armor.

Conditions were ideal for a stealthy night attack: low clouds, no moon, visibility ten to twenty yards, temperature a comfortable 65 degrees. As the Japanese tanks approached the main Soviet defense line, lightning from a passing thunderstorm lit the sky. Yasuoka's seventy tanks, their guns blazing, descended upon the startled men of the Soviet 149th Infantry Regiment. It was an awesome sight before which the stunned defenders scattered in disarray.[36] The battle had begun.

When Zhukov got word of Yasuoka's tank attack, he still was unaware that Komatsubara had crossed the Halha. Unsure of the situation or of Yasuoka's strength or intentions, Zhukov ordered his 11th Tank Brigade, 7th Mechanized Brigade, 24th Mechanized Infantry Regiment, and elements of the 6th MPR Cavalry Division to advance northeastward and concentrate at a hill called Bain Tsagan. Bain Tsagan stood on the west bank of the Halha, roughly opposite the Fui Heights, the starting point of Yasuoka's attack. It already was occupied by Komatsubara's troops. In the faint early morning light of July 3, the lead elements of Komatsubara's infantry began advancing southward from Bain Tsagan and ran directly into the vanguard of the 11th Tank Brigade, which was moving north to its assembly point. Both sides were surprised by this encounter. The Soviet armor immediately went over to the attack, but the tanks and armored cars were deployed awkwardly and were badly mauled. The Japanese 37-mm rapid-fire antitank guns, firing armor-piercing shells, were especially effective.

At last Zhukov realized that a large Japanese force had crossed the Halha and menaced his entire position. He hurled the remainder of the 11th Tank Brigade, 7th Brigade, 24th Regiment, and an armored battalion of the 8th Mongolian Cavalry Division against Komatsubara's infantry in an attempt to hold them at Bain Tsagan and prevent them from capturing the Soviet bridge near the river junction. The main punch of the Soviet counterattack was delivered by the 150 tanks of Mikhail Yakovlev's 11th Tank Brigade, plus some 154 armored cars mounting 45-mm guns. But they were supported by only 1,200 infantrymen. As each Soviet unit reached the combat zone, it was thrown into the attack directly off the march. The result was a series of uncoordinated assaults with which the Japanese could deal in succession. Because the Soviet armor had little infantry support, Japanese infantry literally swarmed over the Soviet vehicles, some of whose hatch lids were pried opened from the outside. Many tanks and armored cars were knocked out by primitive gasoline bombs and explosive charges carried by "human bullet" tank-killer teams, as well as by antitank guns. However, these repeated tank attacks threw the Japanese advance off balance.[37]

Generals Komatsubara and Yano and their staff narrowly escaped death around noon. The headquarters party pushed ahead a bit too rapidly. Suddenly, the troop truck accompanying Komatsubara's black Buick sedan stopped and the soldiers jumped out. A squadron of Soviet light tanks was bearing down on them and opened fire at about three hundred yards. The two generals and their staff hit the dirt as enemy shells roared overhead. The headquarters escort had no antitank weapons. The officers piled into the Buick and raced off, with the Soviet tanks in pursuit. Luckily for the fleeing Japanese, their peril was spotted by a Japanese artillery officer. Captain Kusabe Sakae, commander of a battery of the obsolete Type 38 75-mm guns, observed some fifteen Soviet tanks closely pursuing the general's sedan. At a range of seven hundred yards, Kusabe wondered if his guns would knock out the tanks or kill his general. Kusabe "closed his eyes" and gave the order to fire. The second round hit the lead tank, which burst into flames. The rest of the armored squadron abandoned the chase and turned to attack the artillery. Kusabe's venerable old guns gave a good account of themselves, knocking out or driving off all the attacking vehicles.[38]

Japanese infantry and artillery west of the Halha, with some tactical air support, succeeded in beating off each successive attack and knocking out many Soviet tanks. The latter, whose poorly shielded gasoline engines were running hot under the blazing sun, were easily ignited by Japanese gunners and gasoline bombs. The Soviet tankers, who had never experienced this sort of combat, at first did not use their machine guns much, concentrating instead on firing their cannons against enemy heavy weapons. This facilitated the Japanese "human bullet" attacks.

However, although Komatsubara's troops were inflicting heavy losses on Soviet armor, Japanese offensive momentum was checked. By the afternoon of July 3, the repeated Soviet counterattacks and increasing effective artillery fire forced the Japanese infantry to dig defensive positions in the loose sand west of the Halha, not far south of Bain Tsagan. Zhukov's gamble with his armor had paid off.

The inability of the Japanese to transport their armored vehicles across the pontoon bridge proved crucial, for Zhukov had massed more than 450 tanks and armored cars in the area. Komatsubara's infantry had no real chance of breaking

Part of Mongolian Border Outpost No. 7, viewed from the outpost observation tower, looking east toward Manchuria, July 2009. Author's collection.

Semi-arid grassland at Nomonhan. Battlefield debris in foreground, Remizov heights in background. Courtesey M. Saandari, MonMap Engineering Services Co.

Left (west) bank of the Halha River dominates the east bank, July 2009. Author's collection.

Lieutenant General Komatsubara Michitaro, commander, 23rd Division (left); Major General Yano Otosaburo, deputy chief of staff, Kwantung Army (right). Mainichi Newspaper/AFLO.

Major Tsuji Masanobu (foreground pointing) China, 1937. Mainichi Newspaper/AFLO.

From left to right, General Yakov Smushkevich (smoking cigarette), Soviet air force commander at Nomonhan; General M. S. Nikishev (looking over Smushkevich's left shoulder); General Georgy Zhukov; and General Grigori Shtern (far right). RIA Novosti/AKG-images.

Soviet BA-10 armored car with 45 mm gun turret. Tracks on rear wheels removable for road travel. Author's collection.

Restored Japanese Type 89 medium tank, Tsuchira, Japan tank museum, 2007. Author's collection, courtesy Max Smith.

Soviet BT 5 tank at Yakovlev Memorial on Bain Tsagan. Inscription claims this is the tank Colonel Yakovlev was commanding when he was killed on July 12. Author's collection.

Soviet Polikarpov I-16 fighter at air museum in Moscow. Author's collection.

Rendering of a Japanese Type 97 fighter (Nakajima Ki-27) with Soviet Polikarpov I-16 in background Photo credit: ICM Holding, Kiev, Ukraine.

through such a force, and as the day wore on, it was all they could do to keep from being overrun by the weight of the Soviet counterattacks. The temperature rose to well over 100 degrees Fahrenheit that afternoon, and the Japanese troops, who had not been able to refill their canteens since crossing the Halha, were thirsty and tired. With the offensive energy of his own force spent, Komatsubara's best hope for salvaging the attack rode with the Yasuoka detachment. If General Yasuoka, moving south, parallel to Komatsubara's force but on the eastern side of the Halha, could achieve a striking success, it would relieve the Soviet pressure on the 23rd Division commander. If Yasuoka with his two tank regiments could seize the Soviet bridge and link up with Komatsubara, the attack might yet succeed. The western bank of the Halha is somewhat higher than the eastern side and commands a fine view of the eastern bank and the arid plain sloping gently away to the east and south. From their position on the western bank, Komatsubara and his men could watch the progress of the Yasuoka detachment on the opposite side. It was not a heartening sight.

Yasuoka's initial predawn tank attack pierced the lines of the Soviet 149th Infantry Regiment and 9th Mechanized Brigade. Japanese tanks literally overran a Soviet artillery unit that was unable to depress its guns to a low enough angle to engage the attackers. Japanese tanks shot up, and in some cases crushed, the enemy guns and scattered the defenders. But with daybreak, the Yasuoka detachment encountered increasingly determined resistance from Soviet infantry, tanks, and artillery. Japanese armor had performed well enough since 1937 against the Chinese, who had few tanks of their own and little effective antitank weaponry. But on this battlefield, the Japanese faced a more potent foe and their tanks suffered heavy losses.

Yasuoka's advance was spearheaded by his two tank regiments, the mainstay of which was the Type 89 medium tank. The Type 89, designed primarily for an infantry support role, had relatively thin armor, 17-mm (about 2/3 inch), which was easily penetrated by Soviet antitank guns and the long-barreled, high-velocity 45-mm cannons of the Soviet BT-5/7 tanks and armored cars, whose armor-piercing shells were deadly at 1,500 yards and could score hits at 2,000 yards. The Type 89's short-barreled, low-velocity (350 meters/second) 57-mm cannon, designed to attack pill boxes and concrete defenses with high-explosive shells, proved utterly ineffective against the Soviet tanks, which could engage the Japanese machines at long range with impunity.

Zhukov's antitank defenses east of the Halha also employed an innovation the Japanese had never encountered: piano wire. The Soviets strung coils of almost invisible fine strands of steel as part of their defensive works. Imported from Japan and intended for pianos, the wire was thin, flat, and extremely strong. When coiled, it resembled the giant mainspring of a wristwatch. The wire was drawn into the gears and boggie wheels of tank tracks that tried to cross it. A few strands were often enough to ensnare a tank, as one survivor recalled, "like butterflies in a spider web." Once enmeshed in the wire entanglements, the tanks were pounded by Soviet gunfire. Even immobilized, many of the Japanese tanks continued to fire their guns as long as they were able, which won the admiration of Japanese infantry. But soon, many were reduced to scorched wrecks.

Japanese army regulations forbade a tank crew to abandon their vehicle under fire, even if it was knocked out of action. This was partly because of Japan's resource scarcity—not enough steel, not enough tanks, each one precious. It was also a throwback to Japanese samurai concepts of martial honor. Retreat and surrender were not merely dishonorable, they were literally impermissible. In some cases they could be capital offenses punishable by death. The leader of one Japanese tank unit in this battle explained to his men that tank crews must share the fate of their tank, saving their last bullet for themselves.[39]

The consequences for Japanese tankers were devastating. In one relatively short engagement that afternoon, twenty of the Type 89 tanks were put out of action. Casualties among tank crews were high. The Japanese Type 95 light tank mounted a 37-mm gun, effective against soft targets up to seven hundred yards. They were quicker and more agile than the medium tanks, but they had even less armor protection and fared poorly. They not only were vulnerable to enemy armor and antitank guns, but they also suffered casualties from Soviet heavy machine gun fire.

Lieutenant Tomioka Zenzo, who commanded a squadron of light tanks, lost five to antitank guns. His own machine was dented by 130 machine gun slugs. Tomioka kept his hatch closed and was peering through the six-inch vision slit when a burst of machine gun fire hit the slit. One bullet struck him in the forehead, blinding him. His machine gunner took command of the tank and Tomioka was evacuated to a first aid station and later a hospital in Harbin. He regained partial vision after two months, carrying bullet fragments in his head for the rest of his life. But he remained a lucky survivor. As a captain in 1945, he was evacuated from Iwo Jima with typhus on the last Japanese plane to leave before the U.S. invasion. A few months later he survived the atomic bombing of Hiroshima, about eight miles from ground zero.[40]

The core of Yasuoka's infantry, the 64th Regiment (23rd Division), on foot, was unable to keep up, or catch up, with the tank regiments, which suffered from lack of infantry support. The infantry, in turn, complained that once the battle began they never saw friendly tanks, only swarms of Soviet armor. The solution, of course, would have been truck transport for the infantry, but Kwantung Army did not have nearly enough trucks, and that day the 64th Regiment had none, so Japanese infantry and armor fought independently, each less effective than they would have been in concert. By late afternoon, Yasuoka's advance was stopped far short of the river junction and the Soviet bridge. Soon the infantry was forced to dig in for protection against deadly Soviet bombardment. By nightfall, the Japanese tank regiments withdrew to their initial jump-off points, having lost about half their tanks.[41]

The situation of the Japanese attackers was imperiled further by the appearance of Soviet aircraft, which had not been seen over the Halha River since June 27. By the afternoon of July 3, however, furious air combat was raging over the battlefield and the Japanese flyers on occasion were outnumbered.[42]

Tsuji's operational plan called for Komatsubara and Yasuoka to envelop the enemy troops and to trap and destroy them in the vicinity of the river junction. The strength of the enemy's resistance, particularly his armor and artillery, frustrated that plan. Komatsubara then found himself in the dangerous position of having his forces divided on opposite sides of a river, with powerful enemy forces between them. This was a classic military dilemma, and the Japanese began to realize that if they did not move quickly, disaster might overtake them. On the evening of July 3, General Yano, Colonel Hattori, and Major Tsuji conferred with General Komatsubara and his divisional staff. They reached the unanimous decision that Komatsubara's troops should be withdrawn to the east bank of the Halha as soon as possible. The urgency of this decision was underlined by the fact that Kwantung Army had no more bridge-building materiel. If the Japanese pontoon bridge were captured or destroyed, Komatsubara's forces east of the Halha (approximately eight thousand men) would be isolated in enemy territory and in danger of annihilation. Zhukov had begun to direct air and artillery bombardment against the bridge, but it remained intact by nightfall.

The withdrawal would have to be effected swiftly, preferably before dawn. It also was decided that in view of enemy strength, which KwAHQ had failed to foresee, General Komatsubara should not be held responsible for the failure of the offensive. Of course, in view of Japanese air superiority before the battle, Kwantung Army *should* have foreseen Soviet strength, especially 450 armored vehicles. But that was a matter for after-action assessment. At that moment, Japanese commanders had to focus all their efforts on averting disaster.[43]

Fortunately for Komatsubara, Zhukov had been caught off guard by the daring river crossing and did not immediately recognize the vulnerability of the Japanese position. On the night of July 3, Zhukov was still thinking in terms of repulsing the enemy, rather than of encircling and destroying him.

Komatsubara ordered his troops to prepare to withdraw across the Halha that very night. Colonel Sumi Shinichiro's 26th Regiment (7th Division), which still was relatively fresh, was ordered to secure Bain Tsagan and protect the withdrawal of the battered 71st and 72nd Regiments. By dawn of July 4, the two exhausted regiments had recrossed the pontoon bridge and reassembled at Fui Heights. However, a delay developed in withdrawing the 26th Regiment from its covering position. When the Soviets discovered that the main Japanese strength had withdrawn across the river, they pressed their assault on the 26th Regiment with greater intensity. Colonel Sumi's men soon found themselves very heavily engaged and unable to break off the action and withdraw across river. The 26th Regiment suffered heavy losses throughout the day but fought off repeated Soviet attempts to overrun their position. The high ground to which they were pinned on Bain Tsagan at least afforded a strong defensive position. The Japanese pontoon bridge miraculously survived every Soviet attempt to destroy it throughout the day, but that was a situation that could change at any moment.[44]

During July 4, Zhukov brought up several batteries of heavy artillery, which soon were pounding Komatsubara's troops on and near Fui Heights. These were German-made 152-mm Rheinmetall pieces acquired by the Red Army during the long years of clandestine cooperation with Weimar Germany. They had a range of over 20,000 yards, more than twice that of Komatsubara's few 150-mm guns. The Japanese had no effective reply to this long-range bombardment. There was nothing to do but dig in deeper, accept their casualties stoically, and wait for nightfall.[45]

With darkness came a slackening of the Soviet pressure. The fragile pontoon bridge still spanned the river and the 26th Regiment, reduced in numbers, clung tenaciously to Bain Tsagan. Major Tsuji, who had accompanied Komatsubara and the others to the relative safety of the east bank of the Halha on the previous night, now recrossed the river to help Colonel Sumi execute a stealthy withdrawal. In the predawn hours of July 5, the last of Sumi's troops regained the eastern shore. Tsuji was among the last to cross to safety, taking care to see that the pontoon bridge was destroyed behind them. Japanese combat engineers had ample experience in blowing up bridges, but this was the first time the Imperial Army had ever had to destroy one of its own bridges after retreating across it.

Some Japanese stragglers and wounded who had been separated from their units made it to the Halha after the bridge was blown, but few survived the attempt to swim across the swollen and swift-flowing river. One witness to the drownings, Lieutenant Nagami Hiroshi, an Olympic swimmer (Amsterdam, 1928), noted that no ordinary swimmer could have made it across the Halha. Soviet troops watching from the high ground west of the river took a less charitable view. Soviet sources claim that panicky Japanese engineers blew up their bridge prematurely, condemning latecomers to a watery death.[46]

Ten percent of the Japanese troops that crossed the Halha were killed or wounded, half of those from Sumi's 26th Regiment. In addition, nearly 60 percent of the Japanese tanks had been disabled or destroyed, although many were subsequently recovered and repaired. On July 9 KwAHQ decided to withdraw its two tank regiments from the combat zone. Japanese armor would play no further role in the conflict at Nomonhan, a decision that was regretted by Japanese commanders and criticized by analysts for years afterward. Soviet tank losses were much heavier than the Japanese, but Zhukov started with a 6:1 advantage in armor and was able to more than make good his losses with new—and improved—machines. The verdict on the July offensive was inescapable. Kwantung Army had failed again.

Part of the reason for the failure was an unfortunate combination of difficult terrain and inadequate logistics. Unusually heavy rains in late June had turned the dirt roads between Hailar and Nomonhan to a muddy quagmire. Japanese truck transport, limited in the best of circumstances, was so hampered by these conditions that it seriously affected combat effectiveness. Colonel Yamagata's 64th Infantry Regiment, on foot, could not keep up with and support General Yasuoka's tanks on July 3–4. Komatsubara's infantry on the west side of the Halha ran short of ammunition, food, and water.

As was the case in the May 28 battle, however, the main cause for the failure of Kwantung Army's July offensive lay in wholly inadequate military intelligence. Again the enemy's strength had been seriously underestimated. Furthermore, a highly disturbing fact was becoming evident to some at KwAHQ and in the field. Their intelligence error was not merely quantitative, but qualitative as well. The Soviet forces not only were more numerous but were much more powerful than had been anticipated. The attacking Japanese forces actually enjoyed a slight numerical advantage as well as tactical surprise at the outset, but the Red Army fought tenaciously and the weight of Soviet firepower proved decisive.

Because of her relative lack of raw materials and industrial strength, Japan could not hope to match the great industrial powers in the quantitative production of military materiel. Consequently, Japanese military leaders traditionally felt compelled to stress in their doctrine and training the paramount importance of the spiritual superiority of Japan's armed forces. As a corollary they tended to underestimate the relative importance of material factors, including firepower.[47] This was particularly characteristic of the army that carried the tactic of the massed bayonet charge into the Second World War. This "spiritual" battle doctrine was born of necessity, since to admit the superiority of material over human factors in battle was to concede the defeat of Japanese arms. Moreover, Japan's great victories in the Sino-Japanese War, Russo-Japanese War, Manchurian incident, and the China War (not to mention the legendary thirteenth-century victories over the invading Mongol Horde of Genghis Khan), against vastly more numerous foes, seemed ample evidence of the transcendent importance of fighting spirit. Only in such a doctrine could the Imperial Japanese Army find the inner strength and confidence needed to confront powerful enemies.[48] This was especially true vis-à-vis Soviet Russia, whose vast geography, population, and material resources might otherwise have seemed awesome. But what of its spirit? The Japanese military held Bolshevism in contempt as a base and inhuman materialist philosophy utterly lacking spiritual power. Consequently, the Red Army was believed to have very low morale and fighting effectiveness. Stalin's purge of the Red Army only strengthened this conviction.

But Kwantung Army's recent experiences at Nomonhan undermined this whole outlook. Among common soldiers as well as ranking officers, among the 23rd Division Staff and at KwAHQ, terrible questions were beginning to formulate themselves. Had Soviet materiel and firepower proven superior to Japanese fighting spirit? If not, did the enemy possess a fighting spirit comparable to their own?

To some in Kwantung Army, these were grotesque, almost literally unthinkable, ideas. To others, these lines of thought led to conclusions that simply were too painful to contemplate. Perhaps the results of the combat in May and July were an aberration attributable to the inexperience of the 23rd Division.[49] In any case, the conviction took hold at KwAHQ that they faced a situation that absolutely had to be rectified.

The assessment at Zhukov's First Army Headquarters of the recent events was less painful, but it was not without self-criticism and apprehension about the future. That the enemy had succeeded in transporting nearly ten thousand men across the Halha River without being detected, at a time when the Soviet command presumably was at heightened alert because of the June 27 air raid, reflected a carelessness and lack of foresight on the part of Zhukov and his subordinates. Nor did Zhukov capitalize as fully as he might have on Komatsubara's predicament on July 4–5.

Conversely, the Soviet commander and his troops reacted coolly in the first and most critical hours of the crisis. Although he was taken by surprise and outnumbered, Zhukov recognized instantly that "our trump cards were the armored detachments and we decided to use them immediately."[50] Zhukov played his trump quickly and that proved decisive. Some have criticized the uncoordinated and seemingly clumsy manner in which the Soviet armor was hurled against Komatsubara's infantry on the morning of July 3, but the Japanese troops were only a few hour's march from the river junction and the Soviet bridge. By recklessly throwing their tanks without adequate infantry support against Komatsubara's advancing regiments, Mikhail Yakovlev, commander of the 11th Tank Brigade, and A. L. Lesovoi, commander of the 7th Mechanized Brigade, suffered appalling losses. But they halted Komatsubara's southward advance and forced him onto the defensive, after which he was never able to regain offensive momentum. Zhukov did not flinch from incurring heavy casualties to achieve his objectives. He told General Dwight D. Eisenhower after the war, "If we come to a mine field, our infantry attack exactly as if it were not there. The losses we get from personnel mines we consider only equal to those we would have gotten . . . if the Germans had chosen to defend the area with strong bodies of troops instead of mine fields."[51] Zhukov admitted losing 120 tanks and armored cars that day, a high but necessary price paid to avert defeat.

Years later in his memoirs, Zhukov defended his tactics at Nomonhan, saying that he knew his armor would suffer very heavy losses, but that was the only way to prevent the Japanese from taking the bridge at the confluence of the rivers. If Komatsubara's men had been allowed to advance southward unchecked for another two or three hours, they might have fought their way to the Soviet bridge and linked up with the Yasuoka detachment, thus splitting and gravely imperiling Zhukov's forces. For their timely and self-sacrificing counterattacks, Zhukov credited Yakovlev, Lesovoi, and their men with stabilizing a critical situation. The armored car battalion of the 8th MPR Cavalry Division also distinguished itself in this action.

Zhukov and his tankmen learned a good deal in those two days of deadly combat. One important lesson was the successful use of large tank formations as an independent primary attack force. This contradicted orthodox military tactics of the day, which saw armor's role primarily as support for the infantry and called for the integration of armor into every infantry regiment rather than maintaining large independent armored units. The German army would demonstrate the terrible potency of their panzer divisions in Poland shortly after the Nomonhan conflict and a year later in Western Europe, but until their demonstration of blitzkrieg, no other major armies had heeded the theoretical writings of the advocates of tank warfare such as Britain's Basil Liddell-Hart and the young Charles De Gaulle. The leading exponent of large-scale tank warfare in the Soviet High Command had been the gifted Marshal Mikhail Tukhachevsky. With his liquidation in the purge of 1937, his ideas on the utilization of armor perished with him. Misapplying battlefield lessons from the Spanish Civil War, the Red Army then disbanded its armored divisions and dispersed most of the tanks among the infantry divisions.[52] However, Zhukov was learning a different lesson on a different kind of battlefield. The open grassland and low sandy hills of eastern Mongolia was tank country. Zhukov was a quick learner.

There were other, more mundane lessons to be absorbed. Japanese infantry daringly clambering upon their vehicles had taught the Soviet tankmen the necessity of having hatch lids that could be locked from the inside. This deficiency had cost the 11th Tank Brigade dearly on July 3. Also, the Soviet BT-5 and BT-7 tanks were too easily set afire by even primitive hand-thrown firebombs. The exposed ventilation grill and exhaust manifold on the rear deck was especially vulnerable and had to be shielded somehow.

In a broader sense, recalled the future marshal of the Red Army, "The experience of the battle in the Bain Tsagan area showed that tank and motorized troops skillfully cooperating with air force and mobile artillery are a decisive means for carrying out swift military operations."[53] Zhukov was discovering a powerful formula. He was by no means the first to conceive of combining these elements of mobile firepower, but very few men would have his opportunities to apply that formula in such crucial tests.

Finally, the Japanese July offensive confirmed Zhukov's initial judgment that the Nomonhan incident was no mere border clash. To the Soviets it appeared evident that the Japanese, who had initiated the fighting in early May and had escalated the scope and intensity of the combat on May 28, June 27, and July 3, were intent upon further aggression. The highest leadership in Moscow now agreed with Zhukov's assessment. They were privy, through Richard Sorge's espionage ring in Tokyo, to Japan's redoubled efforts to draw Germany into an anti-Soviet military alliance. It was a danger that now had to be taken in deadly seriousness. At this point, Stalin and Vyacheslav Molotov began indicating explicitly to Joachim von Ribbentrop and Adolf Hitler that Berlin's attitude toward the Soviet-Japanese conflict was one of the crucial factors in the Soviet evaluation of a possible rapprochement with Germany.[54]

At the same time, Moscow decided to send Zhukov the additional reinforcements he was requesting. Tens of thousands of men and machines were ordered to Mongolia, many from European Russia. Foreign diplomats traveling the Trans-Siberian Railway reported eastbound trains jammed with military personnel and equipment.[55] The Soviet buildup encountered a serious logistical problem at Borzya, the easternmost railhead in the MPR, some four hundred miles from the Halha River. To prevent men and materiel from piling up in a horrible bottleneck at Borzya, a massive truck transport operation was required. Virtually every truck in the Soviet Far East was commandeered for that purpose. The Trans-Baikal Military District, commanded by the same General Shtern who had led the Soviet troops at Changkufeng, supervised this effort. Thousands of trucks, half-tracks, gun-towing tractors, and other vehicles were organized into a continuous shuttle along the eight-hundred-mile, five-day round-trip route.[56]

Meanwhile, east of the Halha, many Japanese officers both in the 23rd Division staff and at KwAHQ would not and could not accept a verdict of failure for the July offensive that they had launched with such confidence. The balance had to be redressed. General Komatsubara did not return to Hailar but instead established a temporary divisional headquarters at Kanchuerhmiao, where he and his staff wrestled with the problem of overcoming superior enemy firepower. They decided that night combat, a traditional mainstay of Japanese infantry tactics, might provide a solution. At night, they reasoned, the effectiveness of Soviet armor and artillery would be minimized, allowing the incomparable Japanese infantry to come to grips with the enemy at close quarters and prevail.

At 9:30 p.m. on July 7, a thirty-minute Japanese artillery barrage preceded a nighttime assault by elements of Komatsubara's 64th and 72nd Regiments. The Soviet 149th Infantry Regiment and supporting Mongolian cavalry were taken by surprise and forced to fall back toward the Halha and regroup before counterattacking. Reinforcements were brought up by both sides and in the bloody hand-to-hand combat that ensued the Japanese were pushed part way back, but they ended with a net advance. Major I. M. Remizov, commander of the 149th Regiment, was killed in this action. For his bravery under fire, he was posthumously decorated as a Hero of the Soviet Union and his command post that night renamed Remizov Heights.

Since late May, Soviet engineers had built no fewer than seven bridges across the Halha and the smaller Holsten Rivers to support their operations. At least one of these bridges was underwater, invisible to the Japanese except when Soviet trucks were seen to miraculously drive across the surface of the Halha. On the night of July 7–8, Japanese demolition teams blew up two Soviet bridges. Komatsubara believed that if he could destroy the bridges, he could disrupt enemy operations east of the Halha, thus accomplishing his mission of securing the border. His night attacks steadily constricted Zhukov's bridgehead east of the Halha.

This pattern of night attacks was repeated from July 8 to July 12, with Japanese attacks against various points on the Soviet perimeter.[57] Soviet resistance stiffened as the pattern of Japanese action was recognized. Casualties on both sides mounted in these relatively small but bitterly fought actions. In the hours of darkness, Japanese audacity and cold steel prevailed. At daybreak, the forward Japanese positions, especially those just wrested from the Soviets in the previous night's fighting, would be subjected to merciless artillery bombardment, to which the Japanese artillery replied weakly. Soviet artillery barrages were followed by counterattacks by motorized infantry and armor. In this deadly two-steps-forward, one-step-back shuffle, the Japanese were making gradual, albeit costly, progress. Their biggest problem was the superiority of Soviet artillery and the lack of effective countervailing artillery support. Japanese infantry commanders learned that to remain at advanced positions in the low ground, easily spotted by Soviet artillery and tanks, brought death in the daytime. They had to pull back behind heights away from the river and lie low until nightfall.

On the night of July 11–12, all three battalions of Yamagata's 64th Regiment and elements of Colonel Sakai Mikio's 72nd Regiment set out to storm the Soviet bridgehead. Passing grim remains of Azuma's recon unit destroyed May 28,

Yamagata's 1st Battalion charged the bridgehead, knocked out several Soviet tanks, and pushed the defenders back toward the river. By 4:30 a.m. the 1st Battalion was on the downward slope of the high ground 1,500 yards from the Halha. Its lead elements were as close as five hundred yards from the river, but thirty Soviet tanks and armored cars pinned them down there. At that point, two companies of Soviet infantry supported by fifteen tanks counterattacked from the high ground on the left while Soviet artillery hammered the attackers from the right flank and rear. Japanese rapid-fire guns took on the Soviet armor but were struck by Soviet artillery west of the Halha and smashed. Japanese demolition teams approached the main Soviet bridge near the confluence of the two rivers but ran into two groups of Soviet armored vehicles from the 11th Armored Brigade, which threw them back. Soviet infantry and tanks surrounded the 1st Battalion. Soldiers from both sides hurled grenades at each other from thirty yards. Soviet flame-throwing tanks joined the melee. The din of battle was literally deafening. As the day wore on, five successive Soviet counterattacks by two infantry battalions and 150–160 armored vehicles of the 11th Armored Brigade, with powerful artillery support, again pushed the Japanese back nearly to their jump-off point of the night before. Brigade Commander Yakovlev of the 11th Armored personally led the counterattacks, died a "glorious death," and like Remizov, was made a Hero of the Soviet Union.[58] The tank in which he perished stands as a monument on the battlefield today.

The action of July 11–12 would prove to be the high-water mark of Kwantung Army's attempt to expel the Soviet/MPR "invaders" from east of the Halha. Later that day, General Komatsubara decided to suspend the night attacks that had been so costly to his infantry. That night alone the 64th Regiment had suffered eighty to ninety killed and three times that many wounded. Komatsubara's decision would become a controversial one. Months later, the 23rd Division commander claimed that he had not realized how close his 64th Regiment had come to taking the bridge. Other considerations, however, influenced the decision to suspend the night attacks.

Throughout the fighting at Nomonhan, the Soviet advantage in artillery, quantitative and qualitative, had become painfully clear to the Japanese. The Soviet guns had taken a heavy toll and time and again had forced Japanese infantry to pull back from hard-won but exposed positions. Besides their actual destructiveness, there are few things as damaging to the morale of infantrymen as to be subjected to incessant artillery bombardment to which one's own guns do not make effective reply. On July 9 KwAHQ informed General Komatsubara that he would soon receive powerful new artillery reinforcements. Kwantung Army would virtually strip its other divisions of heavy artillery and mass them at Nomonhan. In addition, AGS sent the 3rd Heavy Field Artillery Brigade from Japan to Kwantung Army. It also went to Nomonhan. This brigade consisted of a regiment of sixteen 150-mm howitzers (the 1936 model, the most modern in the Imperial Army) and a regiment of sixteen 100-mm artillery (also modern 1932 models). Both regiments were fully motorized, their guns pulled by tractors and ammunition carried by trucks, unlike the 23rd Division's organic artillery, which was horse drawn. The 3rd Artillery Brigade had been earmarked for Kwantung Army for some time, because heavy artillery was not needed in the homeland and Kwantung Army was known to lack firepower vis-à-vis the Red Army. The fighting at Nomonhan merely speeded the deployment of this unit to Manchukuo.[59]

AGS hoped that Kwantung Army, thus reinforced, would be able to best the enemy in a large-scale artillery duel—and then withdraw from Nomonhan after achieving "satisfaction." Kwantung Army had a more ambitious idea. Their massed artillery would neutralize the Soviets' heavy guns and armor, allowing their infantry to advance to the Halha, expel the invaders, and bring the conflict to a victorious conclusion. In Tokyo and Hsinking, this seemed like a relatively safe and inexpensive way to "even the score" at Nomonhan.

By the third week of July, the Japanese had amassed eighty-six heavy guns—100-mm artillery and 120-mm and 150-mm heavy artillery and howitzers—in the Nomonhan area. This Artillery Corps was commanded by Major General Uchiyama Eitaro, Kwantung Army's senior artillery officer. It was Uchiyama who prevailed upon Komatsubara to halt the 23rd Division's night attacks, so that Soviet artillery would not be pulled back out of range of his guns and his artillery could have a clear field of fire without fear of harming friendly infantry.

Uchiyama planned to overwhelm the Soviet positions by firing as many as 15,000 rounds per day for several days.[60] To Japanese commanders who had not experienced trench warfare and massive artillery bombardments in the First World War, this was an unheard-of volume of shell fire.

Meanwhile, reinforcements and supplies poured steadily into the Zhukov's First Army Group, including two additional artillery regiments and literally thousands of tons of artillery shells.

As the array of Japanese heavy artillery was brought into position along the line, the infantry was heartened. Infantry commanders asked newly arrived artillery officers to fire even if the enemy were out of range, because the big guns were good for the morale of the Japanese troops who had been badly outgunned until then. This was not a moot point, since the Japanese 120-mm howitzers had a maximum range of 5,500 yards and could only reach the enemy if deployed relatively close to Soviet lines, exposing them to deadly counterbattery fire.[61]

On the morning of July 23, the Japanese artillery opened fire with a thunderous sustained barrage that brought cheers from nearby Japanese troops. Before long, the

Soviet guns began to reply, and soon a deadly storm of fire and steel was crashing back and forth across the Halha.

As the day wore on, each side intensified its bombardment. Stripped to the waist, Japanese and Soviet gunners alike sweated profusely at their work. The Japanese were dismayed to find that the rate of Soviet fire, far from slackening, soon reached and then exceeded their own. Many Soviet guns that seemed to have been silenced in the morning had been relocated and rejoined the fight from new firing positions later in the day. From the somewhat higher western shore of the Halha, the Soviet gunners were able to pour a torrent of fire down onto the Japanese. Their big guns outranged the Japanese. Their elevation also gave them an advantage in observing the impact of their shellfire and making corrections to improve accuracy.

The Japanese army had no modern experience with counterbattery firing. They did not receive much help from friendly spotter aircraft, because Kwantung Army's 2nd Air group had lost control of the sky over the battlefield. Soviet fighters sometimes strafed the Japanese gun positions. General Uchiyama's men actually attempted to use artillery spotters in balloons suspended above the battlefield to direct their fire. Naturally, when the balloons went up, Soviet fighter planes attacked and shot them down. This was repeated twice during the day, testimony both to the courage of the balloonists working in open gondolas and to the antiquated techniques of the Japanese army. After having two balloons shot down, the balloon observation unit was withdrawn and returned to service with the China Expeditionary Army, where such methods still could be employed against an enemy that possessed virtually no air force. A Japanese artillery officer estimated that on July 23, Soviet guns fired 30,000 rounds to the Japanese 10,000.[62]

The intense shelling subsided at nightfall, only to be resumed with added fury the following morning. The Japanese hoped that on this second day of the duel, the enemy's store of ammunition would become depleted. This was not the case. Zhukov had used the hours of darkness to bring up all his artillery from the rear as well as a tremendous amount of ammunition. On that day, the rate, volume, and accuracy of the Soviet artillery fire far exceeded that of the Japanese. The Japanese artillerists were stunned. Komatsubara's long-suffering infantry was forced to endure the most terrible bombardment any of them had ever experienced. By the third day of the artillery duel, it became clear that the Soviets held the upper hand. Their ammunition supply seemed inexhaustible and their accuracy improved, especially in counterbattery fire.

In infantry combat at close quarters, fighting spirit counts for a great deal. With artillery, however, it is size and weight that counts. From the start, the Japanese artillery offensive had no chance of success. First, they simply did not have enough ammunition. Never having engaged in such an operation before, they had no idea how much ammunition would be consumed. Kwantung Army allocated 70 percent of its entire artillery ammunition stock to this operation. Two-thirds of that was expended in the first two days. As the Japanese rate of fire slackened, Soviet fire intensified. Zhukov had more ammunition, more guns, and better guns. The Japanese gunners were not trained to fire artillery much beyond 6,000 yards and howitzers not beyond 5,000. They had never conducted live-fire practice at maximum range. But the Soviet heavy guns were deployed in several lines, the closest 8,000–10,000 yards away. Beyond this line were other guns, especially 152-mm artillery that the Japanese guns could not even attempt to engage, but which were able to hit the Japanese gun lines at 14,000–15,000 yards. A Japanese artillery regiment commander said his guns were once attacked by Soviet 152-mm cannons at 18,000 yards. The maximum range of the Soviet heavy artillery was 20,800 yards; of their best 152-mm howitzers, 16,500 yards. In addition, the Soviet artillery commanders, some of whom had been operating in the area since May, knew the east shore of the Halha intimately. Not only did they use good spotting techniques, but they had also preregistered potential targets. To some Japanese officers, the region seemed like one vast Soviet firing range.[63]

On day three, a group of 23rd Division infantry officers in shame-faced dismay asked General Komatsubara if the artillery attack might not be suspended, since the enemy's return fire was "saturating" and "smothering" the positions of their men unfortunate enough to be stationed near their own big guns.[64] A similar conclusion was reached that day at KwAHQ, where the lesson was driven home that they could not match the Red Army in materiel. In a spirit of gloom, on July 25, Kwantung Army ended its artillery attack, which had provided yet another humiliating failure.

As they assessed the results of the fighting in July, the General Staff and Army Ministry in Tokyo recognized the futility of trying to achieve a military victory at Nomonhan and shifted toward pursuing a diplomatic settlement, even if concessions had to be made to the Soviet Union and the MPR. Kwantung Army, however, vehemently opposed such negotiations, fearing that they might lead to a repetition of the "Changkufeng debacle" and be interpreted by the enemy as a sign of weakness. For many in Kwantung Army, Nomonhan had become an issue of honor and pride. In Tsuji's words, Kwantung Army, "insisting that the second phase of the fighting represented a tie because of the heavy losses inflicted on the Soviet side, showed its reluctance to yield even one foot [of the disputed territory]."[65]

The differences in outlook and policy between AGS and Kwantung Army were clear, as was the central army authorities' failure to impose their will on the field army in Manchukuo. Much of the military establishment was abuzz with stories of how deeply *gekokujo* had taken hold within Kwantung Army and in relations between that army and the General Staff. To ensure Kwantung Army's compliance with their latest directives, AGS ordered General Isogai to Tokyo for detailed briefings and instructions regarding Tokyo's attitude toward the Nomonhan incident. At KwAHQ too there was embarrassment about the stories of their undisciplined insubordination. Some were sufficiently sensitive on that score that the Kwantung Army chief of staff pointedly flew to Tokyo without any of his staff officers, making a show of his independence from the middle-echelon staff.[66]

On July 20 General Isogai arrived at General Staff Headquarters for what would be an emotion-charged scene. Before a group of senior General Staff officers, Isogai was told in no uncertain terms that the central authorities had decided to settle the Nomonhan incident "unilaterally," by winter at the very latest. Isogai then was handed a formal AGS document, "Essentials for Settlement of the Nomonhan Incident." These "Essentials" went beyond the earlier prohibition against air strikes into enemy territory. They specified a step-by-step program whereby Kwantung Army was to maintain its defensive position east of the Halha River while the government attempted to settle the dispute through diplomatic negotiations. In the event that negotiations were unsuccessful, Kwantung Army's forces, "would be withdrawn upon the advent of winter to the boundary claimed by the Soviet Union."[67]

General Isogai was the most restrained and circumspect member of that tightly knit Kwantung Army clique of which Tsuji was the spark plug. But on that day, Isogai alone carried Kwantung Army's banner at General Staff Headquarters, and he argued vigorously against the AGS Essentials, asserting that since it was logistically and politically impossible for the Soviets to mount a major military effort at Nomonhan, "localization" of the dispute best could be achieved by Japan maintaining a firm attitude. Furthermore, argued Isogai, from the standpoint of Kwantung Army's honor and dignity, he could not approve of a pullback from the east bank of the Halha, where the blood of thousands of his soldiers already had been shed. Isogai asked sharply if the General Staff had decided, in effect, to capitulate and accept the enemy's claims regarding the boundary. Tension filled the air as General Hashimoto Gun, chief of the Operations Division, answered tersely in the affirmative. A heated argument ensued between the two until General Nakajima, deputy chief of the General Staff, ended the quarrel by declaring that international boundaries could not be determined by the army alone. Isogai pledged to convey the General Staff's opinions to his commander and to take the Essentials back to KwAHQ for diligent study, and on that note the conference ended.[68]

Technically speaking, a General Staff document entitled Essentials was not a direct order. In most Japanese field armies, however, AGS Essentials were received and interpreted as orders. Kwantung Army, however, tended to interpret such documents as suggestions, and reserved their own discretion in implementing them.

AGS had couched its instructions in the form of Essentials in the hope that Kwantung Army's injured pride might be assuaged.[69] The briefing given to General Isogai at General Staff Headquarters was meant to ensure that Kwantung Army understood and would obey. However, the meeting with Isogai had not gone well and after his departure for Hsinking, doubts remained at AGS concerning Kwantung Army's attitude.

These doubts were justified, for on July 22 Kwantung Army commander General Ueda, at the urging of his staff, decided to ignore the Essentials.[70] AGS learned of this a week later, when two General Staff officers who had been sent to Hsinking for this purpose reported that Kwantung Army had no intention of adopting the Essentials. In the face of this defiance, AGS, astonishingly, decided to let the matter drop. Colonel Inada, who was privy to this decision at AGS, wrote three months later that this was a grave mistake on their part and that the central authorities should have replaced the recalcitrant Kwantung Army staff officers then and there. But they had waited, he said, hoping that the coming of "the cold autumn weather would cool the emotions at KwAHQ."[71] Again the General Staff miscalculated. But this time it would be the Red Army rather than Kwantung Army that would turn up the heat at Nomonhan.

As a temporary measure, on August 4 AGS created a new administrative entity within Kwantung Army, which it designated as the Sixth Army. Command of the Sixth Army was given to General Ogisu Rippei, who had distinguished himself as a division commander in China. Komatsubara's 23rd Division and other units in that vicinity were attached to the Sixth Army, under Ogisu's command. Sixth Army also was given primary responsibility for the defense of west central Manchukuo, including the Nomonhan area. Actually, the Sixth Army existed only on paper, a small headquarters staff with no other combat units of its own. It was a device by which AGS endeavored to insert a responsible layer of command between KwAHQ and the Nomonhan combat zone.[72] General Ueda and his staff at KwAHQ resented this latest "interference" in their internal affairs by AGS but could do nothing to prevent the move. However, they did not have to cooperate with the intrusion. In the few remaining weeks before the final battle, General Ogisu and his small staff had no significant effect on the situation at Nomonhan.

Zhukov's August Offensive

Meanwhile, the European crisis over German demands on Poland intensified, moving into a configuration highly favorable to the Soviet Union. By the first week of August, it became evident in the Kremlin that both the Anglo-French powers and the Germans were vying with one another to secure an alliance with Moscow.[73]

Stalin knew now that in all probability he would be able to keep a free hand in the coming war in the West. At the same time Richard Sorge, the Soviet master spy in Tokyo, reported correctly that Japan's top political and military leaders sought to prevent the escalation of the Nomonhan incident into an all-out war.[74] These developments gave the cautious Soviet dictator confidence to commit the Red Army to large-scale combat operations in eastern Mongolia. In early August, Stalin gave the order to prepare a major offensive to clear the Nomonhan area of the "Japanese samurai who had violated the territory of the friendly Outer Mongolian people."[75]

The buildup of Zhukov's First Army Group accelerated still further. Its July strength was augmented by the 57th and 82nd Infantry Divisions, 6th Tank Brigade, 212th Airborne Brigade, numerous smaller infantry, armor, and artillery units, and two Mongolian cavalry divisions. Soviet air power also was greatly strengthened in the area. When this buildup was completed by mid-August, Zhukov commanded an infantry force equivalent to four divisions, supported by two cavalry divisions, 216 artillery pieces, 498 armored vehicles, and 581 aircraft.[76] To bring in the supplies necessary for this force to launch an offensive, General Shtern's Trans-Baikal Military District Headquarters amassed a fleet of more than 4,200 vehicles, which trucked in some 55,000 tons of materiel from the distant railway depot at Borzya.[77]

The Japanese intelligence network in Outer Mongolia was weak, a problem that went unremedied throughout the Nomonhan incident. This deficiency, coupled with the curtailment of Kwantung Army's transborder air operations, helps explain why the Japanese remained ignorant of the scope of Zhukov's buildup.[78] They were aware that some reinforcements were flowing eastward across the Trans-Siberian Railway toward the MPR but had no idea of the volume. Then at the end of July, Kwantung Army Intelligence intercepted part of a Soviet telegraph transmission indicating that preparations were under way for some offensive operation in the middle of August. This caused a stir at KwAHQ. Generals Ueda and Yano suspected that the enemy was preparing to strike across the Halha River. Ueda's initial reaction was to reinforce the 23rd Division at Nomonhan with the rest of the highly regarded 7th Division. However, the 7th Division was Kwantung Army's sole strategic reserve and the Operations Section was reluctant to commit it to extreme western Manchukuo, because Soviet forces in the Maritime Province were being mobilized and the Operations Staff feared an attack in the east, perhaps in the vicinity of Changkufeng. The Kwantung Army commander again ignored his own better judgment and accepted the recommendation of the Operations Section. The main strength of the 7th Division remained at its base near Tsitsihar, but another of its infantry regiments, the 28th, was dispatched to the Nomonhan area, as was an infantry battalion from the Mukden Garrison.[79] Earlier, in mid-July, Kwantung Army had sent Komatsubara 1,160 individual replacements to make up for casualties from earlier fighting. All these reinforcements combined, however, did little more than make good the losses already suffered by Komatsubara's forces: as of July 25, 1,400 killed (including 200 officers) and 3,000 wounded.[80]

Kwantung Army directed Komatsubara to dig in, construct fortifications, and adopt a defensive posture. Colonel Numazaki, who commanded the 23rd Division's Engineer Regiment, was unhappy with the defensive line he was ordered to fortify. He urged the general to pull back a bit from his forwardmost lines to more easily defensible terrain. Komatsubara, however, refused to pull back at all from ground his men had bled so profusely to take. Komatsubara and his line officers still nourished the hope of a revenge offensive. As a result, the Japanese defensive positions proved to be as weak as Numazaki feared.[81] As Zhukov's First Army Group prepared to strike, the effective Japanese strength at Nomonhan was less than one and one-half divisions.

Major Tsuji and his colleagues in the Operations Section had little confidence in Kwantung Army's own Intelligence Section. That is part of the reason why Tsuji frequently conducted his own reconnaissance missions.[82] Also, up to this time it was gospel throughout the Japanese army that the maximum range for large-scale infantry operations was 125–175 miles from a railway. Anything beyond 200 miles from a railway was considered logistically impossible.[83] Since Kwantung Army had only 800 trucks available to it in all of Manchukuo in 1939,[84] the massive Soviet logistical effort involving more than 4,200 trucks was almost literally unimaginable to the Japanese. Consequently, the Operations Staff was confident that it had made the correct defensive deployments if a Soviet attack really were to occur, which it doubted. If the enemy did strike at Nomonhan, it was believed that it could not possibly marshal enough strength in that remote region to threaten the reinforced 23rd Division. Furthermore, the 7th Division based at Tsitsihar, which was on a major rail line, could be transported to any trouble spot on the eastern or western frontier in a few days' time.

KwAHQ advised Komatsubara to maintain his defensive posture and prepare to meet a possible enemy attack around August 14 or 15. Kwantung Army took another highly unusual defensive measure at this time. Attached to Kwantung Army was a secret organization whose code name was Unit 731. Its official designation was the Epidemic Prevention and Water Purification Department of the Kwantung Army. Unit 731 specialized in biological and chemical warfare. Its principal production facilities and laboratories—including a notorious prison-laboratory complex where hideous experiments were conducted on hundreds of mainly Chinese human subjects—were in Harbin. During the early August lull in the fighting at Nomonhan, a detachment from Unit 731 infected the Halha River with bacteria of an acute cholera-like strain. There are no reports in the Soviet or

Japanese accounts of the conflict suggesting that this attempted biological warfare had any effect. In the last days of the war, Unit 731 was disbanded, its Harbin facilities demolished, and most of its personnel fled to Japan—but not before they gassed the surviving 150 human subjects and burned their corpses. The unit's commander, Lieutenant General Ishii Shiro, swore his men to secrecy and threatened retribution to any who blabbed. Ishii and his senior colleagues escaped prosecution at the Tokyo War Crimes Trials by trading the results of their experiments to U.S. military authorities in exchange for immunity.[85]

The Japanese Sixth Army exerted some half-hearted efforts by way of constructing defensive fortifications. The lack of enthusiasm, in part, resulted from the scarcity of suitable building materials. Even wood had to be trucked in from far off. More to the point, Japanese military doctrine despised the concept of static defense and favored offense in virtually all circumstances. Thus, Kwantung Army waited on events.

West of the Halha River, Zhukov accelerated his preparations. Because of the tightness of Komatsubara's perimeter security, the lack of Japanese deserters, and the nearly total absence of a civilian population in the combat area, it was difficult for Soviet Intelligence to obtain detailed information on Japanese defensive positions in depth. Combat intelligence could only discern the Japanese frontline disposition and their closest mortar and artillery emplacements. Aerial reconnaissance provided photographs, but the skillful use by the Japanese of camouflage and mock-ups limited their usefulness. The new commander of the 149th Mechanized Infantry Regiment (successor to the slain Major Remizov) took personal charge of infiltration and intelligence gathering. Under his expert direction, he and a small group of men succeeded in penetrating the Japanese lines on several nights and brought back the information that Zhukov needed—Komatsubara's northern and southern flanks were held by Manchukuoan cavalry and he lacked mobile reserves.[86]

With this information, Zhukov drew up a plan of attack to exploit the enemy's weaknesses. Zhukov's operational plan was uncomplicated. The main Japanese strength was concentrated several miles east of the Halha, on both sides of the smaller Holsten River. Their infantry lacked mobility and armor support and their flanks were weakly held. Zhukov decided to divide his First Army Group into three strike forces. The central force, under his direct command, was to launch a frontal assault and tie down the main Japanese strength. At the same time the northern and southern strike forces, with the bulk of his armor, were to turn in the Japanese flanks and force the enemy into a pocket that then would be reduced and destroyed by the concerted efforts of the three forces. The success of the plan depended on achieving tactical surprise and overwhelming force at the points of attack. The offensive—pending a final green light from Moscow—would begin in the latter part of August.[87]

To ensure tactical surprise, Zhukov and his staff devised an elaborate program of concealment and deception—*disinformatsiya*. Men and materiel arriving at Tamsag Bulak from the USSR and thence toward the Halha River were transported only at night, with vehicles' lights blacked out. Noting that the Japanese were tapping their telephone lines and intercepting radio messages, First Army Headquarters sent a series of false messages in an easily decipherable code, dealing with construction of defensive positions and preparations for prolonged autumn and winter campaigning. Thousands of leaflets entitled, "What the Infantryman Should Know about Defense," were printed and liberally distributed among the troops. Some two weeks before the proposed attack, the Soviets brought in special sound equipment to simulate the noises of tank and aircraft engines and of heavy construction and put on a long, loud performance nightly. At first, the Japanese mistook the sound effects for large-scale enemy activity and fired in the general direction of the loudspeakers. After a few nights, however, the Japanese frontline troops realized that it was only sound effects, became accustomed to the nightly "serenade," and tried to ignore it. On the eve of the attack, the sounds of actual Soviet troop concentration and preattack staging would go largely unnoticed by the Japanese.[88]

On August 7–8 Zhukov executed a series of minor attacks to expand his bridgehead on the east bank of the Halha to a depth of two to three miles. That these attacks were "contained" relatively easily by Komatsubara's troops added to his and to Kwantung Army's false sense of confidence. In addition, the Japanese military attaché in Moscow misinterpreted Soviet press treatment of the incident. In early August, the military attaché sent a message directly to General Isogai at KwAHQ, advising that unlike the situation a year earlier during the Changkufeng incident, the Soviet press virtually was ignoring the present conflict. This meant, he advised, that the Red Army's confidence and morale were low and that they were unsure of the outcome on the battlefield. Therefore, Kwantung Army should do nothing to show undue restraint or lack of confidence. That was precisely what most of the KwAHQ staff wanted to hear, and it lulled them still further into an almost casual mood of self-confidence.[89]

This is not to say that there were no portents of danger. Some three weeks before the Soviet attack, Colonel Isomura Takesuki, chief of Kwantung Army's Intelligence Section, warned the Operations Section staff of what he saw as the vulnerability of the 23rd Division's flanks. Tsuji and his colleagues brushed off this observation and explained disingenuously that that defensive disposition had been made intentionally to lure the enemy into attack. A similar warning from General Kasahara Yukio of AGS also went unheeded. The "desk jockey" General Staff officers commanded virtually no respect at KwAHQ by that time. A more ominous warning came from yet another source. General Hata Yuzaburo was Komatsubara's successor as chief of the Special Services Agency at Harbin and a highly respected intelligence officer. Around August 10 Hata warned that, although he did not know the exact strength of Soviet forces in the Mongolian salient, he believed that enemy strength there was very great and was seriously underestimated at KwAHQ. Even Kwantung Army's Operations Section was disturbed by Hata's report, yet no decisive action was taken prior to Zhukov's attack.[90]

Kwantung Army's inaction and unpreparedness prior to the Soviet offensive appears to be a case of faulty intelligence compounded by hubris. But the explanation may be more complicated than that. According to a perceptive observer at KwAHQ, Major Tsuji and his colleagues were not simply blind fools, but also were subject to a kind of fatalistic wishful thinking that was prevalent in the Japanese military. In this view the army, in accordance with its emphasis on spiritual power, traditionally believed that it *must* prevail over the enemy. Given this categorical imperative, they persuaded themselves that they probably would win. In such a frame of mind they could conclude that enemy strength probably was not as great as was reported, because they expected victory. Furthermore, even if enemy strength was overwhelming, there was little they could do about it in view of their meager resources.[91] Though such an "explanation" may seem circular and illogical to a Westerner, it derived in part from the tendency of Japanese philosophy and culture to stress subjectivism over empiricism.

Meanwhile, in the rational, objective, and scientifically preeminent West, the Nazi war machine stood poised at the Polish frontier, ready to unleash a new dimension of horror. The Wehrmacht was held in check by an impatient Adolf Hitler, who now was urgently importuning Stalin to conclude a nonaggression pact immediately. The German-Soviet Nonaggression Pact would neutralize the Russian threat of a two-front war against Germany and clear the way for Hitler's invasion of Poland. But if the Hitler-Stalin pact was a "green light," the signal flashed in two directions, east as well as west. It also would neutralize the German threat of a two-front war against Russia and clear the way for Zhukov's offensive at Nomonhan.

On August 18–19 Hitler virtually begged Stalin to receive Ribbentrop in Moscow without delay to conclude the pact that would be, in effect, a military alliance. Thus reassured in the West, Stalin dared to act boldly against Japan. Zhukov supervised final preparations for his attack.

Zhukov held back his forward deployments until the last minute. On August 18 he still had only four infantry regiments, a machine gun brigade, and Mongolian cavalry east of the Halha. Operational security was extremely tight. A week before the attack, Soviet radio traffic in the area virtually ceased. Only Zhukov and a handful of key officers worked on the attack plan, assisted by a single typist. Line officers and the chiefs of supporting services received information on a need-to-know basis regarding only their specific functions and goals. The date for the attack was shared with unit commanders from one to four days in advance, depending on seniority. Noncoms and ordinary soldiers learned of the offensive one day in advance and got specific operational orders three hours before the attack began.

Heavy rain grounded Japanese aerial reconnaissance from August 17 to midday on the 19th, but on that day Captain Oizumi Seisho, in a Japanese scout plane, observed the massing of Soviet forces near the west bank of the Halha. Enemy armor and troops were advancing toward the river, not in columns of march but in dispersed combat formations. He saw no new bridges but spotted pontoons stacked among the trees near the river. Oizumi dropped a hastily scrawled warning in a message tube to a frontline Japanese unit and sped back to his base to report. The air group commander sent out additional reconnaissance planes that discovered that the Japanese garrison on Fui Heights, near the northern end of Komatsubara's line, was being encircled by Soviet armor and mechanized infantry—a fact that was also observed by alarmed Japanese officers on and near the heights. These last-minute discoveries on August 19, however, were not reported to KwAHQ and had no effect on the alertness or readiness of Sixth Army and the 23rd Division, whose leaders remained calm on the eve of the storm.[92] As so often happens in militaries the world over, there was a fatal gap between those who gather intelligence and those in a position to act upon it.

On the night of August 19–20, under cover of darkness, the bulk of the Soviet First Army Group crossed the Halha into the expanded Soviet enclave on the east bank. The two weeks of nightly Soviet sound effects shows paid off. Japanese perimeter troops failed to distinguish the rumbling noises of the actual deployment from the oft-heard simulation.

Zhukov's order of battle was as follows:

Northern force, commanded by Colonel Alekseenko—6th Mongolian Cavalry Division, 601st Infantry Regiment (82nd Division), 7th Armored Brigade, 2 battalions of the 11th Tank Brigade, 82nd Artillery Regiment, and 87th Antitank Brigade.

Central force, where Zhukov was located, commanded by his deputy, Colonel Petrov—36th Motorized Infantry Division, 82nd Infantry Division (less one regiment), 5th Infantry Machine Gun Brigade.

Southern force, commanded by Colonel Potapov—8th Mongolian Cavalry Division, 57th Infantry Division, 8th Armored Brigade, 6th Tank Brigade, 11th

Tank Brigade (less two battalions), 185th Artillery Regiment, 37th Anti-tank Brigade, one independent tank company.

A mobile strategic reserve built around the 212th Airborne Regiment, the 9th Mechanized Brigade, and a battalion of the 6th Tank Brigade was held west of the Halha River.[93]

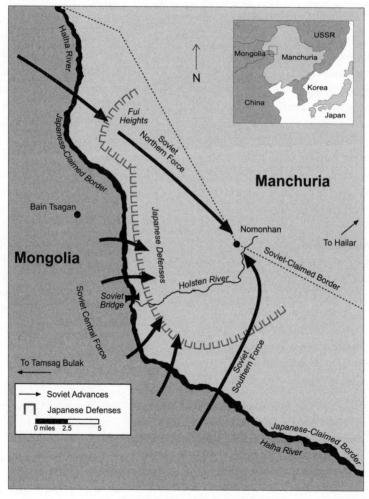

Map 6. August 20–30 Soviet Offensive

The Soviet offensive was supported by massed artillery—a feature that would become a hallmark of Zhukov's operations in the war against Germany. In addition to nearly three hundred antitank and rapid-fire guns, Zhukov deployed over two hundred field and heavy artillery pieces on both sides of the Halha. Specific artillery batteries were assigned to provide supporting fire for each attacking infantry and armored unit at the battalion level and higher.

In the early hours of August 20, the sky began to lighten over the semiarid plain, with the false promise of a quiet Sunday morning. The air was clear as the sun began to warm the ground that had been chilled overnight. General Komatsubara's troops were in no special state of readiness when the first wave of more than two hundred Soviet bombers winged over the Halha River at 5:45 a.m. and began pounding their positions. When the bombers withdrew, a thunderous artillery barrage began, continuing for two hours and forty-five minutes. That was precisely the time needed for the bombers to refuel, rearm, and return to the battlefield for a second run over the Japanese positions. Finally, all the Soviet artillery hurled an intensive fifteen-minute barrage at the forwardmost Japanese positions.[94]

Komatsubara's men huddled in their trenches under the heaviest bombardment to which they or any other Japanese force ever had been subjected. The devastation, physical and psychological, was tremendous, especially in the forward positions. The shock and vibration of incoming bombs and artillery rounds also caused their radio-telegraph keys to chatter so uncontrollably that the frontline troops could not communicate with the rear, compounding their confusion and helplessness.[95]

At 9:00 a.m. Soviet armor and infantry began to move out all along the line while their covering artillery fire continued. A dense morning fog near the river helped conceal their approach, which in some sectors brought them to within small-arms range before they were sighted by the enemy. The surprise and disarray on the Japanese side was so complete, and their communications so badly disrupted, that Japanese artillery did not begin firing in support of their frontline troops until about 10:15 a.m. By that time, many forward positions were overrun.[96] Japanese resistance stiffened at many points by midday and soon fierce combat raged along the front some forty miles from end to end.

In the first day's fighting, Colonel M. I. Potapov's southern force achieved the most striking success. The 8th MPR Cavalry Division routed the Manchukuoan cavalry holding Komatsubara's southern flank and Potapov's armor and mechanized infantry bent the whole southern segment of the Japanese front inward about eight miles in a northwesterly direction.

Zhukov's central force advanced only 500–1,500 yards in the face of furious resistance, but the frontal assault engaged the center of the Japanese line so heavily that Komatsubara could not reinforce his flanks.

Two MPR cavalry regiments and supporting armor and mechanized infantry from Colonel Ilya Alekseenko's northern force easily overran two Manchukuoan cavalry units that guarded the northern flank of the Japanese line, about two miles north of the Fui Heights. But the heights themselves constituted a natural strong point, and there Alekseenko's advance was halted at what became the northern anchor of the Japanese line.[97]

As the first phase of the Soviet offensive gathered momentum, General Ogisu, the brand-new Sixth Army commander, assessed the situation. Still unaware of the strength of Zhukov's forces, he reported reassuringly to KwAHQ that "the enemy intends to envelop us from our flanks, but his offensive effectiveness is weak. . . . Our positions in other areas are being strengthened. Set your mind at ease."[98] This optimistic report contributed to Kwantung Army's delay in reinforcing the 23rd Division. Some at KwAHQ suspected that this might be another limited Soviet push, like that of August 7–8, that soon would end. Others worried that it was a diversionary action prior to a large-scale offensive at some more likely sector of the three-thousand-mile-long frontier. KwAHQ was concerned, but not alarmed, about Komatsubara's position.

On August 21 and 22 Potapov's southern force pierced the Japanese main defense line at several points, breaking the southern sector of the line into a number of segments that the attackers sealed off, encircled, and ground down. Soviet armor, mechanized infantry, and artillery moved swiftly and with deadly efficiency. Survivors described how each pocket of resistance experienced its own individual period of hell. After the Japanese heavy weapons in a pocket were neutralized, Soviet artillery and tanks gradually tightened the ring, with the Soviet guns eventually firing at point-blank range over open sights. Flame-throwing tanks incinerated hastily constructed fortifications and underground shelters. Infantry mopped up with grenades, small arms, and bayonets. By the end of Wednesday, August 23, Potapov had dismembered the entire Japanese defensive position south of the Holsten River. Only one significant pocket of resistance still held out. Meanwhile, Potapov's 8th Armored Brigade looped around behind the Japanese, reached a point southeast of the village of Nomonhan, some eleven miles east of the river junction, on the boundary claimed by the MPR, and took up a blocking position there athwart the most likely line of retreat of Japanese units south of the Holsten.

In those two days, the Japanese center gave up only a few grudging yards, while the northern flank, anchored at Fui Heights, held fast.

Air combat raged over the battlefield. Soviet air force units provided tactical air support for their armor and infantry while Kwantung Army's 2nd Air Group strove to thwart that effort and to hit the attacking Soviet ground forces. Prior to the Nomonhan incident, the Japanese air force had never faced a modern opponent in the air. Japanese fliers had romped largely unchallenged in the skies over Manchuria and China from 1931 to 1939. At Nomonhan, however, the Soviets now enjoyed an advantage of roughly 2:1 in aircraft and pilots. This put an increasingly heavy burden on the Japanese air squadrons, which had to fly incessantly, often against heavy odds. Fatigue began to take its toll and losses mounted. Soviet and Japanese accounts give wildly different, and equally unbelievable, tallies of victories and losses in the air combat, but in the words of an official Japanese air force assessment after the battle, "Nomonhan brought out the bitter truths of the phenomenal rate at which war potential is sapped in the face of superior opposition."[99]

As was the case in tank combat, the Soviet preponderance in the air was qualitative as well as quantitative. In June and early July, the Soviet I-16 fighter plane had not fared well against the Japanese Type 97 fighter.[100] However, in the lull before their August offensive, the Soviets brought in an improved model of the I-16 with armor-plated fuselage and windshield, which made it virtually impervious to the light 7.7-mm machine guns of the Type 97 fighter. The Japanese countered by arming some of their planes with heavier 12.7-mm machine guns, which were somewhat more effective against the new I-16s. But the Soviet flyers discovered that the Type-97's unprotected fuel tank was an easy mark, and Japanese planes soon were being set ablaze in the air with horrifying regularity.[101]

On August 23, as Ribbentrop arrived in Moscow to conclude the pact that would seal Poland's fate and unleash war in Europe, the situation at Nomonhan was deemed sufficiently serious by Kwantung Army to warrant transferring the 7th Division to Hailar for a support mission. Tsuji volunteered to fly to Nomonhan and provide a firsthand assessment. This move was made too late, because August 23–24 proved to be the crucial phase of the battle.

On Tuesday night, August 22, at Japanese Sixth Army headquarters—a safe distance from the battlefield—General Ogisu called for a counterattack to throw back the Soviet forces that were enveloping and crushing the Japanese southern flank. Komatsubara planned the counterattack in minute detail and entrusted its execution to his 71st and 72nd Regiments, led by General Kobayashi Koichi, and the 26th and 28th Regiments of the 7th Division, commanded by General Morita Norimasa. On paper this force looked like two infantry brigades. Only the 28th Regiment, however, was near full strength, although its troops were tired after having marched some twenty-five miles to the front the day before. This regiment's peerless and fearless commander was Colonel Morita Toru (unrelated to General Morita). The chief kendo fencing master of the Imperial Army, Morita claimed to be invulnerable to bullets. The other three regiments were seriously under strength, partly because of combat attrition, partly because several of their battalions were deployed at other parts of the front, unavailable for the counterattack. The forces that Kobayashi and Morita commanded that day amounted to less than one regiment each.

It was not until the night of the 23rd that deployment and attack orders filtered down to the Japanese regiment, battalion, and company commanders. Because of insufficient truck transport capability and the difficulty of navigating in the essentially trackless terrain in darkness, the units were delayed in reaching their assigned positions in the early morning of August 24 and some did not arrive at all. Two battalions of the 71st Regiment did not reach Kobayashi in time, and his attack force that morning consisted of two battalions of the 72nd Regiment. Colonel Sumi's depleted 26th Regiment did not arrive in time, and General Morita's assault force consisted of two battalions of the 28th Regiment and a battalion-equivalent independent garrison unit newly arrived at the front. Because of the delays in assembling the assault force, the Japanese did not have time to reconnoiter enemy positions adequately before the attack. What had been planned as a dawn assault would begin between 9:30 and 10:00 a.m. in broad daylight.

The light plane carrying Tsuji on the last leg of his flight from Hsinking-Hailar-Nomonhan was attacked by Soviet fighter planes and made a forced landing on the battlefield behind the 72nd Regiment's staging area. Tsuji managed to make his way to General Kobayashi's command post by truck and on foot, which would place him closer to the fighting than even he anticipated.

Just before the Japanese counterattack began, a dense fog drifted across part of the battlefield, obscuring visibility and limiting the effectiveness of Soviet and Japanese artillery. Using the fog to mask their movement, lead elements of the 72nd Regiment made straight for a distant stand of scrub pine visible vaguely ahead of them. As they approached the cover of the trees, however, they were astonished to see the scrub pines begin to move away. The stand of trees actually was a well-camouflaged Soviet tank force. At the Japanese infantry's approach, the tanks quickly looped around to the south, jeopardizing any further Japanese advance. As the fog cleared, the Japanese troops found themselves confronting a very large enemy force. Renewed Japanese artillery fire was answered by a vastly heavier Soviet barrage. Kobayashi and Morita discovered, too late, that their counterattack had marched directly into the teeth of far-more-powerful Soviet forces. It is described in one account as "The Charge of Two Light Brigades."[102]

Kobayashi's 72nd Regiment found itself in the path of a massive tank attack and had the misfortune of encountering the very first prototype models of the Soviet T-34 tank, which, with its thick sloping armor and its high-velocity 76-mm gun, was the most powerful tank in the world in 1939. In addition, the Soviet BT-5/7 tanks had been improved since early July, when so many had been set aflame by gasoline bombs and small explosive charges. New model BT-7s powered by diesel, rather than gasoline, engines were less easily ignited. On the gasoline engine vehicles, the Soviets installed wire netting over the ventilation grill and exhaust manifold, which reduced the effectiveness of hand-thrown gasoline bombs.

The Japanese infantry regiments were lacerated that day, with casualties near 50 percent. Nearly every battalion and company commander was lost in the action. General Kobayashi was gravely wounded by a tank shell fragment and nearly trampled to death by some of his fleeing, panic-stricken troops. He was saved by a wounded young lieutenant who dragged him to safety and commandeered a truck to carry the general to the rear. Kobayashi survived the battle and the Pacific War but died in a Soviet POW camp in 1950.

General Morita's 28th Regiment fared little better. It was pinned down some five hundred yards from the Soviet front lines by intense artillery fire. Unable to advance but unauthorized to retreat, Morita's men dug into the loose sand and attempted to withstand the murderous Soviet bombardment. They were cut to pieces. Shortly after sunset, the remnants of the Japanese attack force received orders to withdraw, but by then the two regiments had been shattered. Tsuji, ever a survivor, managed to rejoin Komatsubara at his command post. Upon receiving combat reports from the 72nd and 28th Regiments, General Komatsubara "evinced deep anxiety." Sixth Army chief of staff Major General Fujimoto Tetsukuma, at Komatsubara's command post, "appeared bewildered," announced that he was returning to his headquarters, and asked if Tsuji would accompany him. The major declined and later recalled that he and Komatsubara could barely conceal their astonishment at Fujimoto's abrupt departure at such a time.[103]

Meanwhile, at the other end of the line, Colonel Alekseenko's northern force had been hammering at Fui Heights for three days without success. That vital position was held by a mixed force of some eight hundred men led by Lieutenant Colonel Ioki Eiichiro, consisting of two infantry companies; one company each of cavalry, armored reconnaissance, and combat engineers; and three artillery batteries (37-mm and 75-mm guns). Although the attacking Soviet forces were far more powerful, the heights and their defensive works—barbed wire surmounting deep bunkers connected by trenches—constituted a strongpoint to which the defenders clung tenaciously, inflicting heavy losses on Alekseenko's men. The unexpectedly strong Japanese defense at Fui Heights disrupted the timing of the entire Soviet offensive. By August 23 Zhukov was exasperated and losing patience with the lack of progress in the north.

Some of Zhukov's comrades-in-arms recall a personable chief who, in happy times, played the accordion and urged them to drink and sing along with him. But now, as so often when under stress, his harshness and short temper came to the fore. Zhukov summoned Alekseenko to the telephone. When the commander of the northern force expressed doubt about being able to storm the heights immediately, Zhukov berated him, relieved him of his command on the spot, and entrusted the attack to Alekseenko's chief of staff. After a few hours, Zhukov called again, and finding that the man he had just appointed also was slow in executing the attack, fired the second commander as well and sent over a member of his own staff to take charge. We do not know exactly what epithets may have been ringing in the ears of the two officers Zhukov dismissed, but later firsthand accounts of his temper record that "useless bag of shit" was not the harshest term he flung at subordinates, even generals, who did not measure up.[104] That night, reinforced by the 212th Airborne Regiment, more heavy artillery, and a detachment of flame-throwing tanks, the northern force renewed its assaults on Fui Heights.

The battered Japanese defenders by then were completely overmatched. Soviet artillery fire came pouring in at the rate of two rounds per second. When the last of the Japanese artillery was knocked out, they no longer had effective defense against the flame-throwing tanks. From several miles away, Colonel Sumi could see the heights enveloped in clouds of black smoke, penetrated by spurts of red flame "spitting like the tongues of snakes."[105]

After the night of August 22, trucks carrying ammunition, food, and water could no longer get through to Fui Heights. The next afternoon, Colonel Ioki's radio, his last link to the 23rd Division, was destroyed. His remaining men fought on with small arms and grenades and that night repulsed Soviet infantry with bayonet charges. By the morning of the 24th, Ioki had about two hundred able-bodied men left of his original eight hundred. Soviet tanks and infantry had penetrated his defenses at several points, forcing him to constrict his perimeter. Red flags flew on the eastern edge of the heights. Ioki gathered his few remaining officers at his command tent to discuss last measures. With very little ammunition and almost no food and water left, their situation was hopeless. But Ioki held that even though they were cut off from the division and might only be able to hold out for a few more hours, his orders were to defend Fui Heights to the last man. Several of his subordinates argued that further defense was not only hopeless but meaningless. They urged Ioki to attempt to break out that night and, with reinforcements and fresh supplies, retake the heights later. Faced with these two awful choices, the young lieutenant colonel drew his pistol and attempted to shoot himself but was restrained by an officer who begged him to order a pullout. Rather than see his men blown to bits and incinerated, Ioki decided to abandon Fui Heights, without orders, and retire to the east. Those who were unable to walk were issued hand grenades with the unspoken instruction to blow themselves up rather than be captured. On the night of August 24–25, after the moon went down, with active resistance on the heights quelled and Soviet attention drawn to hot spots further south, Ioki's battered remnant slipped out and encountered a Manchukuoan cavalry patrol the next morning, which summoned trucks that carried them to Chaingchunmiao, forty miles away. The Russians who occupied Fui Heights on August 25 counted the corpses of over six hundred Japanese officers and men.[106]

After capturing the strategic Fui Heights, the Soviet northern force began to roll up and envelop the Japanese northern flank in a wide, sweeping movement south and east from the heights toward Nomonhan. A day after the fall of Fui Heights, elements of the northern force's 11th Tank Brigade linked up with the southern force's 8th Armored Brigade near Nomonhan. A steel ring had been forged around the Japanese Sixth Army.

As the Japanese northern and southern flanks dissolved under the pressure of Zhukov's relentless assaults, General Komatsubara's command as an integrated force ceased to exist. By August 25 the Japanese lines were completely cut and organized resistance continued only in three encircled pockets. The remnants of two battalions of General Morita's "brigade" tried to renew their ill-fated offensive on August 25 and actually managed to advance 150 yards but were hammered by Soviet artillery and tanks and suffered even heavier casualties than the day before.

The only hope for the surrounded Japanese troops lay in a relief force breaking through the Soviet encirclement from the outside. However, Kwantung Army was spread thin in Manchuria and because of its shortage of trucks, was unable to transport even the 7th Division from Hailar to the combat zone in time to affect the decision.

By August 26 the encirclement grew thicker and the three main pockets of Japanese resistance were tightly invested, making a large-scale breakout all but impossible. Potapov unleashed a two-pronged assault with his 6th Tank Brigade and 80th Infantry Regiment. Artillery from the Japanese 28th Regiment managed to check the left wing of the armored attack, but the Soviet right wing overran elements of Sumi's 26th Regiment, and the Japanese were forced to pull back into a tighter enclave. The 28th Regiment's Colonel Morita, the fencing master who claimed to be immune to bullets, like a character in an Akira Kurosawa film, was killed by a burst of machine gun fire while standing boldly atop a trench to encourage his men.[107]

The Japanese 120-mm howitzers became so overheated as they blasted away under the scorching August sun that their breech mechanisms swelled and would no longer eject spent shell casings. Sweating Japanese gunners had to leap from behind the shelter of their gun emplacements after each round and ram wooden rods down the howitzers' barrels to eject the fouled shell casings, thus greatly reducing both their rate of fire and their life expectancy.[108] All of Komatsubara's artillery units suffered a bitter fate. Most were deployed well behind the front lines with their gun emplacements facing west, toward the Halha. As the Soviet offensive developed, however, the attackers, after piercing the Japanese lines at many points and loop-ing behind them, often attacked the Japanese batteries from the east, that is, from their rear. Even when gun crews were able to turn some of their pieces around to face east, they had not preregistered fields of fire in that direction and were not very effective. Furthermore, most of their supporting infantry had already been drawn off for counterattacks and to defend the perimeter. One by one the Japanese gun batteries were smashed by Soviet artillery and tank fire and overrun by armor and infantry. Japanese gun crews, like their tanker comrades, were expected to defend their guns to the last man. The guns themselves, like regimental battle flags, were considered the "soul" of the unit, never to be taken intact by the enemy. In *extre-mis*, the guns, especially sensitive parts like optics, were to be destroyed. Crews were expected to share the fate of their weapons. Few survived. Among those who did was a PFC from an annihilated howitzer unit who was ordered to drive one of the few surviving vehicles, a Dodge sedan loaded with seriously wounded men, east-ward to safety during the night. Near dawn, he came to a Holsten River bridge that he had to cross before daylight if he were to have any chance of reaching Japanese lines. Soviet sentries guarded the bridge. The terrified PFC approached the bridge cautiously and then floored the gas pedal. The sentries jumped forward, raised their rifles to fire, and shouted at him. Out of sheer instinct, the driver honked his horn at them, whereupon the guards stepped back and saluted the sedan as it sped by and kept racing east.[109]

With their supply of drinking water consumed, and unable to reach the Halha or Holsten Rivers for replenishment, the commander of the easternmost of the Japanese enclaves ordered his men to drain the water from the radiators of their vehicles.[110] Drinking that foul liquid at the expense of immobilizing their remaining transport meant the defenders knew their situation to be hopeless.

On August 27 the rest of the Japanese 7th Division—two fresh infantry reg-iments, an artillery regiment, and their supporting units, barely five thousand men—finally reached the northeastern segment of the ring that Zhukov had forged around Komatsubara's forces. One day's hard fighting revealed that the relief force lacked the strength to break the Soviet encirclement. General Ogisu ordered the 7th Division to pull back and redeploy around his own Sixth Army headquar-ters, about four miles east of the village of Nomonhan and of the border claimed by the enemy.[111] There would be no outside relief for Komatsubara's forces.

Throughout August 27–28, Soviet aircraft, artillery, armor, and infantry pounded the three Japanese strong points, compressing them into ever-smaller pockets and gradually grinding them down. The surrounded Japanese fought fero-ciously and inflicted heavy casualties on the Soviet infantry, but the issue was no longer in doubt. The outcome was inevitable and close at hand. After the remaining

Japanese artillery batteries were silenced, Soviet tanks held free sway over the battlefield. One by one the major pockets of Japanese resistance were overrun. Numerous small and medium-size groups of Japanese infantry did manage to slip through the fluid Soviet lines and make it back to safety east of the border claimed by the MPR, where they were unmolested by the Red Army. Effective large-scale Japanese combat operations, however, soon came to an end.

Elements of Potapov's 57th and 82nd Divisions eliminated the last remnants of Japanese resistance south of the Holsten by the evening of August 27. North of the Holsten, during the night of August 28–29, a group of about four hundred Japanese tried to slip eastward through the Soviet lines along the river bank. They were detected by the 293rd Regiment (57th Division), which swooped down on them. The fleeing Japanese refused to surrender and were wiped out attempting to recross the Holsten.[112]

Japanese soldiers' refusal to surrender is well documented throughout the Second World War. Surrender was so unspeakably dishonorable that the Japanese Army Field Manual was silent on the subject of proper conduct if captured. For officers, death was not merely preferable to surrender, it was expected, and in some cases, required. According to the army's penal code (promulgated in 1908 and not revised until 1942), it was dereliction of duty for a commander to surrender, whether or not he "did his best" to resist. If he did his best, he was subject to imprisonment; if not, the punishment was death.[113]

Stemming from the same samurai concept of martial honor (Bushido, "the way of the warrior") was a special fanaticism concerning regimental colors. Upon formation, a regiment received its battle flag from the emperor. According to Shinto, the state religion, the emperor was divine. Regimental colors were not merely symbolically revered, they were treated literally as sacred objects. On the afternoon of August 28, with what remained of his 64th Regiment ripped apart by Soviet gunfire, Colonel Yamagata saw no alternative to burning the regimental colors—his highest priority—then committing suicide. Part of the flag pole had been shattered by an artillery shell and the imperial chrysanthemum ornamental crest had been damaged. Yamagata, Colonel Ise, an artillery regiment commander, an infantry captain, a medical lieutenant, and a foot soldier, the last survivors of the headquarters unit, faced east, gave three "banzai" shouts for the emperor, soaked the pennant in gasoline and lit it. Yamagata, Ise, and the captain then shot themselves. The flag and standard, however, were not entirely consumed by flames and the two survivors buried the unburned remnants beneath the unmarked body of Yamagata, whose insignias of rank had been stripped off. The medical officer and soldier managed to escape and eventually report these last rites to Sixth Army headquarters, where the deaths of the two colonels was regretted but great agitation ensued over whether the regimental colors had been entirely destroyed and thus kept from falling into enemy hands. The uncertain fate of the imperial crest was also a source of anxiety and vexation.[114]

On August 29 Lieutenant Colonel Higashi Muneharu, who had taken over command of the 71st Regiment, faced the same dilemma Yamagata had a day earlier. The regimental standard was broken into four pieces and, together with the flag and chrysanthemum crest, were drenched with fuel and set afire. The fire kept going out and the tassels proved especially hard to burn. It took forty-five minutes to finish the job, all the while under enemy fire. That done, Higashi asked all who were able to join him in a suicide charge, and the severely wounded to "please kill themselves bravely when the enemy approached." Soviet machine gun fire and grenades felled Higashi and all his followers within moments.[115]

When on August 29 it became clear to Komatsubara that all hope was lost, he resolved to share the fate of his 23rd Division. Entrusting his last will and testament to his personal aide, the general stripped off and buried his epaulets and insignia, had his code books burned, and prepared to commit suicide. Just then, General Ogisu, Sixth Army commander, summoned Komatsubara to the radio. Learning of the latter's intent, Ogisu ordered Komatsubara to save himself and attempt to lead as many of his men as possible out of the encirclement. Shortly before midnight on August 30, the bulk of the Soviet armor temporarily pulled back to refuel and take on more ammunition. Some of the Soviet infantry that had been in continuous action for ten days also pulled back a bit. Komatsubara and some four hundred survivors of his command seized that opportunity to slip through the Soviet lines. Carrying their wounded with them and guiding themselves by the stars, this remnant of the 23rd Division managed to reach the safety of Chiangchunmiao on the morning of August 31. Again Major Tsuji was among the survivors. En route, Komatsubara was so distraught he had to be physically restrained from taking his own life. A fellow officer took his pistol and two husky corporals "helped" the general walk by holding on to his arms, preventing him from drawing his sword.[116]

Aftermath

On August 31 Zhukov declared the disputed territory between the Halha River and the boundary line that ran through Nomonhan to be cleared of enemy troops. The Sixth Army had been annihilated, with between 18,000 and 23,000 men killed and wounded from May to September (not counting Manchukuoan losses). The casualty rate in Komatsubara's 23rd Division was 76 percent. Sumi's 26th Regiment (7th Division) suffered 91 percent casualties. In addition, Kwantung Army lost many of its tanks and heavy guns and nearly 150 aircraft. It was the worst military defeat in modern Japanese history up to that time. The Soviet side later claimed that total Japanese casualties exceeded 50,000, undoubtedly an inflated figure.[117]

For years, Soviet-MPR authorities claimed to have sustained 9,284 casualties, surely an underestimate. A detailed unit-by-unit accounting of losses published in Moscow in 2002 puts the Soviet total at 25,655 (9,703 killed, 15,952 wounded), plus 556 MPR casualties.[118] That Soviet casualties may have exceeded Japanese can be taken as a tribute to the fierceness of the Japanese defense or a critique of profligate expenditure of blood by Zhukov. Nevertheless, there was no escaping the fact that the Red Army had given an impressive demonstration of its strength and that Kwantung Army had suffered a serious defeat. Knowledgeable Japanese and Soviet sources agree that in view of the annihilation of General Komatsubara's forces and the predominance of Soviet air power in the area, if Zhukov had pressed his advantage beyond Nomonhan toward Hailar, local Japanese forces "would have fallen into uncontrollable confusion," Hailar would have fallen, and all of western Manchuria would have been gravely threatened.[119] But while that may have been possible militarily, there was no such intent in Moscow. Zhukov's First Army Group obediently halted at the boundary line originally claimed by the MPR. At this point, says a Japanese military historian, "Kwantung Army completely lost its head."

KwAHQ was literally enraged by the developments on the battlefield. Besides the mauling of the Sixth Army at Nomonhan, there was tremendous anxiety about the fate of regimental colors. In particular, it was feared that Colonel Yamagata might not have had time to destroy the imperial crest of the 64th Regiment's colors, which might then have wound up in Soviet hands. Thousands of dead and wounded had been left on the battlefield. To preserve "face" and regain leverage against the enemy, a swift and powerful counterstroke was required.[120]

At Hsinking, they decided to launch an all-out war against the USSR then and there. They would throw the 7th, 2nd, 4th, and 8th Divisions into the Sixth Army, along with all the heavy artillery in Manchukuo, in order to crush the enemy. Recognizing their deficiency in armor, artillery, and air power, they hastily conceived a plan that called for a series of successive night attacks beginning on September 10. This plan was preposterous for a variety of reasons: September 10 was a totally unrealistic target date in view of Kwantung Army's limited logistical capacity. What did Kwantung Army planners think the Red Army would be doing during the *daytime*, with their superior tank, artillery and air power? Furthermore, it was madness to begin a major strategic offensive in northwest Manchuria in the autumn, when extreme cold weather soon would immobilize all forces. (The weather turned very cold and heavy snow began to fall at Nomonhan on September 9.) And finally, Japan's "ally" Germany had just concluded an alliance with Soviet Russia, isolating Japan diplomatically.

These facts all were known at KwAHQ, but they pushed ahead with their plans anyway. Recognizing that if they began an offensive in the autumn, "severe cold weather will soon make major operations impossible," Kwantung Army notified AGS that it should use the winter months well, so that it would, "kindly be prepared to mobilize the entire Japanese Army to engage in the decisive struggle against the USSR in the spring."[121]

This time, however, Kwantung Army would not plunge Japan into another huge conflict with unforeseeable consequences. The military debacle at Nomonhan coincided with the more far-reaching diplomatic disaster of the Hitler-Stalin pact. The course of action that Kwantung Army and its hawkish supporters in Tokyo had been advocating so vigorously—close military cooperation with Germany against the Soviet Union—was dramatically discredited in a single week. Defeated by the Red Army and deserted by Hitler, the civilian and military proponents of the pro-German, anti-Soviet policy were bewildered and infuriated. The government of Premier Hiranuma Kiichiro resigned abruptly on August 28. At AGS and the Army Ministry, more cautious elements rose to the fore, temporarily.

Upon receiving Kwantung Army's proposal for an all-out attack against the Soviet Union, authorities in Tokyo finally concluded that Kwantung Army command had overstepped all permissible bounds and had to be brought back into contact with reality and under strict control. General Nakajima, deputy chief of AGS, flew to Hsinking with Imperial Order 343, commanding Kwantung Army to hold its position near the disputed frontier with "minimal strength" to ensure a quick end to hostilities and a prompt diplomatic settlement. But in meeting with Nakajima, the KwAHQ Staff, led by the Operations Section, clung passionately to its convictions. Incredibly, Nakajima was won over by the staff's fervent spirit and gave verbal approval for Kwantung Army's general offensive to begin on September 10. The emotional atmosphere at KwAHQ was fantastic and spirits soared that night as the officers toasted the great victory they predicted.[122]

General Nakajima was treated to a sobering reception in Tokyo when he returned with the news from Kwantung Army. He was sternly rebuked by his colleagues and sent back to Hsinking on September 4 with a still more strongly worded Imperial Order commanding Kwantung Army to stand down at once. Predictably, the Kwantung Army Staff now felt betrayed and pleaded with the unfortunate Nakajima for a reversal of the order, or at least for permission to reenter the battlefield in force for the ostensible purpose of recovering the bodies of their fallen comrades, sensitive equipment, and regimental colors that may have been left behind. This time, Nakajima would not be swayed. Head in hands, he turned aside their adamant requests and arguments with the repeated declaration, "It is an Imperial Order. It must be obeyed."[123]

General Ueda felt this placed him in an intolerable position. He appealed over Nakajima's head to the chief of the General Staff, Prince Kanin, indicating that unless Kwantung Army were granted permission to "clear the battlefield" and recover the bodies of its fallen dead, he would respectfully request removal from command. On September 6, General Ueda received a "rigid and stern" confirmation that the Imperial Order would stand, with an "insulting" directive added by AGS Colonel Inada that "with respect to implementation, you will submit prompt reports on your actions."[124] A day later Ueda was relieved of his command. He promptly retired. Central authorities then conducted a general house cleaning of KwAHQ. Generals Isogai and Yano, Colonels Hattori and Terada, and Major Tsuji, among others, were transferred out. The inner clique at KwAHQ was broken and scattered—at least temporarily.[125]

At the same time, the Japanese Foreign Ministry instructed Ambassador Togo Shigenori in Moscow to open negotiations with the Soviet government for a speedy settlement of the incident. Togo was authorized to accept the boundary claimed by the Soviet/MPR side as the basis for a temporary cease-fire agreement, pending a formal redemarcation of the boundary. After an initial show of coolness, Foreign Commissar Molotov responded favorably to the Japanese overture and in a few days the details were worked out. Meanwhile, the world's attention was fixed on Germany's invasion of Poland (September 1) and the outbreak of war in Europe.

In the agreement that was concluded on September 15, Molotov did not even insist on Japan's formal recognition of the Soviet/MPR version of the boundary as the basis for a cease-fire. Instead, both sides agreed to accept the frontline positions of their troops in the area as the temporary frontier, a line that, in fact, roughly corresponded to the Soviet/MPR claim. The Molotov-Togo agreement further stipulated that all hostilities cease at 2:00 a.m. (Moscow time) September 16, and that a commission with representatives from the USSR, the MPR, Japan, and Manchukuo be established to redemarcate the boundary.[126]

At 4:00 on the afternoon of September 18, in a tent set up in the no-man's-land between the opposing forces, Soviet and Japanese military delegations met to work out details of the truce. The delegates on both sides were courteous and cooperative, and the discussions proceeded smoothly. At a second meeting the next day, they concluded the local arrangements, which provided for exchange of prisoners and corpses and stipulated that the cease-fire line established by local commanders would have no official bearing on the ultimate determination of the boundary.[127] The new Kwantung Army leadership and the well-disciplined Red Army leadership scrupulously observed these provisions. Prisoners were exchanged and the military episode was closed.

KwAHQ ordered troops to be very cautious in discussing or writing home about the conflict. Company commanders were directed to censor their men's mail. But the magnitude of the battle was too great to be hushed up and soon news of the defeat became common knowledge throughout Manchuria and the home islands.[128]

The reputation of the Kwantung Army was further sullied by a series of episodes in which KwAHQ took harsh measures against certain field officers who were deemed to have performed unsatisfactorily under fire at Nomonhan. Colonel Takatsukasa Shinki, an artillery regiment commander, was forced to retire for having allowed his guns to be captured. Colonel Sakai, who commanded the 72nd Infantry Regiment, committed suicide under pressure prior to being court-martialed for an unauthorized retreat. Several pilots, who had been shot down and captured and then repatriated, were hounded into shooting themselves. Colonel Hasabe Riei, who commanded two battalions of the 8th BGU that were driven from a strategic position south of the Holsten, was called to Sixth Army headquarters, where Generals Ogisu and Komatsubara "suggested" that he cleanse himself of shame by committing suicide, which he did. Most controversial of all was the case of Lieutenant Colonel Ioki, who had commanded the small force that was driven from the strategically important Fui Heights on August 23 after having held out against overwhelming odds for three days. While hospitalized for wounds received in battle, Ioki was ordered to commit suicide to atone for his unauthorized retreat and to "uphold the dignity of the army." At first he refused, insisting that such a judgment was unjust under the circumstances and that he and his men had fought valiantly against a greatly superior force. His accusers were unmoved, however, and Ioki eventually did as he was directed, thus joining his comrades who had died on Fui Heights.[129] Nor was he the last casualty. General Komatsubara, utterly dejected and forlorn, his previously black hair now shockingly white, languished for several months at KwAHQ, an unwanted reminder of defeat. In December, he was recalled to Tokyo and a month later officially retired, after thirty-five years of military service. He served briefly in a defense policy research institute. A broken man at age fifty-four, he died of stomach cancer on October 6, 1940, little more than a year after the destruction of his 23rd Division.[130]

In the opposite camp, of course, the atmosphere was quite different. The terrible purge of the Red Army had come to an end and now with victory at Nomonhan came legitimate cause for self-confidence and congratulation. Zhukov's First Army Group had performed admirably. They and their commander knew it. Appropriate outside recognition soon was forthcoming. The Soviet press continued to treat the Nomonhan incident in a relatively restrained manner, especially in contrast to the trumpeting a year earlier at the time of the Changkufeng incident. Nonetheless, countless citations and decorations were awarded to the Heroes of Khalkhin-Gol, as they were called, including a liberal number of the coveted Order of Lenin and Hero of the Soviet Union medals. Zhukov and Shtern were among the recipients of the latter. Scores of individuals and some whole units were decorated. The MPR leader Khorloogiin Choibalsan visited the First Army Group in late September 1939 and showered them with praise, with promises of the eternal gratitude of the Mongolian people, and with still more decorations. In early May 1940 Zhukov again was summoned to Moscow. By the time he arrived, a new government decree had reestablished the rank of General of the Army, which had been abolished some years earlier. Zhukov was among the first group of five officers named to that rank. He was further honored by a personal interview with Stalin, the first meeting between the two men. During the interview, Zhukov gave a detailed account of the battle and received Stalin's praise and appointment to the command of the strategically vital Kiev Special Military District. Years later, Zhukov paid the highest tribute of all to the veterans of his First Army Group when he noted in his memoirs that "the units which had fought in Mongolia in 1939 . . . when moved to the Moscow area in [December] 1941, fought against the Germans so well that no praise is too high for them."[131]

The large-scale shifting of Red Army forces from Europe to Asia and back again to Europe in a short period of time illustrates that Russia is a geostrategic connecting link between Europe and East Asia. That linkage is examined in the next chapter, highlighting the relationship between the seemingly isolated conflict at Nomonhan and the outbreak of the Second World War in Europe.

CHAPTER 6

NOMONHAN, THE NONAGGRESSION PACT, AND THE OUTBREAK OF WORLD WAR II

W e have seen that Soviet foreign policy alone was not primarily responsible for ending Moscow's diplomatic isolation in the late 1930s. After the Munich Conference seemed to signal the failure of the popular front/united front policy, Neville Chamberlain, Adolf Hitler, and Poland's Joseph Beck all inadvertently strengthened Josef Stalin's hand in the early months of 1939. However, once the high cards were put into his hand, Stalin made the most of them. His conduct of the negotiations with Britain and France and with Germany from April to August was masterful.

The negotiations among the European powers in that fateful spring and summer are well documented and have been thoroughly analyzed from a variety of perspectives. It is unnecessary to reconstruct them all here in detail. However, in May 1939, when Stalin appeared to have things going his way in Europe, but before Hitler had given a clear indication that a German-Soviet agreement was possible, the Nomonhan incident erupted—a conflict initiated and escalated by the Kwantung Army. For a few months, the possibility of Soviet-Japanese war was revived, and with it the specter in Moscow of a two-front war. It is illuminating to review Soviet negotiations with Britain, France, and Germany in the spring and summer of 1939 with an eye toward East Asia, a perspective that provides new insight into the events leading to the German-Soviet Nonaggression Pact and the outbreak of the Second World War.

Nomonhan and the Nonaggression Pact

In the second week of May, when the fighting began at Nomonhan, negotiations between Germany and the USSR scarcely had passed beyond a cautious sniffing out of one another's position. Moscow dropped several hints that an understanding with Nazi Germany was possible. Most notable was the announcement on May

4 that Maksim Litvinov had been removed as foreign commissar and replaced by Vyacheslav Molotov. Litvinov, an urbane diplomat of Jewish origin and married to an Englishwoman, had long been the foremost Soviet spokesman for the united front policy and an implacable critic of Nazi Germany. If an accommodation were sought with Hitler, Litvinov was a poor choice to lead the effort. Molotov had little international experience but possessed a certain gravitas. As chairman of the Council of Commissars, he was the nominal head of government. More important, he was one of Stalin's closest lieutenants. This shift in personnel seemed to have the desired effect in Berlin, where the press was directed on May 5 to cease all polemical attacks against the Soviet Union and Bolshevism.[1]

On the same day, Karl Schnurre, head of the German Foreign Ministry's East European trade section, informed the Soviet chargé d'affaires, Georgie Astakhov, that the German-controlled Czech arms manufacturer Skoda would honor existing contracts for arms deliveries to Russia. Astakhov inquired if, with Litvinov's departure, Germany might be interested in resuming the negotiations for a trade treaty that Berlin had broken off months earlier. On May 17 Astakhov was again discussing trade relations with Schnurre when he declared, as noted above, that "there were no conflicts in foreign policy between Germany and the Soviet Union and that therefore there was no reason for any enmity between the two countries" and that Russia's negotiations with Britain and France appeared unpromising. The next day Ribbentrop personally instructed his ambassador to Russia, Count Friedrich Werner von der Schulenburg, to flash a green light for trade talks. Having baited the hook, the Soviet reply was, in effect, "not so fast." Molotov insisted that first a "political basis" had to be established for economic negotiations.[2]

There remained, understandably, tremendous suspicion on both sides. Stalin feared that Berlin might use reports of German-Soviet negotiations as a wedge to break up a possible triple alliance between the USSR, Britain, and France. The perfect mirror image was Hitler's fear that Stalin might use reports of German-Soviet negotiations as a wedge in Tokyo to break up a possible Germany, Italy, Japan alliance.

Conclusion of the tripartite military alliance among Germany, Italy, and Japan in 1939 was stymied by their conflicting views of who was the primary enemy. Berlin wanted the pact aimed at Britain and France; Tokyo wanted it directed against the Soviet Union. These talks, however, continued through August 1939. And Japan's continued efforts to draw Germany into an anti-Soviet military alliance were reported in detail to Moscow by the Soviet spy Richard Sorge in Tokyo.

Frustrated with Japanese objections to their designs, Hitler and Benito Mussolini first concluded the bilateral "Pact of Steel" on May 22. The next day, the führer treated his assembled generals to one of his rambling politico-military discourses. He stressed the inevitability of war with Poland, which would not be bloodless, as in the case of Czechoslovakia. English opposition, if it arose, would be crushed militarily. Hitler then noted, "It is not impossible that Russia will show herself to be disinterested in the destruction of Poland. Should Russia take steps to oppose us, our relations with Japan may become closer." Uncharacteristically, Hitler's words were leaked to the press almost immediately.[3] Five days later, on May 28, the first pitched battle of the Nomonhan campaign began. The timing of Hitler's speech with the foray of the Yamagata detachment was quite accidental, but that coincidence may have seemed ominous in Moscow.

Hitler and Joachim von Ribbentrop may have pondered Molotov's statement that a "political basis" had to be established before moving forward with economic negotiations, but they made no prompt reply. To move things along, on June 14 Astakhov provided a broad hint to Parvan Draganov, the Bulgarian ambassador in Berlin who both the Russians and Germans used as an unofficial intermediary. Astakhov explained that the USSR must choose among three alternatives: sign a treaty with England and France, continue inconclusive negotiations with them, or reach an agreement with Germany. The third, said Astakhov, "was closest to the desires of the Soviet Union." Astakhov further stated, according to Draganov, that "if Germany would declare that she would not attack the Soviet Union or that she would conclude a non-aggression pact with her, the Soviet Union would probably refrain from concluding a treaty with England." As expected, Draganov informed the German Foreign Ministry of this conversation the next day.[4] Two days later, Schulenburg met with Astakhov in Berlin and informed the Soviet chargé that Germany recognized the connection between economic and political relations, that Germany was ready for far-reaching conversations, and that he had this directly from Ribbentrop, who fully reflected Hitler's views.[5]

The diplomatic situation was complicated. The Soviets were conducting overt and laborious negotiations with Britain and France, and while Stalin may have been fairly sure of his ground, there was still room for doubt. After all, the French guarantee to Czechoslovakia had been no less unequivocal than the recent Anglo-French pledge to Poland. The democracies had knuckled under to Hitler's threats before; no one could be absolutely certain it would not happen again, least of all the chronically suspicious Soviet dictator. Nor can it be said, even at that late date, that Stalin's suspicions were groundless. Chamberlain's reluctance to ally with the USSR was not merely ill-disguised, but undisguised, perhaps intentionally so. By June Chamberlain was forced to concede grudgingly that an alliance with Moscow would at least have a considerable "psychological value at the present time." But having bent that far, he was determined to "drive a hard bargain," because he "did not think that Russia could now afford to break off negotiations."[6] This attitude was reinforced by William C. Bullitt, the American ambassador in Paris, who advised the British that, while he was convinced of the need of an agreement with the Soviets, he was "still more convinced that we shall never reach it if we give them the impression that we are running after them."[7] Bullitt's advice was well received in London, partly because of his personal experience as his country's first ambassador to the USSR, partly because of his presumed closeness to President Franklin D. Roosevelt, and partly because it was exactly what the prime minister wanted to hear, since it confirmed his own antipathy toward the USSR. The depth of Chamberlain's negative attitude toward Moscow at this time is revealed in declassified British documents. On July 2 he wrote confidentially that "I am so skeptical of the value of Russian help that I should not feel our position was greatly worsened if we had to do without them."[8] Some two weeks later, despite having received intelligence information concerning secret German-Soviet talks, the minutes of the cabinet meeting of July 19 show that "the Prime Minister said that he could not bring himself to believe that a real alliance between Russia and Germany was possible."[9]

Still, despite his distaste for the business, Chamberlain recognized that the negotiations with Moscow were necessary. Even if ultimately no real Anglo-Soviet alliance were reached, the appearance of progress in that direction was deemed indispensable, both as a deterrent to Hitler's aggression against Poland and to satisfy the growing revulsion in the British public and in Parliament against the now-discredited policy of appeasement. And so the talks limped on.

The halting pace of these negotiations, however, was not entirely the result of British half-heartedness. Stalin too was intent on driving a hard bargain, and in his own way was responsible for protracting the talks. The negotiations were conducted in Moscow, and the Soviet side almost invariably replied more promptly to queries and proposals than did the British, who often took several weeks to respond. But the Soviet replies, while prompt, were problematic. Time and again Molotov asked questions, raised issues, and made demands that resulted in delay. "Would Britain and France pledge to defend the Baltic states of Estonia, Latvia, Lithuania, and Finland?" "Would Britain and France come to Russia's aid if she were attacked by Japan?" "Would Britain and France fight Germany if Hitler bullied Poland or Romania into accepting a German takeover?" These questions were not irrelevant or trivial, but in each case issues were raised that resulted in long deliberations and delay.

On July 23 Molotov made the highly unusual demand, undoubtedly on Stalin's instruction, that plans for coordinated military action by the three powers in the event of war against Germany be worked out in detail and a military agreement signed before conclusion of a political pact. The British and French accepted the Soviet terms on most of the important political issues, and an Anglo-French military mission finally arrived—by slow boat and train—in Moscow on August 11.

The chief British military negotiator was the magnificently named Admiral Sir Reginald Plunket-Ernle-Erle-Drax. Though this sounded like a character from a Gilbert and Sullivan operetta, Drax was a highly intelligent and capable naval officer who would distinguish himself in the coming war. But he was sent only to conduct staff talks and not authorized by London to conclude or sign a military agreement. In talks with the Soviet military team headed by Defense Commissar Kliment Voroshilov, Drax appeared second rate. His French counterpart, General Joseph Doumenc, at least was authorized to conclude an agreement on behalf of his government—but not to sign it.[10]

By the time the Anglo-French military mission arrived, it was probably too late. Hitler had already set August 26 as the deadline for war with Poland.[11] With the growing prospect of having to fight Britain and France as well, Hitler, belatedly, was eager to secure Soviet neutrality—or better yet, cooperation—in the coming war. In the quickening but highly secret Soviet-German negotiations in July and August, it was the Germans who pressed for a speedy conclusion and made almost all the concessions. Still, it served Stalin's interests to keep the British and French in play. This strengthened Stalin's hand in dealing with Hitler. It also provided an insurance policy in case the German-Soviet talks failed. Stalin's fallback position would be an Anglo-French-Soviet alliance, assuring himself of allies in the event of war.

To prolong the talks with the Anglo-French military mission but forestall resolution, there was the Polish problem. The USSR had no common border with Germany. To come to grips with the Wehrmacht in defense of Poland, Voroshilov demanded that the Red Army be allowed to operate on and through Polish territory. This Moscow knew the Polish government would not allow.[12] And if somehow London and Paris succeeded in pressuring Warsaw into allowing the Red Army to enter Poland (which they were never able to do),[13] Moscow had a further demand that was politically and militarily preposterous. On August 15 Voroshilov informed Drax and Doumenc that in the event of war, the British and French fleets would be expected to enter the Baltic Sea and occupy islands and ports belonging to Latvia, Estonia, and Finland.[14] In the era of the U-boat and the Luftwaffe, such an operation could only have been suicidal. Furthermore, the Baltic states on whose behalf this operation presumably was intended would have protested, and one of them, Finland, would have fought to resist it.[15] Such a proposal can scarcely have been meant seriously by the Soviet side, but it was introduced at what would have been a crucial stage in the negotiations, if Stalin meant for them to succeed. And so the talks dragged on. For Stalin too, the negotiations were necessary. For Stalin too, at least the appearance of progress toward an Anglo-Soviet alliance was indispensable. In all likelihood, Chamberlain and Stalin both conducted these negotiations primarily with an eye toward their effect in Berlin. And in Berlin, in late July, their effect finally was felt.

It was the British decision to send a military mission to Moscow, which finally aroused Hitler to action. The Germans had what they believed to be a very reliable and highly placed informant in the British Foreign Office who had been keeping them informed on the progress of the Anglo-Soviet talks. The informant, John Herbert King of the Foreign Office Communications Center, was actually a Soviet NKVD agent who provided Moscow with detailed information on the evolving British negotiating position. He also fed selected information, and disinformation, to Berlin, designed to exaggerate British enthusiasm for an alliance with Russia and to play down any eagerness on Moscow's part for such a pact.[16]

When the British government abandoned its reluctance and decided to send a military mission to the USSR, Ribbentrop, armed with this information, convinced Hitler, who until then had insisted on dealing cautiously with the Russians, that they must make a dramatic demarche in Moscow. Ribbentrop instructed Ambassador Schulenburg to "pick up the threads" of the German-Soviet talks that had been allowed to fall to the ground the previous month.[17] Hitler finally took the bait that Stalin had been dangling before him for months.

The German-Soviet talks progressed so swiftly that on July 27 Astakhov cabled Molotov that "I have no doubt that if we wanted to, we could involve the Germans in far-reaching negotiations and get from them assurances about the problems that interest us."[18] Two days later, Molotov instructed Astakhov on how to respond to the German overtures. "If the Germans . . . really want to improve relations with the USSR they are obliged to state what this improvement represents in concrete terms."[19] At a crucial meeting on August 2, Ribbentrop dropped all pretenses and told Astakhov that their countries could come to terms on all territorial issues from the Baltic to the Black Sea. "Danzig will be ours," he said, and soon. The conquest of Poland would take a week to ten days. But before going further, Ribbentrop said, he had to know whether the Soviet government was prepared to enter into such talks.[20] Indeed it was. On August 11 Stalin convened a Politburo meeting, which authorized talks with Germany on the issues raised by Ribbentrop.[21]

At last Stalin's patience was rewarded. Britain and Germany had both come a' courting in Moscow, vying with one another for a Soviet alliance. Stalin could choose between them, and he chose alliance with Hitler. More than a nonaggression pact, the treaty and its secret protocols signed in Moscow on August 23 was, in fact, a military alliance. It provided for the USSR to invade Poland from the east and for the partners to divide Poland between them. It also divided the Baltic region between the predators, with Estonia, Latvia, and Finland consigned to the Soviet sphere and Lithuania reserved for Germany. Their respective spheres in the Balkans were more vague. Moscow agreed to provide Germany with vital raw materials, negating the naval blockade that Britain would be expected to clamp on Germany. (On June 21, 1941, the last Soviet trainload of supplies rolled west across the border into German-occupied Poland. The next morning, the German army roared across the border in the opposite direction.)

Scholars have adduced a variety of explanations for Stalin's choice of alliance with Hitler. Yet, in the voluminous Western literature on this subject, one factor is consistently overlooked or underrated: the East Asian component.[22] If Stalin was in a position to choose between an Anglo-French alliance and one with Germany, clearly one of the factors that inclined Stalin toward the pact with Hitler was the Nomonhan incident. Logic dictates that if Stalin had opted for an antifascist alliance with the Western democracies, he would have run a high risk of war against Germany. Even if a major Soviet-German war did not erupt, the Red Army would have to be concentrated in the West. That would have driven Germany into an alliance with Japan and might have encouraged the Japanese to press home an attack against the vulnerable Soviet eastern flank. The danger of a two-front war had to be avoided. Conversely, Stalin's option of the nonaggression pact with Germany allowed him to stand aside from the coming war in Europe and to deal forcefully with Japan at Nomonhan, after having cut the Japanese off from their nominal European ally, Germany. When viewed in its global context, the Soviet decision in August 1939 seems rather obvious.

If this contention that the conflict at Nomonhan influenced Stalin's decision for the pact with Hitler were based solely on circumstantial evidence and speculation, it still would be noteworthy. However, the documentary record shows clearly that the Nomonhan conflict was a factor, and not an unimportant factor, in Soviet calculations in the summer of 1939. In a speech before the Supreme Soviet on May 31, Molotov stressed the resolve of the Soviet Union to defend the borders of the MPR as its own. Without referring specifically to the recent battle, he mildly admonished the Japanese that "it would, therefore, be best for them [Japan] to drop, in good time, the constantly recurring provocative violations of the USSR and the MPR by Japanese-Manchurian military units."[23] The Soviet press played down the Nomonhan fighting to such an extent that the first official references to the incident did not appear until June 26, one and one-half months after the initial clash. Thereafter, the few battle reports were written in a relatively restrained tone and were relegated to the inside and back pages of Soviet newspapers. According to the editor of the First Army Group's newspaper, Stalin personally forbade detailed reporting about the battle.[24]

It would seem that the Kremlin was embarrassed by the Nomonhan incident. A really serious conflict with Japan might jeopardize the negotiations with Japan's nominal ally, Germany. It might also increase doubts in Anglo-French minds about the ability of the Red Army to assist in operations against Germany. Stalin sought to neutralize the German threat by joining it. If an agreement with Hitler materialized, the Japanese threat probably would dissipate.

The evidence indicates that Stalin was not merely embarrassed by the Nomonhan incident, but was alarmed as well. Although he knew through Richard Sorge that the Japanese army was not yet prepared for a large-scale war with the USSR, and that the leaders in Tokyo were striving to avoid such an occurrence, he could not be certain that Kwantung Army would act rationally or obey the instructions from Tokyo. Had not Japanese field armies taken the bit in their mouths in 1931 and 1937 and launched military campaigns with far-reaching consequences? After a seemingly interminable period of diplomatic sparring, in which the Germans and Soviets attempted to ascertain one another's "sincerity," Molotov finally got around to discussing specific outstanding issues between the two nations. One of the first issues he raised was that of German "encouragement and support" of Japanese aggression against the USSR. When the German ambassador, Schulenburg, attempted to turn this charge aside, Molotov insisted that Berlin must prove its good faith not only with words, but with deeds.[25]

In describing this interview in more detail to Weizsacker a few days later, Schulenburg summarized Molotov's sentiments as follows: "Finally—and this seems to me the most important point—M. Molotov demanded that we cease to support Japanese 'aggression'."[26] On August 12 Astakhov reminded Molotov—as if it were necessary—"By the way, the prospect of drawing Japan into the German-Italian alliance remains a reserve option for Berlin in the event of our agreement with England and France."[27] When Molotov learned a few days later that Ribbentrop was anxious to fly immediately to Moscow to lay the foundations for a final settlement of German-Soviet relations, he asked forthwith "how the German Government were disposed toward the idea of concluding a non-aggression pact with the Soviet Union, and further, whether the German Government were prepared to influence Japan for the purpose of improving Soviet-Japanese relations and eliminating border conflicts."[28]

Upon receipt of this momentous news on August 16, Ribbentrop immediately instructed Schulenburg to inform Molotov and Stalin that Germany was prepared both to conclude a nonaggression pact and "to exercise influence for an improvement and consolidation of Russian-Japanese relations."[29] Molotov reacted favorably to this statement, which Schulenburg reported to Berlin. Ribbentrop then ordered Schulenburg immediately to arrange another meeting with Molotov at which he was to explain the extreme urgency of the Polish situation and the need for quick action. Schulenburg was instructed to tell Molotov that "we are in complete agreement with the idea of a nonaggression pact, a guarantee of the Baltic states, and Germany exercising influence on Japan."[30]

With this exchange of messages, Hitler and Stalin knew that there was no obstacle to the conclusion of their pact. Two days later, Georgy Zhukov launched his general offensive across the Halha River. In another three days, Ribbentrop was in Moscow, drinking toasts with Stalin and Molotov to the nonaggression pact and the "new era" in German-Soviet relations.

During the fateful night of August 23–24, while the nonaggression pact was being drafted and the Japanese Sixth Army was being smashed, Stalin, Molotov, and Ribbentrop discussed a wide variety of issues affecting German-Soviet relations. An official on Ribbentrop's staff preserved the substance of this conversation in a detailed memorandum. Seven broad topics were discussed. The first was the question of Soviet-Japanese relations. Ribbentrop repeated his readiness to use his influence to affect favorably the strained relations between the Soviet Union and Japan. At that moment the events in Moscow and on the battlefield both pointed toward a satisfactory resolution of the Nomonhan incident—from the Soviet point of view—and this is reflected in Stalin's reply.

> M. Stalin replied that the Soviet Union indeed desired an improvement in its relations with Japan, but that there were limits to its patience with regard to Japanese provocations. If Japan desired war she could have it. The Soviet Union was not afraid of it and was prepared for it. If Japan desired peace—so much the better! M. Stalin considered the assistance of Germany in bringing about an improvement in Soviet-Japanese relations as useful, *but he did not want the Japanese to get the impression that the initiative in this direction had been taken by the Soviet Union* (italics added).[31]

The assertion that the Soviet Union was prepared for and unafraid of a war with Japan was a bit of an overstatement, although Stalin certainly had cause for optimism in the battlefield situation and the larger East Asian strategic balance. It is interesting to note, however, that in spite of the immediate diplomatic and military victories the USSR then was achieving over Japan, Stalin was still anxious to conceal from Tokyo that any peace initiative had originated in Moscow. That might be interpreted in Tokyo or Hsinking as a sign of Soviet weakness or lack of confidence. The Japanese danger, it would seem, was not completely erased from Stalin's mind.

Even at the moment of his stunning diplomatic coup, Stalin was determined to burn no bridges prematurely. On August 21, while Stalin was inviting Hitler to send Ribbentrop to Moscow, he still did not break off the talks with Britain and France. Instead, Voroshilov asked for a temporary postponement of the talks on the grounds that his colleagues in the Soviet delegation were high-ranking officers whose presence was required at the autumn army maneuvers. Not until August 25, after Britain had reiterated its determination to stand by Poland despite the German-Soviet pact, did Stalin send the Anglo-French military mission home.[32] Fortified by the nonaggression pact, which he hoped would frighten Britain and France into inaction, Hitler unleashed his army on Poland on September 1. Two days later, while Zhukov's First Army Group was finishing its mopping-up operations at Nomonhan, Hitler suffered a setback as Britain and France declared war. He had hoped to destroy Poland in 1939 and not have to fight Britain and France until 1940. The Second World War had begun.

The Soviet-Japanese conflict at Nomonhan was not the exclusive, nor even the principal, factor that led Stalin to conclude the alliance with Hitler. Standing aside from a war in Europe in which the principal capitalist powers might tear themselves apart could well have been reason enough. However, the Soviet-Japanese conflict was also on Stalin's mind and was a factor in his calculations that received little attention in standard historical accounts of the outbreak of the war. This analysis, focusing on those East Asian events, is an attempt to clarify the record. This is not a revolutionary reinterpretation of Soviet foreign policy. Rather, it puts an important piece into place that previously has been overlooked or misplaced in the jigsaw puzzle called "the origins of the Second World War." In so doing, it makes that puzzle less confusing.

One final episode illustrates the correlation between Soviet European and Far Eastern policy in connection with the outbreak of the war. The agreement between Germany and the USSR provided for the Soviet Union to occupy the eastern half of Poland soon after Germany attacked. As early as September 3, forty-eight hours after the German invasion, and the day that Britain and France declared war, Ribbentrop urged Moscow to invade Poland from the east.[33] But for two more weeks Poland's eastern frontier remained inviolate. Soviet divisions were poised at the border. There were few Polish army units capable of offering effective resistance, because the main strength of the Polish army was fighting for its life against Germany. As the days passed, the Germans repeatedly inquired as to when the Soviet invasion would begin, but still the Red Army did not move. This inactivity generally has been attributed to Stalin's well-known caution and suspicion, but that caution and suspicion was not restricted, as is generally assumed, to events in Europe. Throughout the first two weeks of September, sporadic ground and air combat continued in the Nomonhan area. Elements of Kwantung Army's 2nd Division conducted offensive operations September 8–9. Large-scale aerial combat occurred September 1–2, 4–5, and 14–15.[34] Not until September 15 was the Molotov-Togo agreement concluded, arranging for a cease-fire to go into effect at Nomonhan on September 16. The very next morning, September 17, the Red

Army was sent crashing across the Polish frontier into a country that had lain virtually prostrate at its feet for days. It would seem that Stalin, among other things, wanted to be sure that the fighting on his eastern flank definitely had ended before committing himself to battle in the West. Through such policies as this, Stalin assiduously avoided the two-front war that would have spelled disaster for him and for the Soviet Union.

Each of the principals in the complex diplomatic maneuvers of 1939 had its own primary and secondary objectives. The British sought an arrangement with the USSR that would deter Hitler from attacking Poland, and if he were not deterred, would bind Russia to the Anglo-French alliance. Hitler ultimately sought an alliance with the USSR that would deter Britain and France from going to Poland's assistance, and if they did honor their commitment to Poland, would guarantee Soviet neutrality in the ensuing struggle. Japan sought a military alliance with Germany directed against the USSR, and failing that, a general strengthening of the Anti-Comintern Pact. Stalin sought an outcome in which Germany would fight the Western democracies, leaving him a free hand in the West and East, and failing that, military reassurance from Britain and France in case he had to fight Germany. Of the four, only Stalin achieved his primary objective. Hitler obtained his secondary goal; the British and Japanese got neither.[35]

Stalin won the diplomatic war in 1939. But in September diplomats gave way to generals, and the brilliance of Stalin's achievement was eclipsed by the awesome display of German military power in Poland and the following spring in Western Europe. In playing off Germany against Britain and France Stalin got more than he bargained for.

Soviet-Japanese Detente

As was the case after the conclusion of the Treaty of Portsmouth in 1905, Russo-Japanese relations improved rapidly after the cessation of hostilities at Nomonhan. The Molotov-Togo agreement of September 15 and the supplementary local truce agreements arranged at Nomonhan on September 19 were observed scrupulously by both sides. On October 27 the two nations settled another vexing dispute when they agreed to a mutual release of fishing boats that had been detained on charges of fishing illegally in one another's territorial waters. On November 6 the USSR sent a new ambassador, Konstantin Smetanin, to Tokyo, after having been represented there for sixteen months by a chargé d'affaires.[36]

Ambassador Smetanin's first meeting with the new Japanese foreign minister, Nomura Kichisaburō, in November 1939, received broad and favorable coverage in the Japanese press. Contrary to normal diplomatic practice, that first meeting was not confined to formalities. Before Smetanin presented his credentials, Nomura handed the ambassador a draft proposal for a new fisheries agreement and a memo concerning the functioning of the joint border commission that soon was to begin work in the Nomonhan area. On December 31 an agreement was reached concerning the final payment by Manchukuo to the USSR for the sale of the Chinese Eastern Railway, and on the same day the Soviet-Japanese Fisheries Convention was renewed for the year 1940.[37]

In due course, the boundary near Nomonhan was formally redemarcated. An agreement between Molotov and Togo in November 1939 established a mixed border commission representing the four parties to the dispute. After much wrangling, the border commission achieved a final redemarcation of the border on June 14, 1941. The actual construction of new border markers was completed in August 1941. The new border conformed generally to the line claimed all along by the Soviet-MPR side, running ten to twelve miles east of the Halha River. With that, the Nomonhan incident finally was closed.

Meanwhile, during the course of the border commission's deliberations, the international scene underwent a remarkable transformation. The Rome-Berlin-Tokyo Axis was strengthened in September 1940 with the conclusion of the Tripartite Pact. Then, in April 1941 Japan and the USSR concluded a neutrality pact, only nine weeks prior to the German invasion of the Soviet Union. By the end of the year Japan had struck at Pearl Harbor, bringing the United States into the war in Europe and the Pacific. In scope and intensity it was the most total and terrible of all wars. Japan and the Soviet Union, however, remained at peace until the war's final days.

CHAPTER 7

NOMONHAN CASTS A LONG SHADOW

Lessons of Nomonhan: Learned and Not Learned

Kwantung Army and Red Army leaders alike strove to "teach a lesson" to their foe at Nomonhan. The phrase recurs again and again in documents and memoirs from both sides—"we must teach them a lesson." The Nomonhan incident provided lessons to both sides, but not all were well learned.

For the Red Army, the lessons of Nomonhan were intertwined with the laurels of victory, a gratifying, although sometimes distracting, combination. Georgy Zhukov fully appreciated the lessons from his initiation into modern warfare that summer. He had been given the rare opportunity of relatively unhampered command in an intense but narrowly circumscribed conflict and he made the most of it. Zhukov came away from Nomonhan with more than an enhanced reputation and a promotion. He gained invaluable command experience and confidence. At Nomonhan he demonstrated the characteristics and employed the techniques that later would become his hallmarks: the ability swiftly to grasp complex strategic problems; decisiveness in moments of crisis; painstaking attention to detail, especially in logistics and elaborate deceptions; patience in methodically building up superior strength and then striking with devastating force at his enemy's weakest point; coordination of massed artillery, tanks, and mechanized infantry with tactical air support; and employment of all these elements in large-scale double vertical envelopment. All these lessons were later applied in battle at Moscow, Stalingrad, and Kursk, among others, leading ultimately to Berlin. We will never know how well Zhukov would have performed, especially in the crucial autumn and winter of 1941 when the Red Army seemed to be disintegrating under the hammer blows of the blitzkrieg, if he had not had the experience at Nomonhan. Also, had he not distinguished himself at Nomonhan, would the relatively young and inexperienced Zhukov have been entrusted with the command of the Moscow front in 1941?

Although Zhukov may have learned a great deal from his experiences that summer, his superiors in the Soviet High Command overlooked an important and obvious lesson of Nomonhan. Despite Zhukov's success in employing large independent tank formations and tanks accompanied by mechanized infantry, the Soviet High Command, misapplying experiences from the Spanish Civil War, disbanded its armored divisions and seven mechanized corps and redistributed its tanks among the infantry divisions to serve as infantry support. Not until after it had absorbed the German demonstration of tank warfare in 1940 did the Soviet High Command begin to reconstitute its armored divisions and corps, a process that was still under way when the German invasion struck in 1941.[1]

The Red Army's show of strength at Nomonhan went almost totally unnoticed in the West. The military intelligence community and Western military establishments in general continued to believe that the Red Army was "rotten through and through." This oversight was due, in part, to the remoteness of the battlefield. There were virtually no foreign military observers at Nomonhan. Also, both sides played down the incident. The Japanese sought to hush up their defeat. Stalin's negotiating posture that summer with the Anglo-French team and with the Germans would have been weakened if it were apparent that he had a major fight on his hands with the Japanese. Western eyes, meanwhile, were riveted on the Polish crisis and then the outbreak of war in Europe. Nomonhan received scant attention. Then, just a few months after Nomonhan, the miserable performance of the Red Army against Finland, in a conflict much more accessible to Western observers, reconfirmed negative Western opinions of Soviet military capability. Few noted, as did the U.S. military attaché in Moscow, Colonel Raymond Faymonville, that the Soviets, expecting a quick and easy victory against little Finland, had initially relied upon hastily called-up reserve divisions ill equipped for winter fighting. The Red Army, said Faymonville, would be better judged by its performance at Nomonhan. Even in Washington, this assessment made little impression. After the Winter War in Finland, Hitler told his army chief of staff that the Red Army was "a paralytic on crutches."[2] Later that year, he ordered the Wehrmacht to prepare for the invasion of the Soviet Union.

In war, defeat is often a better teacher than victory. Defeat highlights error and weakness and spurs remedy. However, since the Nomonhan incident was a limited war, Japan's defeat also was limited, as was its impact on authorities in Tokyo. Nomonhan did cause the Japanese to revise fundamentally their previous assessment of the Red Army and left the Japanese with a healthy respect for Soviet strength. Shortly after the Nomonhan incident, the Imperial Army abandoned its strategic Plan Eight-B as utterly unfeasible. Soon Kwantung Army adopted a defensive posture toward the Soviet Union.[3]

Kwantung Army conducted an official inquiry into the causes of the debacle. The report, submitted on November 29, 1939, was an objective assessment of the

Red Army's superiority in materiel and in firepower and urged an intense Japanese effort to match and surpass the enemy in those categories. The new Kwantung Army leadership, which still faced the Red Army across a three-thousand-mile-long frontier, had been brought back in touch with military reality at least in this limited sense. Ironically, the Army Ministry and AGS, which had been so critical of Kwantung Army's emotional and "unprofessional" conduct during the Nomonhan incident, were unable or unwilling to act on this recommendation. Despite the bitter lesson of Nomonhan, the army leadership continued the time-honored traditions, doctrines, and policies emphasizing the transcendence of spiritual over material factors.[4] Two years later the army leadership, still clinging to its outmoded doctrine, would commit Japan to war against the United States, the world's leading industrial and technological power.

Furthermore, even after Nomonhan, the army leadership failed to exorcise the spirit of *gekokujo*, that tendency of local forces and middle-echelon staff officers to try to dominate central authorities. This type of self-righteous insubordination recurred time and again in the Japanese army up to the very moment of surrender in 1945. Nor did Tokyo succeed in cleaning house thoroughly after Nomonhan. While the top level of command in Kwantung Army was forced into retirement, the middle-echelon staff officers were not dealt with so harshly. The very Kwantung Army operations officers who played so central a role in the outbreak and expansion of the Nomonhan incident, after a brief "banishment," returned like prodigal sons to key posts at Imperial General Headquarters, where they played a significant part in Japan's decision for war in 1941.[5]

Nomonhan and the Road to Pearl Harbor

The defeat suffered by Kwantung Army at Nomonhan, together with the Stalin-Hitler pact and the outbreak of war in Europe, led to a reorientation of Japanese strategy and foreign policy. The new government headed by the politically inexperienced and unimaginative General Abe Nobuyuki conducted a cautious foreign policy. Chiang Kai-shek's retreat to Chungking in western China led to a stalemate in which the Japanese Expeditionary Army might still enjoy military successes against the Chinese nationalist forces, but it had no means to bring the conflict to a satisfactory conclusion and no prospect for victory.

The China War remained the principal focus of Japan's energy and attention. However, the policy option of forcibly cutting off Soviet aid to China and of northward expansion into Outer Mongolia and Siberia was discredited in Tokyo by the double defeat in August 1939. The policy of northward expansion never again regained the ascendancy, although it was briefly revived in mid-1941 following the German invasion of the Soviet Union.

Germany's alliance with the USSR during the Nomonhan incident was perceived in Tokyo as a betrayal and led to a cooling of German-Japanese relations. Japan also backed away from its confrontation with Great Britain over Tientsin. Tokyo recognized the outbreak of the European war as a momentous development that might also alter the East Asian situation, as the First World War had done. The short-lived Abe government (September–December 1939) and its successor, headed by Admiral Yonai Mitsumasa (December 1939–July 1940) adopted a cautious wait-and-see attitude toward the European war. That changed in the summer of 1940 after the German victories in the West.

With Germany's conquest of France and the Low Countries and with Britain fighting for its life, Tokyo reassessed the worldwide balance of power. Less than a year after Zhukov effectively barred the way to Japanese expansion northward, Hitler's victories seemed to open the way to expansion toward the south. Not only were the resource-rich Dutch, French, and British colonies in Southeast Asia tempting targets in themselves, but they might provide a key to the China problem as well. Many Japanese leaders became persuaded that the stalemate in China finally might be broken in Southeast Asia. If the economic and military aid being funneled to Chiang by the Western democracies via Hong Kong, French Indochina, and Burma could be cut off, reasoned some in Tokyo, then perhaps Chiang would abandon his futile resistance. If not, new military operations could be launched against Chiang from Indochina and Burma, in effect turning China's southern flank. To facilitate her southward advance, Japan took steps to improve relations with Germany and the USSR. Foreign Minister Matsuoka Yosuke brought Japan into the Tripartite Pact with Germany and Italy in hopes of neutralizing the United States and concluded a neutrality pact with the Soviet Union to ensure calm in the north.

Because of the European military situation, only the United States was in a position to check Japan's southward expansion. President Franklin D. Roosevelt appeared determined to do so and to be confident that he could. If the Manchurian incident and the Stimson Doctrine caused an estrangement in U.S.-Japanese relations, and the China War and U.S. aid to Chiang deepened the resentment on both sides, it was the Japanese decision to move south against the French, British, and Dutch colonies, and Roosevelt's determination to prevent such a move, that put the two nations on a collision course.

In July 1941 the Japanese army occupied southern Indochina. The Roosevelt administration responded by freezing Japanese assets in the United States and imposing an embargo on all oil and gasoline exports to Japan. Britain followed suit. Japan had virtually no domestic oil production; nearly 80 percent of its oil imports came from the United States. Virtually all major sources of oil accessible to Japan at that time were controlled by the Anglo-Americans and their friends and allies. Japan's military leaders feared that, with their limited oil reserves, the embargo would force them to curtail military operations in less than a year. That was what Roosevelt and his advisers were counting on—that the embargo would compel Japan to halt its aggression in China. In Tokyo, however, that was intolerable. Japan's military and political leaders alike would not be brought to their knees by the American oil embargo. And there was one major source of oil that was within their reach. The Dutch East Indies—modern day Indonesia—was a major oil producer. The Netherlands had already been conquered by Germany; only a weak Dutch force held the fort in the East Indies. But the Japanese believed that the United States would not acquiesce in their seizure of the Dutch East Indies. The U.S. Pacific Fleet, based in Hawaii, stood in the way. This was the underlying reason for the Japanese attack on Pearl Harbor.

America's industrial strength dwarfed Japan's in some estimates by a factor of 10:1. Imperial General Headquarters concluded that the only chance for success against the United States lay in a sudden attack that crippled the U.S. Pacific Fleet at the outset. This would enable Japan to seize the resource-rich areas in the south, build a powerful defense perimeter, and then negotiate a settlement with Washington that would allow the Americans to defend their true vital interests— which were imperiled by Nazi domination of Europe. This was the reason for Japan's surprise attack at Pearl Harbor.

Because of the huge disparity between U.S. and Japanese military/industrial potential, and with the Japanese army stuck in a seemingly interminable war in China, Roosevelt and his advisers did not believe that Tokyo would be foolish enough to attack the United States. That, they felt, would be not only stupid, but suicidal. What they feared in Washington was a Japanese move against the vulnerable French, Dutch, and British possessions. Although the Japanese believed America would fight to prevent Japan from taking them, Roosevelt was not at all sure he could win U.S. public support and congressional approval for going to war with Japan to defend European colonial holdings in Asia. What Roosevelt dreaded in early December 1941 was further Japanese aggression in Southeast Asia. That is why America was surprised at Pearl Harbor.

Japan's decision to expand southward, as we have seen, was the result of many factors: the search for a solution to the stalemate in China, the quest for economic security (including, but not limited to, oil), Japan's sense of "manifest destiny," the desire to lead a pan-Asian expulsion of Caucasian imperialists, unbridled militarism, and army-navy rivalry. Another factor, often underestimated or ignored in Western assessments of the coming of the Pacific War, was the Nomonhan incident.

Most Japanese studies agree that the lesson learned by Kwantung Army at Nomonhan made a deep impression and figured prominently in deflecting Japanese expansion from a northward to a southward course.[6] After the impressive show of Soviet strength at Nomonhan, the south appeared to be the path of least resistance—even after factoring in the danger of war with the United States. It is not inevitable that Japan's military leaders would have made that assessment if there had been no showdown at Nomonhan, or if that confrontation had ended differently.

This question is especially pertinent in the context of mid-1941, when the final decisions were made in Tokyo. By then, it was acknowledged by Japanese leaders that further expansion to the south probably meant war with the United States and Great Britain, a risky undertaking at best. Just then the whole question was thrown open again by Hitler's invasion of the USSR. In three months German armies plunged more deeply into the heart of Russia than they had in three years from 1914 to 1917. Whole Soviet armies were being destroyed or captured en masse; more than a half-million Soviet troops were lost at Kiev alone. Ukraine lay open, Leningrad was besieged, and German armies were marching on Moscow. The Soviet regime appeared to be disintegrating under Nazi hammer blows. By early autumn, some Western military experts were predicting the collapse of Soviet military resistance within a matter of weeks.

Again Japan's leaders were compelled to choose between the northern and southern paths, between war with the Soviet Union and war with the United States. Which course held the greater promise, the lesser risk? Berlin urged Tokyo to change course and attack and seize the Soviet Far East—and to do it soon, while Germany still needed Japanese assistance. By implication, there might be less booty for Japan if the Soviet Union capitulated before Japan entered the fray.[7] The provisions of the Tripartite Pact did not obligate Japan to join in the war against the USSR. The Soviet-Japanese Neutrality Pact of April 1941, of course, specifically ruled out such action. But the German blandishments and the German victories were seductive. On July 1 Joachim von Ribbentrop cabled Foreign Minister Matsuoka that "the impending collapse of Russia's main military power and thereby presumably of the Bolshevik regime itself offers the Japanese the unique opportunity" to seize the Soviet Far East and keep going. "The goal of these operations," said Ribbentrop, "should be to have the Japanese Army in its march to the west meet the Germany troops advancing to the east halfway even before the cold season sets in."[8]

Foreign Minister Matsuoka, the architect of the Soviet-Japanese Neutrality Pact, urged scrapping the pact and joining Germany in the war against Russia. A minority at Imperial General Headquarters agreed, but most of Japan's military leaders rejected the idea. Japanese military intelligence was quick to note that the

Red Army continued to offer stubborn resistance despite its huge losses, that the German invasion was falling behind schedule despite its great victories, and that the defense of the Soviet central front had been entrusted to Georgy Zhukov, a soldier they had learned to respect. General Tojo Hideki, the powerful army minister and future premier, who commanded the Kwantung Army at the time of the Amur River Islands incident, opposed attacking Russia at that time. Between July and September 1941, amidst internal wrangling in which Foreign Minister Matsuoka was forced to resign, the decision was reconfirmed in Tokyo to hold to the southern course, even if that meant war with America.

Major General Eugene Ott, the German ambassador in Tokyo, persistently pressed his government's arguments that Japan's interests would be served best by striking swiftly at the Soviet Far East. His early optimism that Japan would enter the war against Russia was tempered by Matsuoka's fall. On September 4, Ott sent a long telegram to Ribbentrop describing the situation in Tokyo. Ott explained that the Japanese General Staff was doubtful of its ability to achieve decisive results against the Soviet Union before the onset of winter, and that it was influenced "by the thought of Nomonhan, which is vividly remembered especially by the Kwantung Army."[9] By November, the Japanese decision to move south was irrevocable. Ott summarized the Japanese decision for Ribbentrop as follows: "In my reports I have repeatedly pointed out that after the experiences at Nomonhan and in view of the Russian resistance to an army such as the German Army, the activists [in the Japanese army] consider participation in the war against the Soviet Union too risky and too unprofitable."[10]

General Ott, who was in close contact with the military men who were the real rulers of Japan by then, clearly believed that the Nomonhan incident had a significant influence on the Japanese decision to move south, rather than north, in 1941. Surprisingly few Western scholars have recognized this factor,[11] although it has not been ignored by Soviet and Russian historians.[12]

From the Japanese perspective, the relationship between Nomonhan and the decision to move south is obvious. Colonel Inada Masazumi, the former head of the AGS Operations Section, was forced out of the General Staff in the aftermath of the Nomonhan incident. Ten years after the end of the Pacific War, in a long retrospective magazine article, Inada had this to say about Nomonhan:

> Although very heavy casualties and the dishonor of defeat were among the high prices that we paid, what was more difficult for me to accept was that the Nomonhan incident destroyed our guiding principle of preparing for global conflict by consolidating our position in the North, which would have been achieved by settling the China War and building up our strength against the

Soviet Union. Instead, after the Nomonhan incident Japan unexpectedly drifted toward the decision to move south, the invasion of French Indo-China, and finally the Pacific War. It was this change of policy which I regretted most after being expelled from the Army General Staff. The Nomonhan incident was a turning point which had a great influence on the history of Japan. Even now, when I look back, I think so from the bottom of my heart.[13]

There is another dimension to the relationship between Nomonhan and Japan's decision to move south: the matter of personnel changes at AGS. This was hinted at by Inada when he spoke of the regrettable change in army policy after his expulsion from the General Staff. Colonel Hayashi Saburo, another former General Staff officer, writes in his history of the Japanese army in the Pacific War, that "it is generally acknowledged by those who held contemporaneous High Command posts that the officers responsible for the Nomonhan debacle became strong advocates for launching the Pacific War."[14] The officers referred to are none other than the former Kwantung Army Operations Staff officers, Hattori Takushiro and Tsuji Masanobu. Less than a year after the Nomonhan incident, Colonel Hattori's "exile" as an infantry school instructor ended and he was assigned to the Operations Section of the General Staff (October 1940). By July of the following year, Hattori was elevated to chief of the Operations Section, the powerful post formerly held by Colonel Inada. One of Hattori's first acts in that post was to request the transfer of his friend and colleague, Tsuji, who was languishing in the research staff of the Japanese army on Formosa. Tsuji, by then a lieutenant colonel, joined Hattori in the Operations Section in July 1941 as head of the logistics unit.

From their pivotal position in the Operations Section of the General Staff, using all the leverage afforded by *gekokujo*, Tsuji and Hattori vigorously pressed for southward expansion and for war. An important reassessment of the road to war published in 2006 by a group of Japanese scholars (*From Marco Polo Bridge to Pearl Harbor: Who Was Responsible?*) concludes that Hattori, Tsuji, and a third hardliner "were in charge of operations planning for the Army, and they advocated that Japan should go to war with the United States."[15] Tsuji, rarely constrained by conventions, went so far as to hatch a plot with the ultranationalist leader Kodama Yoshio to assassinate the premier, Prince Konoye, if the latter succeeded in his eleventh-hour attempt to arrange a personal meeting with Roosevelt in order to avert war.[16] General Tanaka Ryukichi, who was chief of the Military Service Bureau in the Army Ministry in 1941, wrote after the war that "the most determined single protagonist of war with the United States had been Tsuji Masanobu."[17]

It would be a colossal overstatement to claim here that Tsuji and the Nomonhan incident were the principal factors responsible for war between Japan and the United States. However, a plausible argument can be made that they were significant contributing factors. Inada's view of Nomonhan as a turning point in Japanese policy is a point worth pondering.

What If . . . ?

To those who believe, as I do, that men choose, whether rationally or not, among alternative courses, and that historical developments are not predetermined and inevitable, it is interesting to look back at Soviet-Japanese relations and consider some of the roads not taken.

What if there had been no immediate Japanese military threat to the Soviet Far East in 1939? If there had been no serious Soviet-Japanese conflict in 1939 and tension along the frontier had declined, perhaps as a result of deeper Japanese penetration into Southwestern China or an irreconcilable Japanese confrontation with British and French interests in Asia, developments in Europe might have been different. If Stalin did not face the immediate danger of a two-front war in the summer of 1939, he would have enjoyed an even freer hand in Europe. To the extent that the Japanese threat was lessened, the pressure on Stalin to conclude an agreement with Hitler—thus isolating Japan—was reduced. In that case, Stalin might have tilted less in favor of Hitler and given greater encouragement to the Anglo-French-Polish forces. Without the assurance of Soviet neutrality in 1939, Hitler might have hesitated to risk war. If Stalin had given the appearance of joining the antifascist powers, even if only nominally and cynically (which seems to be the sort of "alliance" sought by Chamberlain as well) Germany might have been deterred. Conversely, it is possible and perhaps likely that even without an immediate Japanese threat on his eastern flank, Stalin would have played the same game in Europe, promoting conflict between the fascist-militarist capitalists and the bourgeois democratic capitalists—a conflict from which Stalin could stand aside and eventually profit.

What then if the Nomonhan incident had not occurred, or if it had ended differently—say in a stalemate or a limited Japanese victory, and Stalin then signed the nonaggression pact enabling Hitler to launch his attack against Poland? Under such circumstances it is quite possible, and perhaps likely, that the train of events resulting in Japan's decision to expand southward would have been derailed, or at least delayed. If the Japanese had not been thrashed by the Red Army at Nomonhan, and were not committed so irrevocably to a course of southern expansion by the time of the German onslaught against the USSR, then the fateful decisions of 1941 might have turned out very differently. A Japan still confident of its superiority over the despised Bolsheviks in 1941 and faced with choosing between joining Germany in the war against Russia or attacking the Anglo-American powers might have found the northern course less risky, more attractive.

At the very least the Japanese might have adopted a more opportunistic wait-and-see attitude toward the German-Soviet war, rather than plunging down the road to Pearl Harbor. As it was, the decision reached at the Imperial conference of July 2, 1941, which confirmed Japan's determination to advance southward into French Indochina even at the risk of war with the United States, contained an important caveat: "In case the German-Soviet war develops to our advantage, we will settle the Soviet question and guarantee our northern border militarily."[18] Operationally, this was taken to mean that if the Soviet Union transferred 50 percent or more of its Far Eastern forces to the European front, conditions would be favorable for a Japanese attack. To prepare for this contingency, Imperial General Headquarters authorized *Kan Toku En*, Kwantung Army Special Mobilization, in which Kwantung Army's strength, for a brief period, was built up to an all-time high of nearly 700,000 men, with the majority deployed near the Soviet frontiers.[19] To meet this threat, the whole Red Banner Far Eastern Army was mobilized. According to a Western estimate, twenty-five Soviet infantry divisions with full armor and air support waited to meet the Japanese onslaught which was "hourly expected."[20] A more recent Soviet account said that despite the desperate efforts to halt the German onslaught, more than one-fifth of Soviet ground forces and one-third of all Soviet tanks were held in the Far East at this time.[21]

The Japanese attack, of course, never came. Richard Sorge, the peerless Soviet spy in Tokyo, rendered the most valuable service of his career at this juncture, providing Moscow with the most reliable and up-to-date intelligence on the great debate in Tokyo as to whether to move north or south. In July Sorge reported that Japan would send its troops into French Indochina but would also build up its strength in northern Japan and Manchuria to prepare for a strike north if the Red Army were defeated. At the bottom of this document, General Aleksei Panfilov, acting deputy head of Soviet Army General Staff Intelligence, wrote, "In consideration of the high reliability and accuracy of previous information and the competence of the information sources, this information can be trusted."[22] The translations of several of Sorge's messages from this period, found in the Soviet archives, bear Stalin's and Vyacheslav Molotov's signatures, indicating that the actual texts, not just summaries, were read by the top leaders. After having ignored Sorge's warnings in May and June of the coming German attack, Soviet leaders, belatedly, believed him. Thus forewarned, Moscow took care not to weaken the Red Banner Far Eastern Army during the period of *Kan Toku En*.[23]

On August 9 Imperial General Headquarters secretly rejected the option of attacking northward that year. In the next few weeks Sorge and his key Japanese collaborator, Ozaki Hotsumi, an adviser to Premier Konoye, confirmed this decision. On August 25–26 Sorge drafted this message to Moscow: "Invest [Ozaki's code name] was able to learn from circles closest to Konoye . . . that the High Command . . . discussed whether they should go to war with the USSR. They decided not to launch the war within this year, repeat, not to launch the war this year."[24]

At an Imperial conference on September 6, the decision to advance southward was reconfirmed. Tokyo began withdrawing some of the forces poured into Manchuria during the *Kan Toku En*. Sorge learned from Ozaki and Ambassador Ott (who was briefed by the Japanese foreign minister) what decisions had been reached. Ott confided to Sorge the total failure of his efforts to persuade the Japanese to attack Russia. On September 14 Sorge reported even more emphatically to Moscow that "in the careful judgment of all of us here . . . the possibility of [Japan] launching an attack, which existed until recently, has disappeared at least until the end of winter. There can be absolutely no doubt about this."[25] Only then did the Soviet High Command undertake a massive transfer of forces from east to west. Fifteen infantry divisions, three cavalry divisions, 1,700 tanks, and 1,500 aircraft—more than half the strength of the Soviet Far Eastern Army—were shifted from the east to European Russia in the autumn of 1941. The majority went to the Moscow front.[26] It was these powerful forces, commanded by the hero of Khalkhin Gol, that turned the tide in the Battle of Moscow.

According to conventional wisdom, the Battle of Stalingrad (August 1942–February 1943) was the crucial turning point and the most decisive battle on the eastern front, and hence the most important battle of the Second World War. Without gainsaying the enormity of the struggle at Stalingrad, an argument can be made that the Battle of Moscow a year earlier was the real turning point: the biggest, the most important, and the most decisive battle of the war.[27] It was then (October–December 1941) and there (across the entire eastern front, with Moscow at the epicenter) that Germany came closest to defeating the Soviet Union. Some seven million German and Soviet troops were involved in some portion of this battle. Of those, 2.5 million were killed, captured, missing, or seriously wounded—1,896,500 on the Soviet side, 615,000 Germans. Stalingrad, by comparison, involved 3.6 million men, with total losses on both sides of 912,000.

Stalin, unlike Tsar Alexander I in 1812, made a decision to stand and fight at Moscow. Not just to make a fight of it, but to hold Moscow at all costs. Moscow was a far greater prize in 1941 than in 1812. By 1941 Moscow was the political, strategic, and industrial center of the country and also the hub of its highly centralized transportation system. The loss of Moscow would have been a devastating blow to the Soviet war effort. To prevent that, Stalin committed the bulk of his reserves. If the Germans had been able to break the back of the Red Army at Moscow, they might have won not just the battle, but the war. The orthodox view of Soviet historians has been that even if Moscow had fallen, the Red Army would have continued the fight to final victory. But the distinguished Russian military historian Boris Nevzorov states flatly "If they had taken Moscow, the war would have ended with a German victory."[28] It is an open question.

Averell Harriman, the U.S. ambassador in Moscow, recalled a conversation with Stalin after the battle. "Stalin told me that the Germans had made a great mistake. They tried a three-pronged drive" toward Leningrad, Moscow, and the south. "Stalin said that if they had concentrated on the drive toward Moscow, they could have taken Moscow; and Moscow was the nerve center and it would have been very difficult to conduct major operations if Moscow had been lost. . . . So Stalin said they were going to hold Moscow at all costs."[29]

It was a very close thing. By the first week of December, the lead German panzer units, the tip of the spear, stood twelve miles from the Kremlin. German officers could see some of Moscow's main buildings in their binoculars. Then, on December 5–6, Zhukov launched a massive counteroffensive, spearheaded by "the Siberians," the fresh reserves recently arrived from the Soviet Far East—including many of the units he had commanded at Nomonhan. Using the same combined arms tactics he had honed at Nomonhan, but on a much grander scale and with vastly more at stake, Zhukov threw the Germans back about one hundred miles and held them there through the winter. It was a do-or-die effort. The reserves from the east, clad in full winter gear, were decisive. The visiting British foreign minister, Anthony Eden, recalled Stalin telling him plainly in December 1941, "The bringing in of fresh reinforcements was the cause of the recent success."[30]

A day after Zhukov began his counteroffensive, Japan attacked Pearl Harbor. Germany declared war on the United States and vice versa, bringing America into the war in the Pacific and in Europe. It was the most decisive week of the war—the week that doomed the Axis.

However, if Japanese army leaders in 1941 still held their overoptimistic pre-Nomonhan attitude about the Red Army, things might have been very different. A Japanese decision in July or August 1941 to attack northward would probably have brought about the collapse of the Soviet Union. A rapid Japanese victory in the east would not even have been necessary to achieve that result; the mere existence of a large-scale Asian front would have prevented Moscow from shifting those eighteen army divisions, 1,700 tanks, and 1,500 aircraft to the European theater. The economic contribution of the Soviet Far East to the overall Soviet war effort also was substantial, particularly in light of the massive disruption of industry in the western portions of the USSR in the first year of the war. The Soviet margin of victory at Moscow in 1941, and again at Stalingrad a year later, was exceedingly slim. A determined Japanese foe in the east might well have tipped the balance against the

USSR. Many military analysts, including Russian generals, assert that the Soviet Union could not have survived a two-front war in 1941–42.

During the height of the fighting in 1941, Major General Arkady Kozakovtsev, chief of operations of the Soviet Far Eastern Army, confided to his comrade, General Petro Grigorenko, "If the Japanese enter the war on Hitler's side . . . our cause is hopeless."[31] Furthermore, if Japan moved against the USSR in 1941, she certainly could not also have attacked the United States that year. The United States might not have entered the war until a year later, under circumstances perhaps even less favorable than the grim conditions that prevailed in the winter of 1941–42. If the Soviet Union had been defeated in 1941–42, how then would Nazi domination of Europe have been broken? Would the continent be speaking German today?

As we have seen in the preceding chapter, the beating that the Red Army inflicted on the Japanese at Nomonhan made a deep impression. It was well remembered at Imperial General Headquarters in 1941 and was one of the factors that entered into Japan's decision for war with the United States rather than joining Germany and attacking the Soviet Far East. That decision was not inevitable. It could conceivably have gone the other way, altering the course of the war and—if the Soviet Union had been defeated in 1941–42—possibly altering world history.

Playing this game of what-might-have-been involves piling conjecture upon hypothetical conjecture. Plausibility declines in proportion to the accumulation of conjectures. The object here is not to rewrite the history of the Second World War, but to suggest some of the implications of the Nomonhan incident as a turning point, or even more modestly, as a small but significant—and oft overlooked—factor in a profoundly important sequence of events.

Nomonhan and Limited War

Since 1945 there have been a number of conflicts that can be called limited wars. Without attempting to develop a comprehensive definition, limited war here is understood to be international military conflict involving strategic-size forces over a substantial period of time, with at least one of the belligerents refraining from the use of its full war-fighting capability.[32] Implicit also is that the belligerents' objectives must be limited. Similarly, for a limited war to remain limited, at least one party must be willing to accept a compromise settlement or a limited defeat; otherwise the war will escalate or continue interminably.

Since the Korean conflict of 1950–53, a good deal has been written about limited war and about the prospects for limited warfare between great powers. Much of this writing has been theoretical and speculative, given the small number of modern limited wars among the major powers. It is noteworthy that the Nomonhan incident was the first instance in modern (post-Napoleonic) history of limited war between great powers. It represents a neglected but illuminating case study of the character of limited war.

One of the most interesting aspects of this case is its unusual juxtaposition of civilian versus military control of decision making. Never in modern history has the military establishment of a great power been so utterly and ruthlessly subordinated to the political leadership as the Red Army in the 1930s after the purge. By contrast, Japan in the era of the Pacific War was as close as any modern great power has come to an actual military dictatorship. During the Soviet-Japanese conflicts of 1937–39, the two belligerents were polar opposites on the continuum of civil-military relations, virtual caricatures of the two most extreme outcomes of the struggle for control between civilian and military elites. Consequently, the Soviet-Japanese conflict can be useful in evaluating the relative utility of civilian versus military control of decision making in a limited-war situation.

In the Amur River incident of 1937, the Soviet Union was trying to uphold the principle of unimpaired sovereignty over islets around which the main navigable river channel had shifted, which gave the Manchukuoan/Japanese side a plausible claim to the islets. The principle was significant primarily because of its implications for the strategically important Heihsiatzu Island near Khabarovsk. Both sides indulged in a provocative game of tit-for-tat, leading to the Japanese shelling of three Soviet gunboats on June 30. Kwantung Army followed up its attack by unilaterally occupying the disputed islets on July 6, in violation of the diplomatic arrangement reached days earlier in Moscow. One day later the Marco Polo Bridge incident erupted on the outskirts of Peking. A narrowly military assessment of the situation by the Soviet High Command would have called for forceful retaliation on the Amur to back up their interpretation of the riverine border and maintain the credibility of the Red Army while the Japanese were preoccupied by the military confrontation with China. A forceful Soviet thrust toward Northern Manchuria at that time is one of the few things that might have deterred Japan from plunging into war with China. The political leadership in Moscow eschewed such a course, preferring to back down on the Amur so as not to distract the Japanese from escalating in China. This was an intelligent Soviet calculation, contributing to the expansion of the China War, which resulted in a fundamental shift in the East Asian balance of power to Moscow's advantage.

In Japan in mid-1937, where the military was in the ascendancy, although not yet in full control, the situation was viewed differently. Even though Japan "won" the military showdown on the Amur River, the incident gave rise to disharmony between local and central army authorities. Kwantung Army resented what it perceived as General Staff interference in its local command prerogatives, a harbinger of the feuding between KwAHQ and AGS that would contribute to the debacle at Nomonhan. More important was the interpretation put on the outcome of the Amur River incident. Soviet acquiescence in the face of Japanese force was seen by the Japanese as a sign of weakness, a timely test of Soviet intentions and capabilities which influenced Japanese policy in China following the Marco Polo Bridge incident: Russia was not to be feared.[33]

After the outbreak of the China War, Japan's military leaders showed a striking inflexibility in planning vis-à-vis the USSR. Some persisted in believing that the Soviets would remain intimidated and irresolute, as in the early 1930s, despite Japan's entanglement in the China War. Others, more conscious of the sapping of Japan's strength in China, felt that especially because of the China War, Japan must maintain its tough posture toward Moscow so as not to betray any sign of weakness, which might embolden the Russians. It was the relatively cautious Colonel Inada at AGS who conceived the plan of a reconnaissance-in-force by General Suetaka Kamezo's 19th Division at Changkufeng to retest Soviet intentions prior to the Wuhan operation in Central China.

In the Changkufeng incident, both sides exercised considerable restraint, ensuring that the conflict would not escalate seriously. The Japanese refrained from reinforcing the 19th Division, despite its mounting losses, while the Soviets refrained from expanding the breadth of the battlefield, despite the unfavorable terrain at Changkufeng. This is an excellent example of tacit mutual agreement between belligerents to keep a conflict limited. But again, the Soviet political leadership earns higher marks. Inada's idea of testing the Soviets at Changkufeng has been criticized for faulty timing (the bulk of the Japanese army in China was already committed to the Wuhan operation) and for inadequate preparations in the event that the USSR responded by initiating large-scale combat at that time. Although the terrain at Changkufeng favored General Suetaka, the overall strategic situation was unfavorable to Japan, which apparently was recognized in Moscow. The Soviets gauged the situation accurately, applying enough military pressure to force the Japanese to back down, but not so much as to cause Japan to conciliate Chiang Kai-shek and redirect her military attention toward the USSR.

A year later, at the time of the Nomonhan incident, military men were fully in the saddle in Tokyo.[34] During the tension of that four-month-long limited war, which occurred at a critical phase in worldwide diplomacy on the eve of the World War, the superiority of Soviet political leadership over Japanese military leadership was decisive. Throughout May and June, the central authorities in Tokyo, preoccupied with China, paid little attention to the growing conflict at Nomonhan, leaving it to the discretion of the notably indiscrete Kwantung Army. In Moscow the highest levels of leadership took a direct hand as early as the third week of the incident.[35]

From beginning to end, Kwantung Army authorities dealt with the Nomonhan incident as an isolated event, an irksome, potentially dangerous challenge best nipped in the bud. When Kwantung Army attempted to achieve a "local solution," its idea was to destroy the local enemy forces on the spot, thus eradicating the problem. In escalating the scope and intensity of combat, Kwantung Army authorities became preoccupied to the point of obsession with matters of honor and prestige. They consistently failed to apprehend the international dimensions of the problem. They did not even make a broad military assessment, which would have made clear Japan's strategic weakness vis-à-vis the USSR. Instead, with tunnel vision, they focused on the Halha River, oblivious of the outside factors that would overwhelm them. Throughout the crisis, political authorities in Tokyo were unable, and central military authorities unwilling, to assert effective control over their field army until it was too late.

The Soviet political leadership, however, fully aware of von Clausewitz's dictum that war is the continuation of politics by other means, recognized that the military problem at Nomonhan could best be dealt with in its broadest context. Soviet military action was coordinated with and subordinated to political action, with a fine sense of timing, so that in August their blow struck with double effect. Even at the moment of victory, the Red Army was kept in tight rein. There was no intoxication with success, no attempt to further exploit their victory at Nomonhan, no retaliatory—and in their view, perhaps justifiable—pursuit of the disorganized Japanese forces beyond the frontier. Instead, Zhukov's First Army Group halted at the boundary originally claimed by the Soviet-MPR side, and there courteously treated the vanquished foe to bring the conflict to a speedy conclusion. This led Colonel Inada to observe that, "Kwantung Army's declared policy, 'not to invade, not to be invaded,' actually was followed more consistently by the Soviet Union. One might have to say that despite being our enemies and under the control of a dictatorship, their moderation in command was praiseworthy."[36]

Writing in 1950, only months after receiving amnesty for alleged war crimes, the ubiquitous Tsuji Masanobu, former Operations Staff officer, future Japanese Diet member,[37] offered the following explanation—half apology, half excuse—of events at Nomonhan:

> When I compare without prejudice the opinion of KwAHQ, which dealt with the Nomonhan incident only from the point of view of Manchukuo, with that of AGS, which handled the incident from a global point of view, I have to admit that we at KwAHQ could have acted more wisely, if we and those at AGS had

kept cool heads. However, a commander is not a mathematician. On the battle-field where blood is shed and bones are cracked, men tend to react emotionally rather than rationally. The high command must bear this fact in mind, taking care to issue orders with understanding and sensitivity so that front line units do not become excessively emotional, but will remain willing to obey any instructions from the high command.[38]

However, the high command's most serious error at Nomonhan was not insensitivity or meddling but, that it was too lax in its dealings with KwAHQ. If anything, AGS was too sensitive to and understanding of the proud traditions of Kwantung Army, whose independence gave rise to arrogance and insubordination. First through inattention, then irresolution, AGS allowed Kwantung Army to persist in a course of action known to be fraught with peril, in defiance of the General Staff's avowed policy.

If there is truth to the old adage that war is too serious a matter to be entrusted to generals, then the Nomonhan incident suggests that this is especially true of limited war, which by definition has larger nonmilitary components.

Epilogue

All but one of the five major belligerents in the Second World War fought on two or more fronts. Only the United States proved strong enough to accomplish this successfully, prevailing simultaneously in Europe and the Pacific. The others suffered limited or total defeat. Britain barely survived the early going in Europe and lost most of its Far Eastern holdings to Japan, to have them restored temporarily in 1945 by dint of American arms. Adolf Hitler's armies fought in North Africa, the Balkans, on the Soviet front, and in Western Europe and were defeated in all. Japan fought the United States across the Pacific and multiple enemies in the China-India-Burma theater and, like Germany, was defeated in detail. Of the big five, only the Soviet Union under Josef Stalin avoided the trap of a two-front war,[1] which in 1941–42 would probably have been disastrous for the Soviet Union. For all Stalin's faults as a wartime leader, this stands as one of his greatest accomplishments.

At the Yalta Conference in February 1945, the United States sought Soviet participation in the war against Japan. The first atomic bomb test was still six months in the future. U.S. military planners anticipated having to invade the Japanese home islands, at the cost of perhaps half a million U.S. casualties. Undefeated Japanese armies still occupied Manchuria, Korea, and much of China. The United States wanted the Red Army in the fight. With the defeat of Nazi Germany ensured, Stalin agreed to Franklin D. Roosevelt's request. Noting that it would take several months to transfer sufficient Red Army forces from Europe to the Far East, Stalin pledged to declare war on Japan three months after Germany's capitulation. Germany surrendered unconditionally on May 8, 1945. Exactly three months later, on August 8, the Soviet Union declared war.

At Yalta in February, neither Roosevelt nor Stalin knew for sure that the atomic bomb would work, much less that two days before the Soviet Union declared war, Hiroshima would already have been destroyed. On August 9, the day after the Soviet declaration, the second bomb fell on Nagasaki. But hours before that, at one minute past midnight, the Red Army launched a massive invasion of Manchuria. The three-pronged assault, commanded by Marshal Aleksandr Vasilievsky, comprised 89 divisions, 1.5 million men, 3,700 tanks, and an equal number of aircraft—a battle-hardened force that had defeated the bulk of the German army. This tidal wave crashed upon a Kwantung Army that had long since been hollowed out. Its first-rate divisions had all been sent to fight in the Pacific, along with most of its heavy weapons. On paper, Kwantung Army comprised twenty-four infantry divisions and twelve brigades, but these were scrapings from the bottom of the manpower barrel, mostly raw recruits, the elderly, and infirm. Of its 230 serviceable combat aircraft, only 55 were modern fighters and bombers. What little armor it had consisted mainly of the light tank and armored car types that had proved inadequate six years earlier at Nomonhan. The outcome of this unequal contest was a foregone conclusion. The Japanese did not have a chance.

The Red Army of 1945 had learned the art of mobile combined arms warfare in the most harsh and unforgiving testing ground. Some Kwantung Army units put up stiff resistance for a few days but soon were overwhelmed. The three Soviet army groups advanced an average of sixty miles a day, bypassing some isolated Japanese strong points.

At noon on August 15, the voice of Emperor Hirohito was broadcast on radio throughout the empire, announcing what is understood as the surrender of Japan. That did not immediately end the fighting. The emperor did not use the word "surrender." Instead, speaking in the archaic language of the Imperial Court, he stated that the government had agreed to accept the allies' "Joint Declaration" and called upon his people to pave the way for peace "by enduring the unendurable and suffering what is unsufferable." Few of his listeners comprehended that the "Joint Declaration" was the Potsdam Declaration of July 1945 in which the allies set the terms for Japan's surrender. Some thought he was calling on them for further sacrifice in defense of the homeland. At the end of the speech, a radio announcer tried to clarify that the emperor's message meant that Japan was surrendering.

Not all of Japan's military men were willing to accept this verdict. Imperial General Headquarters did not immediately transmit a cease-fire order to Kwantung Army. Communications were spotty and some elements of that army did not receive the order until much later. Some others either did not understand it or ignored it. Pockets of serious resistance continued, as did the Soviet advance. The last Kwantung Army strongpoint near Hutou on the Ussuri River was wiped out on August 22. Sporadic fighting continued until August 27–30.[2] Meanwhile, the Red Army pushed into northern Korea and made amphibious landings on Sakhalin and the Kurile Islands, pursuing Stalin's aim to retake the territory lost to Japan in 1905.

By the end of August, it was over. On September 2, on the deck of the battle-ship USS *Missouri* in Tokyo Bay, General Douglas MacArthur presided over the formal surrender ceremony. The instrument of surrender was signed by Japan's foreign minister and army chief of staff, by MacArthur and Admiral Chester Nimitz, and by representatives of the allied powers. Lieutenant General Kuzma Derevyanko signed for the Soviet Union.

That autumn approximately 600,000 Japanese troops were marched north into captivity, to toil in labor camps throughout the length and breadth of the Soviet Union. Two hundred thousand worked on the Baikal-Amur Mainline project, a railway to run parallel to, but well north of, the Trans-Siberian. Some 60,000–70,000 Japanese detainees died of disease, exposure, and hunger, most in the winter of 1945–46. Repatriation began in 1946, peaked in 1947–48, and continued in dribs and drabs until 1956.

The Soviets turned over much of the captured Japanese weaponry to the Chinese Communists. Soviet occupation authorities in Manchuria also facilitated the consolidation of Chinese Communist control in that region. These measures contributed to the triumph of Mao Tse-tung's forces over Chiang Kai-shek's Nationalists and the establishment of the People's Republic of China in 1949.

The instrument of surrender signed on September 2 was not a peace treaty. Japan concluded separate peace treaties with the victors—but not with the Soviet Union. That was blocked by disputes over the repatriation of detainees, Japanese fishing rights, and territorial questions. There has been no formal peace treaty between Japan and the Soviet Union or its successor, the Russian Federation. Russia's occupation of what they call the Southern Kuriles, known in Japan as the Northern Territories, continues to poison relations between the two countries to this day.

NOTES

Introduction

1. Tsuji's border principles were promulgated as Kwantung Army Operations Order 1488 on April 25, 1939, Japan Defense Agency, Defense Institute, Military History Office, *Kanto Gun, I, Tai So Sen Bi: Nomonhan Jiken* (*Kwantung Army, Vol. I, War Preparations Against the U.S.S.R.: The Nomonhan Incident*) (Tokyo: Asa Gumo, Shinbun Sha, 1969), 441 (hereafter cited as JDA, *Kanto Gun*); Tsuji Masanobu, *Nomonhan* (Tokyo: Ato Shobo, 1950), 46–47. The full text of Order 1488 in English can be found in U.S. Department of the Army, Forces in the Far East, *Japanese Special Studies on Manchuria*, XI, Pt. 1, 99–102 (hereafter cited as *JSSM*).

2. Nihon Kokusai Seiji Gakkai, Taiheyo Senso, and Genin Kenkyububu, *Taiheiyo Senso e no Michi* (*Road to the Pacific War*), vol. IV, *Nicchu Senso II* (*Sino-Japanese War, Part 2*), by Hata Ikuhiko, Usui Katsumi, and Tomoyoshi Hirai (Tokyo: Asahi Shimbun Sha, 1963), 80, 96 (hereafter cited as Hata, *Taiheiyo Senso e no Michi*).

3. Ibid., 97.

4. Stuart D. Goldman, *Soviet-Japanese Conflict and the Outbreak of the Second World War* (Washington, D.C.: Georgetown University, 1970).

5. *Dokumenty Vneshnei Politiki. 1939 god*, vol. 22, 2 vols. (*Documents on Foreign Policy*) (Moscow: Mezhdunarodnye Otnosheniia, 1992) (hereafter cited as *DVP*).

6. L. Il'ichev et al., eds., *God Krizisa 1938–1939* (*Year of Crisis, 1938–1939*), *dokumenty i materialy v dvukh tomakh* (Moscow: Izd-vo polit. Lit., 1990)(hereafter sited as *God Krizisa*).

7. A. N. Yakovlev, ed., *1941 God Dokumenty* (*The Year 1941: Documents*) (Moscow: Mezhdunarodnyi Fond Demokratiya, 1998), 2 vols.

8. Alvin D. Coox, *Nomonhan: Japan Against Russia, 1939*, 2 vols. (Stanford, Calif.: Stanford University Press, 1985); and Edward J. Drea, *Nomonhan, Japanese-Soviet Tactical Combat, 1939* (Fort Leavenworth, Kans.: U.S. Army Command and General Staff College, 1981).

9. Two Russian writers living abroad have written of this link. Aleksandr M. Nekrich in *Pariahs, Partners, Predators: German-Soviet Relations, 1922–1941*, ed. and trans. by Gregory L. Freeze (New York: Columbia University Press, 1997), 113, after emigrating to the United States, offered this brief passage: "The Japanese Army launched a full-scale attack. . . . Given Japan's alliance with Germany, the Soviet Union suddenly faced the frightening prospect of fighting a two-front war. . . . This danger exerted a strong influence on

thinking in the Kremlin, especially as tensions over Danzig mounted during the summer of 1939." Viktor Suvorov, a former Soviet military intelligence officer and prolific writer living in England, is outspoken in his denunciation of the nonaggression pact and also has a good deal to say about Nomonhan/Khalkhin Gol, but his interpretation of the link between these events is off the mark. See especially Viktor Suvorov, *The Chief Culprit* (Annapolis, Md.: Naval Institute Press, 2008).

10. See for example, A. J. P. Taylor, *The Origins of the Second World War* (Greenwich, Conn.: Fawcett, 1961); Sidney Aster, *1939: The Making of the Second World War* (New York: Simon and Schuster, 1973); Gerhard Weinberg, *The Foreign Policy of Hitler's Germany: Starting World War II, 1937–1939* (Chicago: University of Chicago Press, 1980); Geoffrey Roberts, *The Unholy Alliance: Stalin's Pact with Hitler* (Bloomington: Indiana University Press, 1989); Geoffrey Roberts, *The Soviet Union and the Origins of the Second World War* (New York: St. Martin's Press, 1995); Donald Cameron Watt, *How War Came: The Immediate Origins of the Second World War, 1938–1939* (New York: Pantheon Books, 1989); Andrew J. Crozier, *The Causes of the Second World War* (Oxford, UK: Blackwell, 1997); Victor Rothwell, *The Origins of the Second World War* (Manchester, UK: Manchester University Press, 2001); Robert Boyce and Joseph A. Maiolo, eds., *The Origins of World War Two* (New York: Palgrave Macmillian, 2003).

11. P. M. H. Bell, *The Origins of the Second World War in Europe* (London: Longman, 1986), 199, contains this sentence: "In 1939, the prospect of a war on two fronts, against Japan in the Far East (where battle was already joined) and Germany in Europe, was certainly unwelcome; and the influence of this simple calculation on the making of the Nazi-Soviet pact should not be underrated." Jonathan Haslam, *The Soviet Union and the Threat from the East: Moscow, Tokyo, and the Prelude to the Pacific War, 1933–1941* (Pittsburgh, Pa.: University of Pittsburgh Press, 1992), 133, offers this: "The talks with the Germans that shadowed the negotiations with Britain and France in the late spring and summer of 1939 were guided in no small measure by the lingering concern to outflank the Japanese diplomatically." A Swiss historian little known in the English-speaking world, Walter Hofer, in his *Die Entfesselung des Zweiten Weltkrieges* (The Outbreak of the Second World War) (Frankfurt, FRG: Fischer, 1960), 82ff., saw the Nomonhan incident as contributing to the Soviet decision for the Nonaggression Pact.

12. Most people outside of Japan and Russia, that is. The Nomonhan/Khalkhin Gol conflict is better known in those two countries, although its broader significance is generally overlooked there as well.

Chapter 1: The Legacy of the Past

1. See James W. Morley, *The Japanese Thrust into Siberia* (New York: Columbia University Press, 1957).

2. Japanese companies owned and operated coal mines and oil fields on Northern (Soviet) Sakhalin. These economic concessions were considered significant in Tokyo because of Japan's lack of mineral resources. Japan's fishing rights in Russian waters were written into the 1905 Treaty of Portsmouth and the annual catch from those waters contributed significantly to the diet of Japan's rapidly growing population. For a survey of these negotiations, see George A. Lensen, *Japanese Recognition of the U.S.S.R.: Soviet-Japanese Relations, 1921–1930* (Tallahassee, Fla.: Diplomatic Press, 1970).

3. The CER was a legacy of Tsarist economic imperialism, which "cut-the-corner" of the Trans-Siberian Railway route by connecting Chita with Vladivostok diagonally across Manchuria.

4. George A. Lensen, *The Damned Inheritance: The Soviet Union and the Manchurian Crises, 1924–1935* (Tallahassee, Fla.: Diplomatic Press, 1974).

5. From a speech at the First All-Union Conference of Managers of Socialist Industry, February 4, 1931, printed in *Pravda*, February 5, 1931.

6. Richard Storry, *A History of Modern Japan* (Baltimore: Penguin Books, 1960), 172.

7. Hugh Borton, *Japan's Modern Century* (New York: Ronald Press, 1970), 359.

8. Storry, *Modern Japan*, 174.

9. Until Japan adopted universal manhood suffrage in 1925, only 5 percent of the male population could vote.

10. Richard Storry, *The Double Patriots* (Boston: Houghton Mifflin, 1957), 4.

11. Yoshihashi Takehiko, *Conspiracy at Mukden: The Rise of the Japanese Military* (New Haven, Conn.: Yale University Press, 1963), 78.

12. Hugh Byas, *Government by Assassination* (New York: Alfred A. Knopf, 1942). Besides Hamaguchi, Premiers Inukai Tsuyoshii (1932) and Takahashi Korekiyo (1936) were assassinated, as were a number of other cabinet officers and other senior government officials. Even some generals and admirals who dared oppose the ultranationalists were cut down.

13. Fujiwara Akira, "The Role of the Japanese Army," trans. by Shumpei Okamoto, in Dorothy Borg and Okamoto Shumpei, eds., *Pearl Harbor as History* (New York: Columbia University Press, 1973), 194.

14. Lensen, *Damned Inheritance*, 212–13. Moscow rid itself of this embarrassment and potential source of conflict by selling the CER to Japan in 1936.

15. Hata Ikuhiko, *Reality and Illusion, The Hidden Crisis Between Japan and the U.S.S.R., 1932–1934* (New York: East Asian Institute of Columbia University, 1967), 3–4.

16. USSR Commissariat of Foreign Affairs, *Dokumenty Vneshnei Politiki (Documents on Foreign Policy)* (Moscow: Gosudarstvennoe Izdatel'stvo Politicheskoi Literatury, 1957–), XV (hereafter cited as *DVP*).

17. U.S. Department of State, *Foreign Relations of the United States: Diplomatic Papers, 1933* (Washington, D.C.: U.S. Government Printing Office, 1950), III (hereafter cited as *FRUS*).

18. James B. Crowley, *Japan's Quest for Autonomy, National Security, and Foreign Policy, 1930–1938* (Princeton, N.J.: Princeton University Press, 1966), 184, 204–5.

19. Cited in Lensen, *Damned Inheritance*, 383.

20. Godfrey E. P. Hertslet, *Treaties, Conventions, Etc., Between China and Foreign States*, 3rd edition (London: Harrison & Sons, for His Majesty's Stationery Office, 1908), I, 27.

21. *Proceedings of the International Military Tribunal for the Far East* (Tokyo: 1946–48), 23,006–9 (hereafter cited as *IMTFE*); Clark Tinch, "Quasi-War Between Japan and the U.S.S.R.," *World Politics* 3 (January 1951): 176–77.

22. *JSSM*, X, 32.

23. Figures for Soviet forces are based on Japanese military intelligence estimates, *JSSM*, XIII, 32; and Haslam, *The Threat from the East*, 28. Figures for Japanese forces are from Coox, *Nomonhan*, 84.

24. For example, the Trans-Siberian Railway bridge at Iman was only four kilometers from Japanese artillery at the border near Hutou. *JSSM*, XIII, 25.

Chapter 2: The Global Context

1. One notable exception was the Red Army's illicit cooperation with Weimar Germany's Versailles-limited army. Soviet Russia also had a nominal ally in the Mongolian People's Republic, but few others recognized the MPR as an independent state until after the Second World War.

2. The Comintern was established by delegates from thirty-four mostly embryonic Communist parties meeting in Moscow in March 1919. Its avowed goal was to "fight by all available means to overthrow the international bourgeoisie," spark proletarian revolution, and work for the triumph of socialism and, eventually, communism.

3. The Mongolian People's Revolutionary Party, which joined the Comintern in 1924, was also a ruling party. At first, Lenin and Trotsky ran Comintern proceedings themselves, while Grigory Zinoviev, a member of the CPSU's ruling Politburo, chaired the Comintern Executive Committee. After Lenin's death in 1924, leadership of the Comintern was caught up in the larger succession struggle. In 1934 Stalin appointed the Bulgarian communist Georgi Dimitrov to head the Comintern, a position he held until Stalin dissolved the organization in 1943 as a gesture of friendship to his wartime capitalist allies.

4. Dennis W. Brogan, *The Development of Modern France, 1870–1939*, 2 vols. (New York: Harper and Row, 1966), II, 651–58.

5. This interpretation closely follows the analysis of Soviet foreign policy in Adam Ulam's *Expansion and Coexistence* (New York: Praeger, 1968).

6. This was a concession to the canny French premier, Pierre Laval. Jane Degras, *Soviet Documents on Foreign Policy*, 3 vols. (New York: Oxford University Press, 1951–53) III, 132.

7. VII (Seventh) Congress of the Communist International, *Abridged Stenographic Report of Proceedings* (in English) (Moscow: 1939), 244.

8. Ibid., 592.

9. *World News and Views*, April 29, 1939, 488; May 27, 1939, 628.

10. The most extreme formulation of this thesis is in Suvorov's *The Chief Culprit*.

11. VII Congress of the Communist International, 240.

12. Ibid., 593.

13. Ibid., 291; *International Press Correspondence* (London, 1920–1938), October 1935, 1, 489 (hereafter cited as *Inprecor*).

14. Charles B. McLane, *Soviet Policy and the Chinese Communists, 1931–1946* (New York: Columbia University Press, 1958), 51–60ff.

15. Ulam, *Expansion and Coexistence*, 243n.

16. Ibid., 217.

17. The CCP had actually "declared war" on Japan as early as 1932, although at that time the communists' main base of operations was a thousand miles south of Manchuria.

18. McLane, *Soviet Policy and the Chinese Communists*, 79–82.

19. U.S. Department of State, *Foreign Relations of the United States: Diplomatic Papers* (Washington, D.C.: U.S. Government Printing Office, 1937), III, 827–28 (cited hereafter as *FRUS*).

20. John Erickson, *The Soviet High Command* (London: Macmillan, 1962), 449–509.

21. Coox, *Nomonhan*, 85.

22. Harriet L. Moore, *Soviet Far Eastern Policy, 1931–1945* (Princeton, N.J.: Princeton University Press, 1945), 81–82; Hidaka Noburo, ed., *Manchukuo-Soviet Border Issues* (Harbin: *Manchuria Daily News*, 1938); U.S. State Department Archives, Henderson in Moscow to Secretary of State, July 3, 1937, ser. no. 761.94/973.

23. U.S. State Department Archives, U.S. Consul in Harbin, Manchukuo, Walter A. Adams to Secretary of State, July 6, 1937, ser. no. 893.00 P.R. Harbin/104; Degras, *Soviet Documents on Foreign Policy*, III, 242–43; *JSSM*, XI, Part 1, 65–67; Coox, *Nomonhan*, 105.

24. Hata, *Taiheiyo Senso e no Michi*, 80.

25. Ibid., 80.

26. Ibid., 81; Degras, *Soviet Documents on Foreign Policy*, III, 242–43.

27. Tsuji, *Nomonhan*, 36.

28. These vessels displaced only 25 tons; their main armament was heavy machine guns.

29. JDA, *Kanto Gun*, 335.

30. Degras, *Soviet Documents on Foreign Policy*, III, 243.

31. Ibid., 244–45; Erickson, *The Soviet High Command*, 468; Coox, *Nomonhan*, 111.

32. U.S. State Department Archives, U.S. Ambassador Joseph E. Davies in Moscow to Secretary of State, June 30, 1937, ser. no. 761.9415/1.

33. The Japanese were well aware of the strategic significance of Heihsiatzu Island, and Kwantung Army undertook a serious study of the feasibility of claiming the island. Colonel (then Captain) Nishihara was assigned to conduct monthly reconnaissance of the area, which he did through 1938, disguised as a Manchukuoan border policeman. He found the Soviet defensive positions on the island to be very strong and advised against contesting its ownership. Interview with Nishihara (see note 29, above). This same principle was at issue in the Sino-Soviet battle over Damansky/Chenpao Island in the Ussuri River, which brought the two to the brink of war in March 1969.

34. Haslam, *The Threat from the East*, 92.

35. Coox, *Nomonhan*, 119.

36. *FRUS*, 1937, III, 928; Erickson, *The Soviet High Command*, 468.

37. U.S. State Department Archives, Loy W. Henderson in Moscow to Secretary of State, September 2, 1937, ser. no. 761.94.983.

38. *FRUS*, 1937, III, 635–36.

39. Erickson, *The Soviet High Command*, 490.

40. Conversation described by Sun Fo to Ambassador Bullitt, *FRUS*, 1938, III, 165.

41. *JSSM*, XI, Part 3, 193.

42. In 1938 the Soviet Army in the East, commanded by the illustrious Marshal Vasily Blyukher, was given the distinctive name Red Banner Far Eastern Army.

43. Haslam, *The Threat from the East*, 94.

44. *World News and Views*, June 26, 1939, 719–20.

45. *Documents on German Foreign Policy, 1918–1945*, Series D, 13 vols. (Washington, D.C.: U.S. Government Printing Office, 1949–64), I, 733 (hereafter cited as *DGFP*).

46. Japanese Foreign Ministry archives, cited in Leonid N. Kutakov, *Japanese Foreign Policy on the Eve of the Pacific War*, trans. and ed. by George A. Lensen (Tallahassee, Fla.: Diplomatic Press, 1972), 9.

47. Bradford Lee, *Britain and the Sino-Japanese War, 1937–1939* (Stanford, Calif.: Stanford University Press, 1973), 12.

48. The term "Western democracies" is used here primarily to denote Britain, France, and the United States but also includes the Netherlands, Canada, and others to which the label is appropriate and had significant interests in East Asia.

49. Lee, *Britain and the Sino-Japanese War*, 142.

50. Ibid., 107–8.

51. Ibid., 87, 109.

52. Ibid., 80.

53. August 7, 1937, reported by Anthony Eden in his *Memoirs of Anthony Eden, Earl of Avon*, vol. I, *Facing the Dictators, 1923–1938* (London: Cassell, 1962), 456.

54. Lee, *Britain and the Sino-Japanese War*, 106–7.

55. Pierre Laval, as foreign minister, negotiated the Franco-Soviet treaty. Its conclusion in May 1935 helped propel him into the premiership in June.

56. Cited in Lensen, *Damned Inheritance*, 447.

57. The French General Staff gave this as part of their rationale for postponing the joint staff consultations without which the Franco-Soviet defense pact would remain barren. Keith Eubank, *The Origins of World War II* (New York: Crowell, 1969), 42.

58. Kutakov, *Japanese Foreign Policy*, 1.

59. German Naval Archives, Kr1672/42 geh, U.S. National Archives and Record Service, microfilm reel no. T-79-E.

60. For an account of Soviet policy based on previously secret Soviet documents, see Hugh Ragsdale, *The Soviets, the Munich Crisis, and the Coming of World War II* (Cambridge, UK: Cambridge University Press, 2004).

61. For example, Sidney Aster, a respected Canadian scholar and no Soviet apologist, concluded, "As long as secret intelligence indicated that Hitler's next move would be eastwards, it was considered best in London and Paris to ignore the Soviets, and to leave Hitler to deal with them as he saw fit." Aster, *1939*, 153.

62. Here is an example of that rhetoric from June 1938: "The independence of the French nation is seriously threatened by Fascism.... The best guarantee of this independence would be the strengthening of the bonds between France and the Soviet Union.... The Soviet Union can guarantee its national independence. But it would not dream of isolating itself." *Inprecor*, June 25, 1938, 763.

63. *World News and Views*, April 22, 1939, 453.

64. For a convenient summary, see James E. McSherry, *Stalin, Hitler, and Europe: The Origins of World War II, 1933–1939* (Cleveland, Ohio: World Publishing, 1968), 99–128.

65. *World News and Views*, October 29, December 31, 1938; January 7, February 4, March 11, 1939.

66. Ibid., December 3, 1938, 1,235; February 4, 1939, 42.

67. Ibid., April 2, 1938, 402.

68. Letter from Chamberlain to his sister, cited in Aster, *1939*, 154–45.

69. *DGFP*, V, 104–7.

70. Stalin was aware of the German pressure on Poland thanks to a Soviet agent in the German embassy in Warsaw. Weinberg, *The Foreign Policy of Hitler's Germany*, 533.

71. Degras, *Soviet Documents on Foreign Policy*, III, 312.

72. Gustav Hilger and Alfred G. Meyer, *The Incompatible Allies* (New York: Macmillian, 1953), 288–89, 383–84; *DGFP*, IV, 616–20.

73. Ulam, *Expansion and Coexistence*, 263–64.

74. Great Britain, Foreign Office, *Documents on British Foreign Policy*, 3rd series (London: Her Majesty's Stationery Office), vol. IV, 360–1, 392–93 (hereafter cited as *DBFP*).

75. It is not clear what Beck feared more at this point: Soviet guarantees, implying permission for the Red Army to enter Poland, or the effect that such an alliance might have on Hitler. For a conversation between Beck and the British ambassador in Warsaw on this question, see *DBFP*, IV, 453–54.

76. Keith Feiling, *The Life of Neville Chamberlain* (London: Macmillan, 1946), 403.

77. These discussions are summarized in Aster, *1939*, 80–97.

78. Ibid., 115.

79. Chamberlain at cabinet meeting, April 19, 1939, Ibid., 164.

80. *DBFP*, V, 228–29.

81. Ibid., V, 331; Aster, *1939*, 183, 272.

82. Roberts, *The Unholy Alliance*, 147.

83. In a memorandum to Ribbentrop on May 25, 1939, Weizsacker wrote of the oblique Soviet overture: "A German move in Moscow at the present time is only of value if it is taken seriously by the Russians; otherwise it would be worthless or even dangerous: that is, Moscow would ... play it off against us in Tokyo." *DGFP*, VI, 586. To his ambassador in Moscow, Weizsacker urged prudence, lest unsolicited German cordiality call forth "a peal of Tartar laughter." Ibid., 597–98.

84. Ernst von Weizsacker, *Memoirs* (London: Victor Gollancz, 1951), 126–27.

85. Ernst L. Presseisen, *Germany and Japan: A Study in Totalitarian Diplomacy, 1933–1941* (The Hague: Martinus Nijhoff, 1958), 126–27.

86. *DGFP*, VI, 396–97.

87. Ibid., 337–38.

88. Sorge's chief collaborator was Ozaki Hotsumi, a leftist journalist who was employed at that time as a foreign policy consultant in the office of Japanese premier Konoye Fumimaro. Ozaki was able to provide Sorge with accurate information on the German-Japanese negotiations and Japan's determination to make it an anti-Soviet alliance. Robert Whymant, *Stalin's Spy: Richard Sorge and the Tokyo Espionage Ring* (New York: St. Martin's Press, 1996), 114–15.

Chapter 3: Changkufeng

1. *JSSM*, XI, Pt. 3a, 26–27.

2. Erickson, *The Soviet High Command*, 505–6.

3. Hata, *Taiheiyo Senso e no Michi*, 82–83. For a full discussion of the occupation of alternating hills, see Inada Masazumi, "Soren Kyokutogun to no Taiketsu" ("Confrontation with the Soviet Far Eastern Army"), *Chisei*, Special Issue no. 5, December 1956, 278.

4. Details of Lyushkov's defection are based on Alvin D. Coox, "L'Affaire Lyushkov," *Soviet Studies* 19 (January 1968), unless otherwise noted.

5. From a verbatim transcript of the interrogation of Lyushkov in Tokyo. U.S. Department of the Army, Military Intelligence Reports (Washington, D.C.: National Archives and Records Service), Record Group 165, Maj. Frank W. Hane, Acting Military Attaché in Moscow, to Department of the Army, May 12, 1939, ser. no. 2037-1997/11 (hereafter cited as Military Intelligence Reports).

6. Inada, "Soren Kyokutogun to no Taiketsu," 279; *Gen Dai Shi X* (*Modern History Documents X*) *Nichu Senso*, 3 (*Japan-China War*, Pt. 3), ed. Tsunoda Jun (Tokyo: Misuzu Shobo, 1964), xxxii (hereafter cited as *Gen Dai Shi*).

7. *JSSM*, XI, Pt. 3a, 55–56; Erickson, *The Soviet High Command*, 494–95; Haslam, *The Threat from the East*, 114.

8. Hata, *Taiheiyo Senso e no Michi*, 83.

9. Ibid.; Tsuji, *Nomonhan*, 38–39.

10. Inada, "Soren Kyokutogun to no Taiketsu," 279–80.

11. Hata, *Taiheiyo Senso e no Michi*, 89–93.

12. Ibid., 84; Inada, "Soren Kyokutogun to no Taiketsu," 280.

13. M. V. Novikov, "U Ozera Khasan" ("At Lake Khasan"), *Voprosy Istorii* (August 1968), 205.

14. *The Saionji-Harada Memoirs*, trans. Supreme Commander Allied Powers (Pacific) (Washington, D.C.: National Archives and Records Service), Record Group 331, Pt. XV, 2, 189–91.

15. Alvin D. Coox, "Qualities of Japanese Military Leadership: The Case of Suetaka Kamezo," *Journal of Asian History* 2 (1968), 32–43.

16. *Chokoho Jiken no Keii* (*Development of the Changkufeng Incident*), a Chosen Army Headquarters document, cited in *Gen Dai Shi*, 9–10.

17. JDA, *Kanto Gun*, 349.

18. Hata, *Taiheiyo Senso e no Michi*, 85.

19. *Gen Dai Shi*, xxxi–ii.

20. Hata, *Taiheiyo Senso e no Michi*, 85.

21. *JSSM*, XI, Pt. 3a, 63; V. Ezhakov, "Boi u Ozera Khasan" ("The Battle at Lake Khasan"), *Voenno-Istoricheskie Zhurnal* (July 1968), 124.

22. Ibid., 125.

23. *JSSM*, XI, Pt. 3a, 63; Hata, *Taiheiyo Senso e no Michi*, 86.

24. Ibid., 86.

25. Ibid., 87.

26. JDA, *Kanto Gun*, 367–68. Suetaka "got the message" from Tokyo. The "medium" was a process of indirect communication called *hara ge*, literally, "belly-talk," a highly cultivated practice in Japan.

27. Alvin D. Coox, *The Anatomy of a Small War: The Soviet-Japanese Struggle for Changkufeng/ Khasan, 1938* (Westport, Conn.: Greenwood Press, 1977), 48.

28. This reconstruction of the battle is based on *JSSM*, XI Pt. 3a, 71–94; Hata, *Taiheiyo Senso e no Michi*, 87; Ezhakov, "Boi U Ozera Khasan"; and Novikov, "U Ozera Khasan," 206–8.

29. JDA, *Kanto Gun*, 364; Coox, *Anatomy of a Small War*, 167.

30. In his first message to Chosen Army Headquarters at 5:40 a.m., Suetaka claimed that "since the enemy near Shachaofeng staged an advance, the Sato unit dealt them a counterattack." Hata, *Taiheiyo Senso e no Michi*, 87.

31. Ibid.

32. Ibid., 88.

33. Erickson, *The Soviet High Command*, 498; Novikov, "U Ozera Khasan," 206.

34. N. F. Kuzmin, *Na Strazhe Mirnovo Truda* (*On Guard for the Workers of the World*) (Moscow: Military Publishing House, 1959), 202; *JSSM*, XI, Pt. 3a, 97–98.

35. *JSSM*, XI, Pt. 3a, 98; JDA, *Kanto Gun*, 373.

36. Hata, *Taiheiyo Senso e no Michi*, 89.

37. From the gist of Shigemitsu's memoirs, Litvinov seems to have convinced the ambassador that Soviet forces then held the disputed heights and that the repeated attacks were being launched by the Japanese in an effort to dislodge them. Soviet authorities took pains to create this same false impression in their press. Litvinov himself may have believed this. Shigemitsu Mamoru, *Japan and Her Destiny*, ed. by F. S. G. Piggott, trans. by Oswald White (New York: E. P. Dutton and Co., 1958), 159; Degras, *Soviet Documents on Foreign Policy*, III, 296–98.

38. On August 4, 1938, Litvinov told the U.S. chargé in Moscow that he "knew" Japan did not seek war with the Soviet Union and that the Soviet government had no intention of backing down at Changkufeng. *FRUS, 1938*, III, 470. Moscow's confidence may have been reinforced by intelligence reports from their spy Richard Sorge in Tokyo.

39. Military Intelligence Reports, U.S. Military Attaché in China, Colonel Joseph Stillwell, to Department of Army, August 17, 1938, ser. no. N.A. 2657-H-452/26.

40. *JSSM*, XI, Pt. 3a, 112.

41. State Department Archives, U.S. Chargé in Moscow Kirk to Secretary of State, August 4, 1938, ser. no. 761.93 Manchuria/154.

42. *FRUS*, 1938, III, 463.

43. Hata, *Taiheiyo Senso e no Michi*, 89; State Department Archives, U.S. Consul in Harbin, to Secretary of State, August 5, 1938, ser. no. 761.93 Manchuria/160.

44. *JSSM*, XI, Pt. 3a, 115.

45. Ibid.; JDA, *Kanto Gun*, 399.

46. *Saionji-Harada Memoirs*, 2,219.

47. Shigemitsu, *Japan and Her Destiny*, 163; Hata, *Taiheiyo Senso e no Michi*, 91.

48. Opinion of the editors, JDA, *Kanto Gun*, 406.

49. *JSSM*, XI, Pt. 3a, 121–23; Hata, *Taiheiyo Senso e no Michi*, 92; Haslam, *The Threat from the East*, 119.

50. Ibid., 119–20.

51. On October 15, 1938, Prince Kanin, chief of AGS, met with the emperor, who expressed his praise for the valor of the 19th Division, which had fought under "very difficult circumstances," and his sorrow over the loss of life. He instructed Prince Kanin to tell this to the troops. JDA, *Kanto Gun*, 410.

52. Military Intelligence Reports, U.S. Military Attaché in Moscow Colonel Raymond Faymonville to Department of Army, September 22, 1938, ser. no. N.A. 2037-1833/66.

53. Ibid., Stillwell in China to Department of Army, August 17, 1938, ser. no. N.A. 2657-H-452/26.

54. Shtern commanded the Soviet Eighth Army in the Winter War against Finland in 1939–40. He was executed on Stalin's orders in October 1941, one of many generals purged during the initial phase of the German-Soviet war.

55. Inada, "Soren Kyokutogun to no Taiketsu," 284–85.

56. *Gen Dai Shi*, X, Pt. 3, xxxv–xxxviii.

57. Hata, *Taiheiyo Senso e no Michi*, 94.

58. Ibid.

59. *Saionji-Harada Memoirs*, 2,220.

Chapter 4: Nomonhan: Preliminaries

1. The Japanese call it *Nomonhan jiken* (the Nomonhan incident) after the tiny hamlet of Nomonhan near the battlefield. The Soviet side calls it *Boi u Khalkhin Gol* (the battle at the Khalkhin River), using the Mongol name of the river that figured prominently in the fighting. For reasons of economy and ease of pronunciation for Western readers, the Japanese name is used in this study.

2. Hata, *Taiheiyo Senso e no Michi*, 95–96; *IMTFE* Exhibits 764–66; Military Intelligence Reports, U.S. Military Attaché in Moscow to Department of the Army, July 24, 1939, ser. no. N.A. 2657-H-439/181.

3. Tsuji, *Nomonhan*, 72–73; JDA, *Kanto Gun*, 318–19, 442–44.

4. This interpretation is based on Tsuji's account in *Nomonhan*, 72–73, and on an interview with Colonel Nishihara Yukio (see chapter 2, note 29).

5. JDA, *Kanto Gun*, 321; State Department Archives, U.S. Consul in Mukden, William R. Langdon, to Secretary of State, June 1, 1939, ser. no. 761.9315 Manchuria/118. While at KwAHQ in Hsinking, Langdon shrewdly observed a carelessly displayed Kwantung Army wall map of 1933 showing the Manchukuo-MPR boundary running through the middle of Lake Buir Nor, while the 1936 map showed a boundary that put all of Lake Buir Nor within Manchukuo. Langdon concluded that "the inference is that in the intervening years 'Manchukuo' unilaterally rectified the frontier to its advantage, giving rise to the border conflicts of 1935 and the present time." This cartographic sleight of hand is independently confirmed by a U.S. military attaché report from China and by IMTFE Exhibit 764, which features a map published by the Kwantung Army in 1934 and obtained from the Japanese Imperial Library in 1946, showing the boundary precisely as claimed by the MPR and the USSR, i.e., through the middle of Lake Buir Nor and thence running some miles east of the Halha River.

6. *JSSM*, XI, Pt. 3 b, 197–203; JDA, *Kanto Gun*, 438; Coox, *Nomonhan*, 175. The Special Services Agency was Japan's version of America's World War II–era OSS, responsible for intelligence, counterintelligence, and other clandestine activities.

7. JDA, *Kanto Gun*, 438.

8. Japan Army Ministry Archives, *Kyokai Jiken Toku Hokoku* (*Special Report on Border Incidents*), December 1938, contained in U.S. National Archives and Record Service, Alexandria, Virginia, N.A. 16065, T782, Reel 109, frames 18,732–40. This is General Komatsubara's official report of the incident to army minister Itagaki.

9. *JSSM*, I, 20–32, 105–7.

10. Inada, "Soren Kyokutogun to no Taiketsu," 285; JDA, *Kanto Gun*, 297.

11. Cited in Coox, *Nomonhan*, 188.

12. Tsuji, *Nomonhan*, 40–41. Additional details of Tsuji's unusual diversionary tactics were provided by Colonel Nishihara Yukio in an interview on November 29, 1973.

13. Tsuji's father was a charcoal maker, a lowly occupation in Japan.

14. Tsuji, *Nomonhan*, 40–41; JDA, *Kanto Gun*, 415–17.

15. Ibid., 415–17, 422.

16. Shimada Toshihiko, *Kanto Gun* (Tokyo: Chuo Koron Sha, 1965), 135; Tsuji, *Nomonhan*, 46–47; *JSSM*, XI, Pt. 1, 99–102.

17. Tsuji, *Nomonhan*, 45–46.

18. Hata, *Taiheiyo Senso e no Michi*, 96.

19. JDA, *Kanto Gun*, 436.

20. Ibid., 435–36.

21. Tsuji, *Nomonhan*, 44; JDA, *Kanto Gun*, 436.

22. Hata, *Taiheiyo Senso e no Michi*, 96; *Gen Dai Shi*, X, Pt. 3, 2; JDA, *Kanto Gun*, 420–21, 425–26.

23. *Gen Dai Shi*, X, Pt. 3, xlvii, 72.

24. Tsuji, *Nomonhan*, 42.

25. Soviet and Japanese newspaper accounts from 1939 can be discounted as largely propagandistic fabrications. The indictment by the Soviet prosecutor at the Tokyo War Crimes Trial and the Japanese defense can be found in *IMTFE*, 7,840–54ff. Other official and semiofficial Soviet versions can be found in A. Deborin et al., *Istoriia Velikoi Otechtestvennoi Voiny Sovetskogo Soiuza, 1941–1945 (History of the Great Fatherland War of the Soviet Union, 1941–1945)*, I (Moscow: Akademiia Nauk SSSR, 1960), 237 (cited hereafter as *IVOVSS*); S. N. Shishkin, *Khalkhin-Gol* (Moscow: Military Publishing House, 1954), 10–13; and G. N. Sevost'yanov, "Voenno i Diplomaticheskoe Porazhenie Yaponii v Periode Sobytiy u Reki Khalkhin-Gol" ("The Military and Diplomatic Defeat of Japan in the Period of the Events at the Khalkhin-Gol River"), *Voprosy Istorii* (August 1957), 63–84. Some important Japanese accounts can be found in Tsuji, *Nomonhan*, 67–77; Hata, *Taiheiyo Senso e no Michi*, 96; JDA, *Kanto Gun*, 440–42, *JSSM*, XI, Pt. 3b, 215–18; and numerous records in the Archives of the Japanese Defense Agency, especially the Operations Log of Kwantung Army and *Nomonhan Jiken Keiko no Gaiyo (Summary of the Course of the Nomonhan Incident)*, written by Colonel Hattori Takushiro in November 1939; and *Nomonhan Jiken Kankei Tzuzuri (Nomonhan Incident Files)*. A detailed account based on exhaustive research in Japanese sources is in Coox, *Nomonhan*, 188–89.

26. This reconstruction of events is based on JDA, *Kanto Gun*, 441–42; Sasaki Chiyoko, *Der Nomonhan Konflikt*, unpublished doctoral dissertation (Bonn: Friedrich-Whilhelms-Universitat, 1968), 55–61, which makes use of Mongolian as well as Japanese and Soviet sources; and interviews in July 2011 with R. Bold, Director of the Mongolian General Intelligence Agency and a Nomonhan scholar.

27. JDA, *Kanto Gun*, 441.

28. Ibid., 442; *JSSM*, XI, Pt. 3b, 215–16.

29. Tsuji, *Nomonhan*, 75–77.

30. *IMTFE*, 7,850; *JSSM*, XI, Pt. 3b, 220–21.

31. R. Bold interview, July 2011; Shishkin, *Khalkhin-Gol*, 13–15.

32. Several sources agree that the usually cautious Komatsubara was spurred to action by Order 1488. JDA, *Kanto Gun*, 438; Tsuji, *Nomonhan*, 77; Sasaki, *Der Nomonhan Konflikt*, 72.

33. *JSSM*, XI, Pt. 3b, 204; Coox, *Nomonhan*, 176–80.

34. Ibid., 200; JDA, *Kanto Gun*, 443.

35. *JSSM*, XI, Pt. 3b, 222–23.

36. JDA, *Kanto Gun*, 446–47.

37. Coox, *Nomonhan*, 203; R. Bold interview, July 2011.

38. Shimada, *Kanto Gun*, 140–41; Coox, *Nomonhan*, 203–4.

39. Ibid., 246; Shishkin, *Khalkhin-Gol*, 15–16; R. Bold interview, July 2011.

40. Whether this was a gross error of omission by Yamagata, as Coox implies (Coox, *Nomonhan*, 232), or was due to technical radio problems, the result proved deadly for Azuma.

41. Shishkin, *Khalkhin-Gol*, 16–17.

42. JDA, *Kanto Gun*, 451.

43. Ibid., 454–55; Shishkin, *Khalkhin-Gol*, 17–19; JSSM, XI, Pt. 3b, 232–37; Coox, *Nomonhan*, 209–12.

44. Ibid., 236–39.

45. JDA, *Kanto Gun*, 462.

46. Coox, *Nomonhan*, 248; Shishkin, *Khalkhin-Gol*, 19.

47. Maksim Kolomiets, "Boi u Reki Khalkhin-Gol" ("Battle at the Khalkhin-Gol River"), *Frontovaya Illyustratsiya*, February 2002, 28.

48. This is suggested by an AGS message to KwAHQ on May 30, 1939, congratulating that army on its "recent great success" at Nomonhan. JSSM, XI, Pt. 3b, 243–44.

49. Ibid., 244; JDA, *Kanto Gun*, 445–46.

50. Hata, *Taiheiyo Senso e no Michi*, 98.

51. JDA, *Kanto Gun*, 466.

52. Hata, *Taiheiyo Senso e no Michi*, 97.

Chapter 5: Nomonhan: A Lesson in Limited War

1. Georgy Konstantinovich Zhukov, *Memoirs of Marshal Zhukov* (New York: Delacorte Press, 1971), 147–48.

2. Ibid., 149–50.

3. Ibid., 150–51; Shishkin, *Khalkhin-Gol*, 19–20.

4. *Gen Dai Shi*, X, Pt. 3, 74. All important Japanese accounts of the Nomonhan incident refer to Soviet air raids on June 19. Soviet accounts do not deny them specifically, but make no mention of any such air raids. In the absence of specific evidence to the contrary, it seems reasonable to conclude that the air raids did occur.

5. JDA, *Kanto Gun*, 468–69; interview with Colonel Nishihara Yukio, former Kwantung Army intelligence officer, November 29, 1973. There is some confusion on this last point. Komatsubara's report speaks of "*bakugeki*," which means aerial bombardment. But in the Japanese military lexicon of that day there was no specific word for "strafe." *Bakugeki* was used to denote both bombing and strafing. None of the official reports of this incident mention bombers or the kind of damage usually associated with bombing. JDA, *Kanto Gun*, 478.

6. R. Bold interview, July 2011.

7. Tsuji, *Nomonhan*, 97–99; JDA, *Kanto Gun*, 469.

8. JSSM, XI, Pt. 3b, 249–50.

9. JDA, *Kanto Gun*, 469–71; *Gen Dai Shi*, X, Pt. 3, 75; Tsuji says it was his idea not to inform Tokyo of the planned attack. Tsuji, *Nomonhan*, 99–101.

10. *JSSM*, XI, Pt. 3b, 256–59.

11. Hata, *Taiheiyo Senso e no Michi*, 98–99.

12. JDA, *Kanto Gun*, 475.

13. Coox, *Nomonhan*, 263–64.

14. JDA, *Kanto Gun*, 626.

15. Sevost'yanov, "Voennoe i Diplomaticheskoe Porazhenie Yaponii," 70–71.

16. *JSSM*, XI, Pt. 3b, 286–88; Tsuji, *Nomonhan*, 105–6.

17. Ibid., 108.

18. JDA, *Kanto Gun*, 473, 476; Hata, *Taiheiyo Senso e no Michi*, 99.

19. Ibid.; Tsuji, *Nomonhan*, 110. A Kwantung Army staff officer, Katakura Tadashi, allegedly leaked the information while in Tokyo on June 24. It is not clear whether or not his action was intentional.

20. *JSSM*, XI, Pt. 3b, 267; JDA, *Kanto Gun*, 482.

21. Ibid.; Hata, *Taiheiyo Senso e no Michi*, 99.

22. Tsuji, *Nomonhan*, 117; JDA, *Kanto Gun*, 484. Coox, *Nomonhan*, 276. Sasaki, *Der Nomonhan Konflikt*, 83. Soviet accounts acknowledge the Japanese air raid of June 27 but claim, unbelievably, to have shot down one hundred attacking planes against thirty-three Soviet losses, Shishkin, *Khalkhin-Gol*, 21.

23. R. Bold interview, July 2011; Baabar, *History of Mongolia*, trans. by D. Suhjargalmaa et al. (Cambridge, UK: White Horse Press, 1999), 389; Michael Parrish, *Sacrifice of the Generals: Soviet Senior Officer Losses* (Lanham, Md.: Scarecrow Press, 2004), 211.

24. Inada used the word *"Baka,"* which translates literally as "animal," but carries a far stronger and deeply insulting meaning. For details of this emotional exchange between KwAHQ and AGS, see Tsuji, *Nomonhan*, 118–19; and Inada, "Soren Kyokutogun to no Taiketsu," 291.

25. *JSSM*, XI, Pt. 3b, 270.

26. Tsuji, *Nomonhan*, 119.

27. *JSSM*, XI, Pt. 3, 270–71; JDA, *Kanto Gun*, 486.

28. Coox, *Nomonhan*, 279–81.

29. Ibid., 287; *JSSM*, XI, Pt. 3b, 274–77.

30. Tsuji, *Nomonhan*, 119; Inada, "Soren Kyokutogun to no Taiketsu," 291.

31. Tsuji, *Nomonhan*, 44–45ff.

32. JDA, *Kanto Gun*, 495.

33. Sevost'yanov, "Voennoe i Diplomaticheskoe Porazhenie Yaponni," 78.

34. Zhukov, *Memoirs*, 150–51; Shishkin, *Khalkhin-Gol*, 23.

35. JDA, *Kanto Gun*, 501.

36. Ibid., 503–5.

37. Ibid., 514–15; Shishkin, *Khalkhin-Gol*, 25–26; Zhukov, *Memoirs*, 151–53.

38. Coox, *Nomonhan*, 316.

39. Ibid., 379.

40. Ibid.

41. Hata, *Taiheiyo Senso e no Michi*, 101; *JSSM*, VI, 79–82.

42. Ibid., XI, Pt. 3b, 295; JDA, *Kanto Gun*, 507–10.

43. Ibid., 518.

44. Ibid., 521–22, 524.

45. *JSSM*, XI, Pt. 3b, 306.

46. Coox, *Nomonhan*, 341; Zhukov, *Memoirs*, 153; Shishkin, *Khalkhin-Gol*, 26.

47. JDA, *Kanto Gun*, 173–74.

48. Naturally, there were officers who rejected this doctrine in favor of a more objective, empirical outlook, but they ran against the grain of deep tradition. The most notable such exception was General Nagata Tetsuzan, who reached the powerful post of chief of the Bureau of Military Affairs in the Army Ministry by virtue of sheer intellectual brilliance. Nagata was a believer in materiel and firepower and sought to restructure the army, and indeed the entire nation, on the basis of his vision of "total war." In August 1935 Nagata was assassinated by Lieutenant Colonel Aizawa Saburo, who deplored Nagata's materialist outlook. Aizawa became a public hero and his trial a cause célèbre, the inspiration for the notorious Tokyo Army Mutiny of February 26, 1936. Crowley, *Japan's Quest for Autonomy*, 262–67.

49. In an interview in 1955, Colonel Sumi bitterly recalled the recriminating attitude of KwAHQ, "saying that the defeat was not due to their operational plan, but to the inadequate command of the front line commanders, they decided to punish us, but without formal procedures." *JSSM*, XI, Pt. 3c, 402–3. Sumi held a confidential letter written to him on July 10, 1939, by his commanding officer, General Sonobe Waichiro, the respected commander of Kwantung Army's 7th Division, who was promoted to the command of the China Expeditionary Army in August 1939. In this letter, General Sonobe heaped criticism on KwAHQ for inadequate intelligence and poor planning of the July offensive. Sumi had kept secret for thirty-four years this indiscrete letter written by the venerated Sonobe. Its publication in 1973 was carried as a feature story in Japan's premiere newspaper. *Asahi Shinbun*, August 15, 1973.

50. Zhukov, *Memoirs*, 152.

51. Cited in Andrew Nagorski, *The Greatest Battle: Stalin, Hitler, and the Desperate Struggle for Moscow That Changed the Course of World War II* (New York: Simon and Schuster, 2007), 121.

52. Erickson, *The Soviet High Command*, 567–68.

53. Zhukov, *Memoirs*, 154.

54. *DGFP*, VI, 1,059–62; VII, 67–69. This theme is developed at length in chapter 6.

55. Military Intelligence Report, U. S. Military Attaché in Moscow to Department of Army, July 6, 1939, Ser. No. N.A. 2657-H-452/3.

56. Zhukov, *Memoirs*, 155; Shishkin, *Khalkhin-Gol*, 31, 36–37.

57. JDA, *Kanto Gun*, 536–45.

58. Zhukov, *Memoirs*, 164, 240; Shishkin, *Khalkhin-Gol*, 40.

59. JDA, *Kanto Gun*, 581.

60. Hata, *Taiheiyo Senso e no Michi*, 101.

61. JDA, *Kanto Gun*, 609.

62. Ibid., 572; Coox, *Nomonhan*, 532.

63. Ibid., 544–45.

64. Ibid., 609.

65. Tsuji, *Nomonhan*, 156.

66. Ibid., 163.

67. Ibid., 166–67; Hata, *Taiheiyo Senso e no Michi*, 102.

68. Ibid.; *Gen Dai Shi*, X, Pt. 3, 79–81.

69. JDA, *Kanto Gun*, 582.

70. Tsuji, *Nomonhan*, 168.

71. JDA, *Kanto Gun*, 582–83.

72. Ibid., 597–98.

73. This development is examined in detail in chapter 6.

74. Chalmers Johnson, *An Instance of Treason: Ozaki Hotsumi and the Sorge Spy Ring* (Stanford, Calif.: Stanford University Press, 1964), 150–52.

75. Shishkin, *Khalkhin-Gol*, 31, 34.

76. Ibid., 31, 36, 37.

77. Zhukov, *Memoirs*, 155.

78. *JSSM*, X, 51. Not only was Kwantung Army's air activity restrained by orders from Tokyo, but early August also brought two solid weeks of miserable weather in which virtually all reconnaissance flights were grounded. Hata, *Taiheiyo Senso e no Michi*, 103.

79. *Gen Dai Shi*, X, Pt. 3, 86–87; *JSSM*, XI, Pt. 3b, 353; JDA, *Kanto Gun*, 589, 628–29.

80. Coox, *Nomonhan*, 560.

81. Ibid., 559.

82. Opinion of Colonel Nishihara Yukio, formerly of Kwantung Army Intelligence Section, expressed in an interview on December 7, 1973.

83. JDA, *Kanto Gun*, 245.

84. Inada, "Soren Kyokutogun to no Taiketsu," 293.

85. Kitagami Norio and Nara Hiroshi, "Kanto Gun Tokushu Himitsu 731 Butai ni Yoru Hijindoteki Hanzai" ("Inhuman Crimes of Kwantung Army's Special Secret Troop 731"), *Nichu* 2, no. 12 (December 1972), 26; Tracy Dalby, "Japan's Germ Warriors," *Washington Post*, May 26, 1983, A1, 25.

86. In his memoirs, Zhukov mistakenly attributes this to Remizov, who was killed in action in July. Zhukov, *Memoirs*, 157–58.

87. Ibid., 155–56; Shishkin, *Khalkhin-Gol*, 37–40.

88. Zhukov, *Memoirs*, 156–57.

89. Tsuji, *Nomonhan*, 177–78.

90. Kwantung Army's consistent intelligence failures are summarized in JDA, *Kanto Gun*, 626–27.

91. The author is indebted to Colonel Nishihara Yukio for this idea, which he developed at length in an interview in December 1973.

92. Coox, *Nomonhan*, 585–87.

93. Shishkin, *Khalkhin-Gol*, 37–40.

94. Ibid., 40–42; Zhukov, *Memoirs*, 159–60.

95. *JSSM*, VII, Pt. 2, 102.

96. Shishkin, *Khalkhin-Gol*, 43–44.

97. Ibid., 44–45; JDA, *Kanto Gun*, 632–36.

98. *JSSM*, XI, Pt. 3c, 383.

99. *JSSM*, IV, 64.

100. The I-16, a cantilevered-winged monoplane with retractable landing gear, was introduced in the mid-1930s and formed the backbone of the Soviet air force in 1939.

101. Ibid., 77–78.

102. Coox, *Nomonhan*, 708.

103. *JSSM*, XI, Pt. 3c, 384–89; JDA, *Kanto Gun*, 641–55; Tsuji, *Nomonhan*, 186.

104. Nagorski, *The Greatest Battle*, 121.

105. Coox, *Nomonhan*, 677.

106. Ibid., 678–81; P. Ruslanov (pseudonym?), "Marshal Zhukov," *Russian Review 15*, no. 3 (July 1956), 190; Shishkin, *Khalkhin-Gol*, 47; JDA, *Kanto Gun*, 636–38, 657–59, 685–86.

107. Coox, *Nomonhan*, 752.

108. Imai Takeo, ed., *Kindai no Senso, XV, Chugoku to no Tatakai (Modern Wars, Vol. XV, War Against China)* (Tokyo: Jinbutsu Orai Sha, 1965), 192.

109. Coox, *Nomonhan*, 769.

110. Imai, *Kindai no Senso*, 195.

111. JDA, *Kanto Gun*, 669; Shishkin, *Khalkhin-Gol*, 49.

112. Ibid., 52–53; Zhukov, *Memoirs*, 160–62.

113. Coox, *Nomonhan*, 958.

114. Ibid., 810–11.

115. Ibid., 826–27.

116. Ibid., 836; *JSSM*, XI, Pt. 3c, 431–32.

117. Kwantung Army officially admitted having lost 17,000–18,333 men at Nomonhan, but when Manchukuoan forces and other supporting units are included, the total may exceed 23,000. JDA, *Kanto Gun*, 462, 713; Shishkin, *Khalkhin-Gol*, 56.

118. Kolomiets, "Boi u Reki Khalkhin-Gol."

119. Hata, *Taiheiyo Senso e no Michi*, 133.

120. Coox, *Nomonhan*, 853.

121. Letter from Lieutenant Colonel Terada of Kwantung Army Operations Section to Colonel Inada, chief of AGS Operations Section, cited in Hata, *Taiheiyo Senso e no Michi*, 133.

122. Ibid.; Tsuji, *Nomonhan*, 222. One is reminded of Field Marshal Michel Ney's mission to arrest Napoleon after the deposed emperor returned from St. Helena to France before the Battle of Waterloo.

123. Ibid., 225; Hata, *Taiheiyo Senso e no Michi*, 133–34.

124. Coox, *Nomonhan*, 870–71.

125. *JSSM*, XI, Pt. 3c, 333–36. The subsequent careers of some of these officers, particularly Hattori and Tsuji, and their role in the coming of the Pacific War, are discussed in chapter 7.

126. Hata, *Taiheiyo Senso e no Michi*, 136–37.

127. *JSSM*, XI, Pt. 3c, 456–69.

128. Japanese Army Ministry Archives, September 25, 1939. "Directive of Kwantung Army Chief of Staff: Control of Officers and Men of Kwantung Army Regarding the Nomonhan Incident," U.S. National Archives and Record Service, Microfilm N.A. 16382, T-788, R139, frame 18,886–88.

129. *JSSM*, XI, Pt. 3c, 432–35; Tsuji, *Nomonhan*, 226; Hata, *Taiheiyo Senso e no Michi*, 137.

130. Nihon Kindai Shiryo Kenkyuka, *Nippon Riku-Kaigun no Seido Shoshiki Jinji* (*System, Organization, and Personnel of the Japanese Army and Navy*) (Tokyo: University of Tokyo Press, 1971).

131. P. A. Nevolin, ed., *Geroi Khalkhin-Gola* (*Heroes of Khalkhin-Gol*) (Perm: Perm Publishing House, 1966); Zhukov, *Memoirs*, 162–71.

Chapter 6: Nomonhan, the Nonaggression Pact, and the Outbreak of World War II

1. Weinberg, *The Foreign Policy of Hitler's Germany*, 573.

2. *God Krizisa*, vol. 1, 482–483.

3. *DGFP*, VI, 574–80; Trumbull Higgins, *Hitler and Russia: The Third Reich in a Two-Front War* (New York: MacMillan, 1966), 19–20.

4. *DGFP*, VI, no. 529; Nekrich, *Pariahs, Partners, Predators*, 112–13; Roberts, *The Soviet Union and the Origins of the Second World War*, 77.

5. *DVP*, no. 378, Astakhov's record of the conversation with Schulenburg.

6. Chamberlain spoke thus at the June 9, 1939, meeting of the Foreign Policy Committee of his cabinet, cited in Aster, *1939*, 267.

7. *DBFP*, V, 749.

8. Aster, *1939*, 273.

9. Ibid., 281.

10. Watt, *How War Came*, 380–83.

11. The date was pushed back twice to September 1. Hitler feared that if he postponed the attack beyond the first days of September the autumn rains would bog down his offensive and prevent the rapid victory he needed. Weinberg, *The Foreign Policy of Hitler's Germany*, 634ff.

12. Soviet ambassador Ivan Maisky admitted this to Foreign Minister Lord Halifax on March 31, 1939. *DBFP*, IV, 556–58.

13. The Polish government would not budge on this despite the most intense British and French pressure. In desperation on August 19, Paris instructed General Doumenc to lie to the Russians and claim that Warsaw had agreed to grant access to the Red Army. By then it was a moot point. Stalin agreed that day to receive Ribbentrop in Moscow to conclude the nonaggression pact.

14. *DBFP*, VII, 576–77.

15. Ulam, *Expansion and Coexistence*, 275.

16. Watt, *How War Came*, 231, 376.

17. *DGFP*, VI, 955–56.

18. *God Krizisa*, vol. 2, no. 504.

19. Ibid., no. 511.

20. *DVP*, no. 445, Astakhov's record of the conversation with Ribbentrop.

21. Information revealed by the Russian Commission on the German-Soviet Nonaggression Pact, *Pravda*, December 24, 1989.

22. An early account that attributes to the Nomonhan incident a significant role in the Soviet decision for the nonaggression pact is the Swiss historian Walter Hofer's *Die Entfesselung des Zweiten Weltkrieges*, 82ff. G. N. Sevost'yanov states that among other reasons, the pact with Germany was "necessary" in order to prevent solidification of a German-Italian-Japanese alliance against the Soviet Union. Sevost'yanov, "Voenno i Diplomaticheskoe Porazhenie Yaponii," 83. This point is treated in greater detail in G. N. Sevost'yanov, *Politika Velikikh Derzhav Na Dal' nem Vostoke Nakanune Vtoroi Mirovoi Voini (Policies of the Great Powers in the Far East on the Eve of the Second World War)* (Moscow: Izdatel'stvo Sotsialino-Ekonomicheskoi Literatury, 1961), 514–18. The best treatment of this linkage until now in Western writing is Haslam's *The Soviet Union and the Threat from the East*, 133–34.

23. *World News and Views*, June 3, 1939, 645–48.

24. Suvorov, *The Chief Culprit*, 116.

25. *DGFP*, VI, 1,059–62.

26. Ibid., VII, 67.

27. *God Krizisa*, vol. 2, no. 542.

28. *DGFP*, VII, 77.

29. Ibid., 84.

30. Ibid., 121–23.

31. Ibid., 225.

32. *DBFP*, VII, 114–15, 225, 237.

33. *DGFP*, VII, 540–41.

34. Coox, *Nomonhan*, 880–4.

35. Ulam, *Expansion and Coexistence*, 271–72.

36. F. C. Jones, *Japan's New Order in East Asia: Its Rise and Fall, 1937–1945* (London: Oxford University Press, 1954), 185.

37. Kutakov, *Japanese Foreign Policy*, 154–55, 8.

Chapter 7: Nomonhan Casts a Long Shadow

1. Erickson, *The Soviet High Command*, 567–68; Bell, *The Origins of the Second World War*, 198.

2. Anthony Cave Brown and Charles B. MacDonald, *On a Field of Red: The Communist International and the Coming of World War II* (New York: G. P. Putnam's Sons, 1981), 534.

3. *JSSM*, I, 111.

4. Japan Army Ministry, Chairman, Investigating Committee, "Kwantung Army, Report on Study of Nomonhan Incident," U.S. National Archives and Record Service, Microfilm N.A. 14550, T-803, R109, frames 19,024–27; Hata, *Taiheiyo Senso e no Michi*, 108.

5. Ibid.

6. This idea has made its way into Japanese popular culture. The Nomonhan incident is the climactic event in the sprawling and popular 1973 cinematic dramatization of Japan's road to war, *Senso to Ningen (War and Humanity)*, in which Soviet power at Nomonhan is, if anything, exaggerated. The Japanese defenders, the screen, and the audience are overwhelmed by endless and seemingly unstoppable waves of Soviet tanks.

7. *DGFP*, XIII, 40–41; 61–63; 110–13; 375–79.

8. Cited in Nagorski, *The Greatest Battle*, 157.

9. Ibid., 446–49.

10. Ibid., 798–800.

11. One exception is Gerard M. Friters, who states that "It is perhaps no exaggeration to say that Japanese strategy in World War II might have been different if the miniature war started by Japanese and Manchukuoan troops in the Nomonkhon [*sic.*] area . . . had not resulted in severe defeat." Gerard M. Friters, *Outer Mongolia and Its International Position* (Baltimore: Johns Hopkins University Press, 1949), 240.

12. Kutakov, *Japanese Foreign Policy*, 153–54.

13. Inada, "Soren Kyokutogun to no Taiketsu," 298.

14. Hayashi Saburo, *Kogun: The Japanese Army in the Pacific War*, ed. Alvin D. Coox, trans. Oswald White (Quantico, Va.: The Marine Corps Association, 1959), 117.

15. Watanabe Tsuneo, ed., *From Marco Polo Bridge to Pearl Harbor: Who Was Responsible?* (Tokyo: Yomiuri Shinbun, 2006), 114.

16. John Toland, *The Rising Sun* (New York: Bantam Books, 1971), 114–15.

17. Tanaka Ryukichi, *Nihon Gunbatsu Ante Shi* (*History of the Hidden Feuds Within the Japanese Army*) (Tokyo: Seiwado Shoten, 1947), 143–44; Maxon, *The Control of Japanese Foreign Policy*, 47. Tanaka's trustworthiness as a witness for both the prosecution and the defense at the IMTFE has been questioned. See Robert J. C. Butow, *Tojo and the Coming of the War* (Princeton, N.J.: Princeton University Press, 1961), 492–94.

18. Presseisen, *Germany and Japan*, 307.

19. Shimada, *Kanto Gun*, 155–58.

20. Erickson, *The Soviet High Command*, 599.

21. S. Isaev, "Meropriyatiya KPSS po ukrepleniyu dal'nevostochnykh rubezhei v 1931–1941 gg" ("Measures of the CPSU to Strengthen the Far Eastern Border, 1931–1941"), *Voenno-Istoricheskii Zhurnal* 9 (1981), 67, cited in Haslam, *The Threat from the East*, 143.

22. Whymant, *Stalin's Spy*, 199.

23. Erickson, *The Soviet High Command*, 567–68.

24. Whymant, *Stalin's Spy*, 234. Ozaki Hotsumi, a leftist journalist, was a China expert and a full-time policy adviser to Premier Konoye.

25. Ibid., 244.

26. Erickson, *The Soviet High Command*, 631–32.

27. This idea is supported by experts. See for example, Nagorski, *The Greatest Battle*; and R. H. S. Stolfi, *Hitler's Panzers East: World War II Reinterpreted* (Norman: University of Oklahoma Press, 1991).

28. Cited in Nagorski, *The Greatest Battle*, 5. Nevzorov, a retired army colonel, is a member of the Institute of Military History of the Ministry of Defense of the Russian Federation.

29. Nagorski, *The Greatest Battle*, 311.

30. Ibid., 312.

31. Petro G. Grigorenko, *Memoirs*, trans. Thomas Whitney (New York: W. W. Norton, 1982), 132.

32. This definition excludes civil wars such as Lebanon in the 1970s and 1980s. Such terms as "strategic-size forces" and "substantial period of time" are relative and subjective but are meant to exclude low-intensity conflicts regardless of duration (such as the Arab-Israeli conflict between 1957 and 1966) as well as sharp military clashes of short duration (such as the Sino-Soviet battle on the Ussuri River in March 1969).

33. "The fact that the Japanese Army forged ahead with the dispatch of troops to China after the outbreak of the Marco Polo Bridge incident, without worrying about the Soviet response, derived from such estimates [of the Amur River incident]." Hata, *Taiheiyo Senso e no Michi*, 81.

34. At the end of the war, Baron Hiranuma, a defendant at the IMTFE, was asked by the Soviet prosecutor whether he, as premier, ever gave orders to end the hostilities at Nomonhan. "As the supreme command of the army was not controlled by the government," he replied, "I could not give such orders, but I expressed my views on the necessity of ceasing hostilities to the War Minister, General Itagaki, orally." *IMTFE*, 7,854–56. This was considered a self-serving evasion by the prosecution, but it was the plain truth.

35. Stalin himself may have selected Zhukov for command on the Mongolian frontier in late May. Ruslanov, "Marshal Zhukov," 189.

36. Shimada, *Kanto Gun*, 150.

37. Tsuji Masanobu has been accused of instigating the murder of thousands of pro-British Chinese in Singapore, and of atrocities in the Philippines, including the Bataan "death march." Toland, *The Rising Sun*, 336–37ff. Tsuji was on the mainland at the time of Japan's surrender and went into hiding in Southeast Asia, returning to Japan in May 1948, after the end of the IMTFE. He received amnesty for alleged war crimes in January 1950 and was elected to the Lower House of the Diet in 1952, where he served until election to the Upper House in 1959. While on a fact-finding tour in Southeast Asia, he disappeared mysteriously in the jungles of Laos in April 1961 and officially was declared dead seven years later. Shiro Yoneyama, "Disappearance of Masanobu Tsuji Remains a Mystery," *The Japan Times*, July 26, 2000.

38. Tsuji, *Nomonhan*, 80–81.

Epilogue

1. The Soviet Union fought limited wars against Japan in mid-1939 and Finland in the winter of 1939–40, fought Germany from June 1941 to May 1945, and three months after Germany's surrender, attacked Japan in August 1945.

2. Coox, *Nomonhan*, 1,070–73.

BIBLIOGRAPHY

Unpublished Documents

German Foreign Ministry Archives. Microfilms of documents on German foreign policy, 1937–1939. Washington, D.C.: U.S. National Archives and Records Service.

German Navy Ministry Archives. Microfilms of documents of German Navy Ministry, 1937–1939. Washington, D.C.: U.S. National Archives and Records Service.

Japan Army Ministry Archives. Microfilms of documents of Imperial Japanese Army, 1937–1939. *Kyokai Jiken Toku Hokoku (Special Report on Border Incidents)*. Alexandria, Va.: U.S. National Archives and Records Service. December 1938.

Japan Defense Agency Archives. Operations Log of Kwantung Army, *Nomonhan Jiken Keiko no Gaiyo (Summary of the Course of the Nomonhan Incident)*, Colonel Hattori Takushiro, November 1939; and *Nomonhan Jiken Kankei Tzuzuri (Nomonhan Incident Files)*. Tokyo.

Proceedings of the International Military Tribunal for the Far East. Tokyo: 1946–48.

The Saionji-Harada Memoirs. Trans. by Supreme Command Allied Forces (Pacific). Washington, D.C.: National Archives and Records Service, 1930–1940.

U.S. Department of the Army, Forces in the Far East. *Japanese Special Studies on Manchuria.* 13 vols. Tokyo: 1954–56.

U.S. Department of the Army. Military Intelligence Reports, Record Group 165. Washington, D.C.: U.S. National Archives and Records Service.

U.S. Department of State. Unpublished diplomatic papers, 1935–1939. Washington, D.C.: U.S. National Archives and Records Service.

Published Documents

Degras, Jane. *Soviet Documents on Foreign Policy.* 3 vols. New York: Oxford University Press, 1951–53.

Documents on German Foreign Policy, 1918–1945. Series D. 13 vols. Washington, D.C.: U.S. Government Printing Office, 1949–64.

Dokumenty Vneshnei Politiki. 1939 god. vol. 22, 2 vols. (*Documents on Foreign Policy, 1939*). Moscow: Mezhdunarodnye Otnosheniia (published by the Russian Federation after the dissolution of the USSR), 1992.

Great Britain. Foreign Office. *Documents on British Foreign Policy*, 3rd Series. London: Her Majesty's Stationery Office, 1919–1939.

Hertslet, Godfrey E. P. *Treaties, Conventions, Etc., Between China and Foreign States*, 3rd ed. London: Harrison & Sons, for His Majesty's Stationery Office, 1908.

Hidaka Noboro, ed. *Manchukuo-Soviet Border Issues*. Harbin: *Manchuria Daily News*, 1938.

Il'ichev, L., et al., eds. *God Krizisa, 1938–1939* (*Year of Crisis, 1938–1939*), 2 vols. Moscow: Izd-vo polit. Lit., 1990.

Nihon Kindai Shiryo Kenkyuka. *Nippon Riku-Kaigun no Seido*. *Shoshiki.Jinji* (*System, Personnel, and Organization of the Japanese Army and Navy*). Tokyo: University of Tokyo Press, 1971.

Tsunoda Jun, ed. *Gen Dai Shi X* (*Modern History Documents*), vol. X, *Nichi Senso* (*Japan-China War*), Pt. 3. Tokyo: Misuzu Shobo, 1964.

VII (Seventh) Congress of the Communist International. *Abridged Stenographic Report of Proceedings* (in English). Moscow: 1939.

U.S. Department of State. *Foreign Relations of the United States: Diplomatic Papers*. Washington, D.C.: U.S. Government Printing Office: 1948–present.

USSR Commissariat of Foreign Affairs. *Dokumenty Vneshnei Politiki* (*Documents on Foreign Policy*). Moscow: Gosudarstvennoe Izdatel'stvo Politicheskoi Literatury, (published by the USSR): 1958–1991.

Autobiographies, Memoirs, and Other Primary Sources

Churchill, Winston S. *The Gathering Storm*. Boston: Houghton-Mifflin, 1948.

Craigie, Robert L. *Behind the Japanese Mask*. London: Hutchinson, 1946.

Eden, Anthony. *Memoirs of Anthony Eden, Earl of Avon*, Vol. I, *Facing the Dictators, 1923–1938*. London: Cassell, 1962.

Feiling, Keith. *The Life of Neville Chamberlain*. London: Macmillan, 1946.

Grigorenko, Petro G. *Memoirs*. Trans. Thomas Whitney. New York: W. W. Norton, 1982.

Hayashi Saburo. *Kogun: The Japanese Army in the Pacific War*. Trans. Oswald White, ed. Alvin D. Coox. Quantico, Va.: The Marine Corps Association, 1959.

Hilger, Gustav, and Alfred G. Meyer. *The Incompatible Allies*. New York: Macmillan, 1953.

Inada Masazumi. "Soren Kyokutogun to no Taiketsu" ("Confrontation with the Soviet Far Eastern Army"). *Chisei*, Special Issue no. 5 (December 1956).

Shigemitsu Mamoru. *Japan and Her Destiny*. Trans. Oswald White, ed. F. S. G. Piggott. New York: Dutton, 1958.

Tanaka Ryukichi. *Nihon Gunbatsu Anto Shi* (*History of the Hidden Feuds Within the Japanese Army*). Tokyo: Seiwada Shoten, 1947.

Tsuji Masanobu. *Nomonhan*. Tokyo: Ato Shobo, 1950.

Weizsacker, Ernst von. *Memoirs*. London: Victor Gollancz, 1951.

Zhukov, Georgy Konstantinovich. *Memoirs of Marshal Zhukov*. New York: Delacourt Press, 1971.

Books

Aster, Sidney. *1939: The Making of the Second World War*. New York: Simon and Schuster, 1973.

Baabar. *History of Mongolia*. Trans. D. Suhjargalmaa et al. Cambridge, UK: White Horse Press, 1999.

Bell, P. M. H. *The Origins of the Second World War in Europe*. London: Longman, 1986.

Beloff, Max. *Foreign Policy of Soviet Russia, 1929–1941*. 2 vols. London: Oxford University Press, 1949.

Borg, Dorothy, and Shumpei Okamoto, eds. *Pearl Harbor as History*. New York: Columbia University Press, 1973.

Borton, Hugh. *Japan's Modern Century*. New York: Ronald Press, 1970.

Boyce, Robert, and Joseph A. Maiolo, eds. *The Origins of World War Two*. New York: Palgrave Macmillian, 2003.

Brogan, Dennis W. *The Development of Modern France, 1870–1939*. 2 vols. New York: Harper and Row, 1966.

Brown, Anthony Cave, and Charles B. MacDonald. *On a Field of Red: The Communist International and the Coming of World War II*. New York: G. P. Putnam's Sons, 1981.

Butow, Robert J. C. *Tojo and the Coming of the War*. Princeton, N.J.: Princeton University Press, 1961.

Byas, Hugh. *Government by Assassination*. New York: Alfred A. Knopf, 1942.

Cattell, David T. *Soviet Diplomacy and the Spanish Civil War*. Berkeley: University of California Press, 1957.

Clubb, Edmund O. "Armed Conflict in the Chinese Borderlands." Raymond Gartoff, ed. *Sino-Soviet Military Relations*. New York: Praeger, 1966.

Colbert, Evelyn S. *The Left Wing in Japanese Politics*. New York: Institute for Pacific Relations, 1952.

Coox, Alvin D. *The Anatomy of a Small War: The Soviet-Japanese Struggle for Changkufeng/Khasan, 1938*. Westport, Conn.: Greenwood Press, 1977.

———. *Nomonhan: Japan Against Russia, 1939*. 2 vols. Stanford, Calif.: Stanford University Press, 1985.

Craig, Gordon A., and Felix Gilbert. *The Diplomats*. 2 vols. Princeton, N.J.: Princeton University Press, 1953.

Crowley, James B. *Japan's Quest for Autonomy: National Security and Foreign Policy, 1930–1938*. Princeton, N.J.: Princeton University Press, 1966.

Crozier, Andrew J. *The Causes of the Second World War*. Oxford, UK: Blackwell, 1997.

Dallin, David. *Soviet Russia and the Far East*. New Haven, Conn.: Yale University Press, 1948.

Deakin, F. W., and G. R. Storry. *Richard Sorge: Die Geschichte eines Grossen Doppelspiels*. Trans. Ulrike von Puttkamer. Munich, FRG: R. Piper, 1965.

Deborin, A., et al. *Istoriia Velikoi Otechtestvennoi Voiny Sovetskogo Soiuza, 1941–1945* (*History of the Great Fatherland War of the Soviet Union, 1941–1945*). Moscow: Akademiia Nauk SSSR, 1960.

Dobb, Maurice. *Soviet Economic Development since 1917*. New York: International Publishers, 1966.

Drea, Edward J. *Nomonhan: Japanese-Soviet Tactical Combat, 1939*. Fort Leavenworth, Kans.: U.S. Army Command and General Staff College, 1981.

Erickson, John. *The Soviet High Command*. London: Macmillan, 1962.

Eubank, Keith. *Origins of World War II*. New York: Crowell, 1969.

Friters, Gerard M. *Outer Mongolia and Its International Position*. Baltimore: Johns Hopkins University Press, 1949.

Fujiwara Akira. "The Role of the Japanese Army." Trans. Shumpei Okamoto, eds. Dorothy Borg and Shumpei Okamoto. *Pearl Harbor as History*. New York: Columbia University Press, 1973.

Gartoff, Raymond L., ed. *Sino-Soviet Military Relations*. New York: Praeger, 1966.

Haslam, Jonathan. *The Soviet Union and the Threat from the East: Moscow, Tokyo, and the Prelude to the Pacific War, 1933–1941*. Pittsburgh, Pa.: University of Pittsburgh Press, 1992.

Hata Ikuhiko. *Reality and Illusion: The Hidden Crisis Between Japan and the U.S.S.R., 1932–1934*. New York: East Asian Institute of Columbia University, 1967.

Higgins, Trumbull. *Hitler and Russia: The Third Reich in a Two-Front War, 1937–1943*. New York: Macmillan, 1966.

Hofer, Walter. *Die Entfesselung des Zweiten Weltkrieges* (*The Outbreak of the Second World War*). Frankfurt, FRG: Fischer, 1960.

Imai Takeo. *Kindai no Senso, XV, Chugoku to no Tatakai* (*Modern Wars, Vol. XV, War Against China*). Tokyo: Jinbutsu Orai Sha, 1965.

Japan Defense Agency, Defense Institute, Military History Office. *Kanto Gun I, Tai So Sen Bi: Nomonhan Jiken* (*Kwantung Army, Vol. I, War Preparations Against the U.S.S.R.: The Nomonhan Incident*). Tokyo: Asa Gumo Shinbun Sha, 1969.

Johnson, Chalmers. *An Instance of Treason: Ozaki Hotsumi and the Sorge Spy Ring*. Stanford, Calif.: Stanford University Press, 1964.

Jones, F. C. *Japan's New Order in East Asia: Its Rise and Fall, 1937–1945*. London: Oxford University Press, 1954.

———. *Manchuria Since 1931*. London: Oxford University Press, 1949.

Kutakov, Leonid N. *Japanese Foreign Policy on the Eve of the Pacific War*. Trans. and ed., George A. Lensen. Tallahassee, Fla.: Diplomatic Press, 1972.

Kuzmin, Nikolai Fedorovich. *Na Strazhe Mirnovo Truda* (*On Guard for the Workers of the World*). Moscow: Military Publishing House, 1959.

Lattimore, Owen. *The Mongols of Manchuria*. New York: John Day, 1934.

Lee, Bradford. *Britain and the Sino-Japanese War, 1937–1939*. Stanford, Calif.: Stanford University Press, 1973.

Lensen, George A. *The Damned Inheritance: The Soviet Union and the Manchurian Crises, 1924–1935*. Tallahassee, Fla.: Diplomatic Press, 1974.

———. *Japanese Recognition of the U.S.S.R.: Soviet-Japanese Relations, 1921–1930*. Tallahassee, Fla.: Diplomatic Press, 1970.

Malozemoff, Andrew. *Russia's Far Eastern Policy, 1881–1904*. Berkeley: University of California Press, 1958.

Maxon, Yale Candee. *Control of Japanese Foreign Policy*. Berkeley: University of California Press, 1957.

McLane, Charles B. *Soviet Policy and the Chinese Communists, 1931–1946*. New York: Columbia University Press, 1958.

McSherry, James E. *Stalin, Hitler, and Europe: The Origins of World War II, 1933–1939*. Cleveland, Ohio: World Publishing, 1968.

Moore, Harriet L. *Soviet Far Eastern Policy, 1931–1945*. Princeton, N.J.: Princeton University Press, 1945.

Morley, James W. *The Japanese Thrust into Siberia*. New York: Columbia University Press, 1957.

Nagorski, Andrew. *The Greatest Battle: Stalin, Hitler, and the Desperate Struggle for Moscow That Changed the Course of World War II*. New York: Simon and Schuster, 2007.

Nekrich, Aleksandr M. *Pariahs, Partners, Predators: German-Soviet Relations, 1922–1941*. Ed. and trans. Gregory L. Freeze. New York: Columbia University Press, 1997.

Nevolin, P. A., ed. *Geroi Khalkhin-Gola (Heroes of Khalkhin-Gol)*. Perm, USSR: Perm Publishing House, 1966.

Nihon Kokusai, Seiji Gakai, Taiheiyo Senso, and Genin Kenkyubu. *Taiheiyo Senso e no Michi IV, Nichu Senso 2 (Road to the Pacific War, Vol. IV, Sino-Japanese War, Pt. 2)*. Hata Ikuhiko, Usui Katsumi, and Tomoyoshi Hirai. Tokyo: Asahi Shinbun Sha, 1963.

Nogueres, Henri. *Munich*. Trans. Patrick O'Brian. New York: McGraw Hill, 1965.

Nove, Alec. *An Economic History of the U.S.S.R.* Baltimore: Penguin Books, 1969.

Ogata, Sadako. *Defiance in Manchuria*. Berkeley: University of California Press, 1964.

Parrish, Michael. *Sacrifice of the Generals: Soviet Senior Officer Losses*. Lanham, Md.: Scarecrow Press, 2004.

Presseisen, Ernst L. *Germany and Japan, A Study in Totalitarian Diplomacy, 1933–1941*. The Hague: Martinus Nijhoff, 1958.

Price, Ernst Batson. *The Russo-Japanese Treaties of 1907–1916 Concerning Manchuria and Mongolia*. Baltimore: Johns Hopkins University Press, 1933.

Puzzo, Dante A. *Spain and the Great Powers, 1936–1941*. New York: Columbia University Press, 1961.

Ragsdale, Hugh. *The Soviets, the Munich Crisis, and the Coming of World War II*. Cambridge, UK: Cambridge University Press, 2004.

Reischauer, Edwin O. *The United States and Japan*. New York: Viking, 1957.

Roberts, Geoffrey. *The Soviet Union and the Origins of the Second World War*. New York: St. Martin's Press, 1995.

———. *The Unholy Alliance: Stalin's Pact with Hitler*. Bloomington: Indiana University Press, 1989.

Rothwell, Victor. *The Origins of the Second World War*. Manchester, UK: Manchester University Press, 2001.

Salisbury, Harrison. *The Coming War Between Russia and China*. New York: Norton, 1969.

Sevost'yanov, G. N. *Politika Velikikh Derzhav Na Dal'nem Vostoke Nakanune Vtoroi Mirovoi Voini* (*Policies of the Great Powers in the Far East on the Eve of the Second World War*). Moscow: Izdatel'stvo Sotsialino-Ekonomicheskoi Literatury, 1961.

Shimada Toshihiko. *Kanto Gun.* Tokyo: Chuo Koron Sha, 1965.

Shishkin, S. N. *Khalkhin-Gol.* Moscow: Military Publishing House, 1954.

Stolfi, R. H. S. *Hitler's Panzers East: World War II Reinterpreted.* Norman: University of Oklahoma Press, 1991.

Storry, Richard. *The Double Patriots.* Boston: Houghton Mifflin, 1957.

———. *A History of Modern Japan.* Baltimore: Penguin Books, 1960.

Suvorov, Viktor. *The Chief Culprit.* Annapolis. Md.: Naval Institute Press, 2008.

Swearington, Rodger, and Paul Langer. *Red Flag in Japan.* Cambridge, Mass.: Harvard University Press, 1952.

Tanaka Katsuhiko. *Nomonhan Senso: Mongoru to Manshukoku* (*The Nomonhan War: Mongolia and Manchukuo*). Tokyo: Iwanami Shoten, 2009.

Tang, Peter S. H. *Russian and Soviet Policy in Manchuria and Outer Mongolia, 1911–1931.* Durham, N.C.: Duke University Press, 1959.

Taylor, A. J. P. *From Sarajevo to Potsdam.* London: Thomas and Hudson, 1965.

———. *Origins of the Second World War.* Greenwich, Conn.: Fawcett, 1961.

Toland, John. *The Rising Sun.* New York: Bantam Books, 1971.

Treadgold, Donald. *Twentieth Century Russia.* Chicago: Rand McNally, 1972.

Ulam, Adam. *Expansion and Coexistence.* New York: Praeger, 1968.

Watanabe Tsuneo, ed. *From Marco Polo Bridge to Pearl Harbor: Who Was Responsible?* Tokyo: Yomiuri Shinbun, 2006.

Watt, Donald Cameron. *How War Came: The Immediate Origins of the Second World War, 1938–1939.* New York: Pantheon Books, 1989.

Weinberg, Gerhard. *The Foreign Policy of Hitler's Germany: Starting World War II, 1937–1939.* Chicago: University of Chicago Press, 1980.

Wheeler-Bennett, J. W. *The Nemesis of Power, The German Army in Politics, 1918–1945.* New York: Viking, 1967.

Whymant, Robert. *Stalin's Spy: Richard Sorge and the Tokyo Espionage Ring.* New York: St. Martin's Press, 1996.

Wirtz, John E. *From Isolation to War, 1931–1941.* New York: Crowell, 1968.

Wittfogel, Karl A. "A Short History of Chinese Communism." Seattle: Mimeographed copy of Human Relations Area Files: A General Handbook of China, Vol. II, 1964.

Yoshihashi Takehiko. *Conspiracy at Mukden.* New Haven, Conn.: Yale University Press, 1963.

Articles

Blumenson, Martin. "Soviet Power Play at Changkufeng." *World Politics* 12 (January 1960).

Coox, Alvin D. "L'Affaire Lyushkov." *Soviet Studies* 19 (January 1968).

————."Qualities of Japanese Military Leadership: The Case of Suetaka Kamezo." *Journal of Asian History* 2 (1968).

Crowley, James B. "Japanese Army Factionalism in the Early 1930s." *Journal of Asian Studies* 21 (May 1962).

Dalby, Tracy."Japan's Germ Warriors." *Washington Post*, May 26, 1983.

Eshakov, V. "Boi u Ozera Khasan" ("The Battle at Lake Khasan"). *Voennoe-Istoricheskie Zhurnal* (July 1968).

Inada Masazumi. "Soren Kyokutogun to no Taiketsu" ("Confrontation with the Soviet Far Eastern Army"). *Chisei*, Special Issue no. 5 (December 1956).

Kitagami Norio and Nara Hiroshi. "Kanto Gun Tokushu Himitsu 731 Butai ni Yoru Hinjindoteki Hanzai" ("Inhuman Crimes of Kwantung Army's Special Secret Troop 731"). *Nichu* 2, no. 12 (December 1972).

Kolomiets, Maksim. "Boi u Reki Khalkhin-Gol" ("Battle at the Khalkhin-Gol River"). *Frontovaya Illyustratsiya* (February 2002).

Moses, Larry."Soviet-Japanese Confrontation in Outer-Mongolia: The Battle of Nomonhan-Khalkhin-Gol." *Journal of Asian History* 1 (1967).

Novikov, M. V. "U Ozera Khasan" ("At Lake Khasan"). *Voprosy Istorii* (August 1968).

Pratt, Lawrence. "The Anglo-American Naval Conversations on the Far East of January 1938." *International Affairs* (October 1971).

Roberts, Geoffrey. "The Soviet Decision for a Pact with Germany." *Soviet Studies* 44, no. 1 (1992).

Ruslanov, P. (pseudonym?)."Marshal Zhukov." *Russian Review* 15 (July 1956).

Sevost'yanov, G. N. "Voennoe i Diplomaticheskoe Porazhenie Yaponii v Periode Sobytiy u Reki Khalkhin-Gol" ("The Military and Diplomatic Defeat of Japan in the Period of the Events at the Khalkhin-Gol River"). *Voprosy Istorii* (August 1957).

Tinch, Clark."Quasi-War Between Japan and the U.S.S.R." *World Politics* 3 (January 1951).

Yoneyama Shiro."Disappearance of Masanobu Tsuji Remains a Mystery." *The Japan Times*, July 26, 2000.

Young, Katsu Hirai."The Nomonhan Incident." *Monumenta Nipponica* 22 (1967).

Unpublished Doctoral Dissertations

Goldman, Stuart D. *Soviet-Japanese Conflict and the Outbreak of World War II.* Washington, D.C. Georgetown University, 1970.

Sasaki Chiyoko. *Der Nomonhan Konflikt.* Bonn, FRG: Friedrich-Wilhelms-Universitat, 1968.

Thornton, Sandra. *The Soviet Union and Japan, 1939–1941.* Washington, D.C.: Georgetown University, 1964.

INDEX

Italy: Anti-Comintern Pact, 37, 40; British policy toward, 41; four-power pact, formation of, 45–46; Munich Conference, 45; Pact of Steel, 155–56; Rome-Berlin-Tokyo alliance, 37, 54, 155, 165, 169, 171, 205n22; Spain, aid to from, 25, 26–27, 36

Japan: Anti-Comintern Pact, 36–37, 52–53, 164; anti-Russian German-Japanese pact, 53–54, 194n88; assassination of government officials in, 14, 189n12; atomic bomb use against, 183–84; boundary-line and cease-fire agreements, 151; CCP conflict with, 25, 27–28, 191n17; China, bullying of by, 9; China operations and weakening of threat from, 33; Chinese nationalism and Soviet-Japanese relations, 10–11; communism, hostility toward, 10; democracy in, 13, 189n9; depression and economic crisis in, 12–13; diplomatic isolation of, 149; expansion interests of, 7–9; Germany, alliance with, 43, 52–54, 124, 150, 156, 169, 194n88; German-Soviet nonaggression pact objectives, 164; Great Britain, relations with, 37–39; Manchuria invasion and occupation by, 11, 16, 18, 20; modernization of, 7, 15; nationalism and militarism in, 11, 13–16, 189n12; Nomonhan incident and policy decisions by, 5, 167–74, 177, 178, 206n6, 206n11; nonaggression pact proposal by Russia, 17; nonaggression Pact terms and, 3, 188n11; northward expansion of, 168–69, 174–76; oil and gasoline embargo, 169–70; peace treaty with Soviet Union and Russia, 185; political corruption in, 13; preventive war against Soviets, proposal for, 17; prisoners of war, 185; Rome-Berlin-Tokyo alliance, 37, 54, 155, 165, 169, 171, 205n22; Russia, border disputes with, 9, 16–20, 56–58; Russia, China War, and relations with, 33–36, 53, 180; Russia, cooperation with, 8–9; Russia, deterioration of relations with, 16–20; Russia, joining German war against, 171–72, 174–76, 178; Russia, neutrality pact

with, 165, 171–72; Russia, relations with, 10, 162, 164–65, 188n2; Russia, threat to from, 23, 25; Russian fight against, 183–85, 208n1; Russian-Chinese relations and, 25, 27–28; Siberian expedition and Russian Civil War intervention, 9–10, 17; southward expansion of, 169–73, 174–76; Soviet appeasement of, 16–17, 27, 34; strategic advantage of, 20; surrender of, 184–85; Tientsin, confrontation over, 103–4, 169; Twenty-One Demands, 9; two-front war concerns, 33; United States, decision to go to war against, 5, 168–74, 206n6; United States, relations with, 39; Western democracies, relations with, 37–43

Kanchatzu Island, 32, 33, 56

Kanchuerhmiao, 94, 98, 103, 124–25

Khalkhin Gol. *See* Nomonhan incident/ Khalkhin Gol conflict

Khasan, Lake, 56. *See also* Changkufeng incident/Lake Khasan battle

Kobayashi Koichi, 141–42, 143

Komatsubara Michitaro: appearance and character of, 81; artillery barrage operations, 128–29; border dispute principles (Order 1488), 89; death of, 152; encirclement of by Soviets, 145–46, 148; Halha River bridge and Fui Heights attack, 105, 106, 114, 115–17, 119, 120, 122; Halha River, withdrawal to east bank of, 120; Manchukuo, Soviet air raids in, 103, 199n5; night combat operations, 124–25, 126, 127; Nomonhan area, guidelines to patrol, 82; Nomonhan August operations, 133, 139, 141, 143, 145; Nomonhan border dispute mission, 90; Nomonhan incident, 1–3, 88, 91, 92–93, 94, 98, 100, 198n32; reinforcements for, 132–33; retirement of, 152; Special Services Agency leadership role, 81, 197n6; suicide of officers and soldiers, 148, 152

Konoye Fumimaro, 61, 77, 173, 175–76, 194n88

About the Author

Stuart D. Goldman is a scholar in residence at the National Council for Eurasian and East European Research in Washington, D.C. From 1979–2009, he was the senior specialist in Russian and Eurasian political and military affairs at the Congressional Research Service of the Library of Congress. A resident of Rockville, Md., he holds a Ph.D. from Georgetown University.